D1453556

CHICANO POWER

CHICANO

1974 | New York

POWER

THE EMERGENCE
OF MEXICAN
AMERICA

TONY CASTRO

Saturday Review Press | E. P. Dutton & Co., Inc.

Grateful acknowledgment is made to Rodolfo (Corky) Gonzales for permission to reprint portions of "I Am Joaquin," which was first published in 1967, in honor of Escuela Tlatelolco, Denver. Copyright © 1967 by Rodolfo (Corky) Gonzales.

Library of Congress Cataloging in Publication Data

Castro, Tony.
Chicano Power: the emergence of Mexican America.

Bibliography: p.
1. Mexican Americans. I. Title.
E184.M5C37   301.45'16'872073   73-20428

Published simultaneously in Canada by
Clarke, Irwin & Company Limited, Toronto and Vancouver
ISBN: 0-8415-0321-4 (cloth)
ISBN: 0-8415-0349-4 (paper)
Designed by The Etheredges

FOR DAVID McHAM

CONTENTS

PREFACE

Perhaps I should begin by defining what my book is not. It is neither an apology for the Chicano movement nor an attempt at advocacy journalism for the Chicano cause. On the contrary, this book will probably irritate, maybe even anger, Mexican-American activists and leaders of all persuasions. At the same time, it is not a book decrying the movement or questioning the basic moral principle of equality and civil rights.

It is, instead, a newsman's look at the whole spectrum of the Chicano movement from the *barrio* militants to what I describe as Emerging Brown Middle America. It is critical reporting and analysis of one small segment of America that is calling for attention and is beginning to get it. Above all, I would hope the book represents good journalism.

My editor at Saturday Review Press, Tom Davis, asked for an "Olympian view" of the Mexican-American, and this has been what I have sought to depict. If my approach differs from the dry, scholarly books on the Mexican-American that currently line the shelves of stores and libraries, then I know that I've succeeded in breaking at least one stereotype in the treatment of the Chicanos. The tendency has been to write about the Mexican-American in historical terms, as if he were a phenomenon of the past; and there's nothing like plowing four-fifths of the way through a poorly written book only to find that the one-fifth on the contemporary Chicano has been left dangling, without his role both in Mexican-American history and in America today being clearly defined. My idea was to write with full focus on the contemporary Chicano and through him explain not only where he is today but also where he was in the past.

This book evolved out of a lengthy article I wrote on the Nixon Chicano Strategy for the *Dallas Morning News* in the fall of 1971. After completing the article, I began for the first time to see the Chicano in purely political terms, to sense the Nixon Hispanos' relationship to other Mexican-Americans in the movement; and it gradually began to occur to me that a book about contemporary Chicanos and politics was no doubt as valid and, without question, more interesting than what has been published about Mexican-Americans to date.

So the book was begun, and as I became more involved in analyzing the Chicano movement, it very quickly grew to be not only a book about Mexican-Americans but also a book about America, and in particular about ethnicity and assimilation into American society. In working on the book, my being Mexican-American was both a help and a hindrance. It was an advantage in that I believe myself to be more sensitive to the problems and aspirations of the Chicanos than my fellow Anglo reporters. I had rapport with the Chicanos, and I could go into places and talk to people with whom other reporters would not have been able to get to first base. Being Mexican-American provided me with an immediate sense of credibility among those active in the movement. At the same time, however, being non-white, particularly in Texas, stretches your credibility with Anglos to the limit. In the day of advocacy journalism, I suppose they expect every Mexican-American reporter to be carrying the Chicano cause on his sleeve. For myself and for many other Mexican-American and black reporters, the situation has developed into a man-in-the-middle syndrome: the Chicanos expect you to be much more aggressive—an advocate; the Anglos, including some fellow newsmen and immediate superiors, distrust you and demand that you continue proving yourself on their terms. You can't please both groups simultaneously, and the only viable approach is the one I've tried to follow here: to write as honest a book as I could from a frankly partisan viewpoint.

At the time that I began working on the book, I fortunately already had a wealth of background material on the movement, which I had followed closely with some curiosity since the mid-1960s. In 1970, I started actively covering the movement and other Mexican-American developments for the *Dallas Times Herald.* The following year, while I was a fellow in the Washington Journalism Center's public affairs reporting program, I did extensive research on Mexican-Americans and their role in government and politics, looking ahead to the day when I would write a book on the Chicanos. So when I finally decided to give the book a try, it was not as if I had to begin from scratch.

The book is largely the product of several hundred personal interviews, plus my own observations during the time that I have been covering the Chicanos and my storehouse of research, most of which was done before I decided to write the book. On every subject, I believe it was always a case of putting together enough background material to reach a point when I would decide it was time to write.

Throughout my work on the book, I made a conscious effort not only to avoid personal involvement in any aspect of the Chicanos' story but also to avoid even the appearance of a personal involvement. The one thing I didn't want was to have the book bunched with others about the Chicanos by Chicano authors, whose own activism and involvement has clouded their fairness, judgment, and credibility — and have it written off for those reasons. My intent was not to write a book that would bolster the Chicanos and deflate the Anglos; it was to write a book telling a story the way it happened, regardless of who was exalted and who was humbled. I believe I succeeded in maintaining that sense of professional detachment.

It is notable, however, that of all the Mexican-Americans with whom I dealt as a reporter for the *Dallas Morning News* and while I was working on the book, the ones who were most critical of my reporting were the Nixon Hispanos, the only Chicanos who continually raised questions about my fairness and my own personal political convictions. Their criticism was stirred by my newspaper's close watch of the Nixon Chicano Strategy and how the administration had changed directions in dealing with the Spanish-speaking—all coinciding with the buildup to the 1972 presidential election. It was ironic because it was that long piece on the Nixon Hispanos that launched my book idea in the first place.

In a book like this, which wound up being more comprehensive than I had first envisioned, I am indebted to many people. I am especially grateful to my editors at the *Dallas Morning News*, particularly Bob Miller, Bob Compton, Don Smith, and Buster Haas, who encouraged me to follow the political developments of the Chicanos and whose help and consideration made it possible to write this book. David McHam, a friend and journalism professor at my alma mater, Baylor University, encouraged me to take on this book and, as he has for a number of years, provided some needed advice at important times. J. D. Alexander, assistant national editor of the *Washington Post*, for whom I am a stringer, guided my thinking on some Chicano stories I wrote for the *Post* and, in effect, wisely influenced my judgment in looking at certain aspects from a broader national perspective. Frank del Olmo, a staff writer with the *Los Angeles Times*, was extremely generous in helping me to understand better some aspects of the Chicano movement in California. Dr. Chris Garcia, a professor of political science at the University of New Mexico, provided me with excellent insight into developments in New Mexico and into political theory in the movement. Dave Mc-Neely, with whom I worked at the *Dallas News*, unselfishly shared his broad knowledge of Texas politics, and as I became deeply involved in the book, he served as a constant reminder about the necessity of my remaining a "man in the middle." Judy Elfenbein, a researcher at WFAA-TV, the Dallas ABC affiliate, was generous in allowing me the use of her own material on the Chicanos and in serving as a sounding board for many of the interpretive ideas in the book. I am also grateful for the use of the research facilities of the *Dallas News*, the *Houston Post*, the *Houston Chronicle*, the *San Antonio Express-News*, the *Washington Post*, the *Los Angeles Times*, the *Denver Post*, and the Associated Press. There were, of course, many others who, in the course of my research and my work at the *Dallas News,* offered valuable information, documentation, tips, and advice; their assistance and honesty is greatly appreciated.

My original idea for the book was of a much more limited scope than what I finally wrote. Looking back, I can see that particular major shortcoming of my original outline. I am indebted to Tom Davis, my editor at Saturday Review Press, who suggested the broader approach and helped me formulate the outline from which I finally worked. Tom did an excellent job in smoothing out some of my rough edges.

TONY CASTRO

STRANGERS IN THEIR OWN LAND

1 THE AGE OF LA RAZA

It was midsummer 1972, two weeks after he had turned down a place on his party's presidential ticket, and Senator Edward M. Kennedy, in that flat Boston twang so reminiscent of the voices of the other Kennedys, was recalling the past for a people whose own history on the continent predated that of his New England constituents. But it was the recent past that Kennedy recalled, a past marred by the deaths of two brothers who had symbolized a hope and a promise for the people whose cause Kennedy himself was now taking up. He was encouraging his hearers to make an active commitment to their own betterment, to confront the country's political parties, even his own, and make them respond.

"Robert Kennedy shared that view," Kennedy said. "He walked the streets of the *barrio* in East Los Angeles, he broke the fast with César Chávez in Delano, and he committed himself to alter the conditions of poverty and discrimination in this country. For he believed, as I do, that this nation can never be completely free nor completely whole until we know that no child cries from hunger in the Rio Grande Valley, until we know that no mother in East Los Angeles fears illness because she cannot afford a doctor, until we know that no man suffers because the law refuses to recognize his humanity. It is not for the Chicano alone that we must seek these goals. It is not for the disadvantaged alone that we seek these goals. It is for America's future."

Kennedy was addressing the national convention of the American G.I. Forum, one of the countless Mexican-American organizations organized in the twentieth century to fight the discrimination and injustice inflicted on Mexican-Americans in the Southwest. Unlike the crying child from the Rio Grande Valley and the poor mother in East Los Angeles, the Mexican-Americans whom Kennedy was addressing at Washington's plush Statler Hilton Hotel were white-collar Mexican-American businessmen and professionals. They represented the small fraction of Mexican-Americans who had rid themselves of the poverty that had plagued them or their ancestors in years past. Socially and politically, however, the Mexican-Americans who had gathered at the Statler Hilton remained disenfrachised, even if they were no longer poor. At best, many were tokens in the business and professional worlds. But they were token representatives still highly concerned about the plight of their people.

Four years earlier, Mexican-Americans in California had rushed to Robert F. Kennedy's support in his quest for the Democratic party presidential nomination, and the outpouring of Mexican-American votes helped him win the California primary that for a few moments made the nomination seem secure. In 1960, Mexican-Americans throughout the Southwest were actively and emotionally involved in John F. Kennedy's campaign, organizing Viva Kennedy Clubs that ultimately provided the balance of power in Texas and swung the state's large block of electoral votes to Kennedy, nudging the Democratic ticket just over the number of electoral votes needed to win.

Yet a dozen years after John Kennedy's presidential campaign, living conditions for most of the country's Mexican-Americans had not improved significantly. And since an atmosphere of hope existed even as late as 1968, it was easy to blame the slow progress of the past four years on the Nixon administration, as Democrats already were quick to do in a presidential election year. Ted Kennedy's basic speech for much of 1971 and 1972 had been what reporters traveling with him dubbed the "forgotten promises" speech. In it he enumerated five promises he said Richard Nixon had failed to meet—to end the war and inflation, to cut both welfare and crime, and to reconcile the divisions in the country. But for the Mexican-American audience, Kennedy charged the Nixon administration with a different set of "forgotten promises": the failure to convene a White House conference on the Mexican-American, the proposed cuts in funding for bilingual education, the failure to increase the percentage of Spanish-speaking federal employes, and the covert opposition to the aspirations of migrant workers and César Chávez's United Farm Workers Union. In a rousing but little publicized speech, Kennedy said:

"As a nation, we have marveled at the bounty of our farms but overlooked the men and women who toil in the dust and dirt to harvest that bounty. As a nation, we have been silent partners in the denial of the constitutional right to an equal education for millions of Spanish-speaking school children. As a nation, we have forgotten that if the Chicanos are angry and alienated, it is we, the majority, who have made them strangers in their own land. But no one has to tell this convention that millions of Chicanos live in inadequate housing. No one has to tell this convention that millions receive inferior schooling. No one has to tell this convention that millions endure too often the weight of the law instead of its protection. . . . The callous lack of concern for the disadvantaged by this administration is shown in its strategy of dismembering the Office of Economic Opportunity, in its veto of child-care services for the poor, and its decision to turn back to the Treasury as surplus $699 million that Congress appropriated to feed hungry Americans.

"The challenge is before you. It is a challenge to force the political leadership of this nation to keep its promise to La Raza, to keep its promise to America. It is a challenge to force the system to close the gap between promise and performance. And the only way to do that is to become more active politically today than ever before, and to force the political leaders of both parties to respond."

It was the first month of the 1972 presidential campaign, and Richard Milhous Nixon, in one of his rare personal appearances on the way to a landslide victory, had taken his reelection campaign to South Texas, touching down for three stops in the Lower Rio Grande Valley. In Laredo, where he inspected the government's crackdown operation on heroin smuggling, the President was greeted by a cheering crowd of 36,000. Grandmothers in mantillas. Chicano majorettes. Farmers in denims. They packed the narrow city streets and stood six deep cheering *"Hola Nixon"* and *"Bienvenido,"* as Mr. Nixon, for the first time in thirty-two years, returned to the place where he and Mrs. Nixon spent their honeymoon.

An hour later, courtesy of the presidential helicopters, the President was in dusty Rio Grande City, where he met 1,300 high school students, almost all of them Mexican-American, paying them a visit as he had promised a year earlier. In 1971 the students from Rio Grande High School had washed cars and sold tamales to finance a trip to Washington, where they met the President in the Rose Garden at the White House. Now, in Texas, and much more relaxed than usual, Mr. Nixon told the students they had lived up to the highest tradition of the nation. The students who had gone to Washington, he said, might have sought out a foundation or a wealthy *patron* to finance the trip but they didn't.

"The American tradition," he said, "is that we help ourselves when we can. . . . That's what made this country great."

The President urged the largely Mexican-American student body to take pride in themselves and in the nation's diversity. In an oblique reference to the traditional Democratic voting patterns of Mexican-Americans, he urged them to "let your minds become as open as they can" to all facets of the political process. "I am not going to talk about whether you become Democrats or Republicans," he said. "The future of the country is more important than any party label. . . .

"Be for your school, be for your team, but above all, be for your country, for America."

Then, to everyone's surprise, the President turned around and marched to the back of the stage, sat down at the piano, and gave both the students and the horde of reporters travelling with him a view of Richard Nixon that is rarely seen. Smiling, the President led the student body in singing

"Happy Birthday" to U.S. Representative Eligio de la Garza, the local Democratic congressman (running unopposed in the forthcoming election), who was celebrating his forty-fifth birthday. Nixon praised de la Garza for proving that Mexican-Americans from any background can "go right to the top."

The next day a photograph of the President at the piano appeared on the front page of almost every paper in the country, along with a news story about his campaign itinerary that made the obvious comment on his trip to South Texas: Richard Nixon was making a strong bid for the area's Democratic Mexican-American vote.

But what none of the stories mentioned was what a careful plan the President had worked out for wooing the Mexican-American vote. In the summer of 1971, the President gave his cabinet officers the word: begin naming Spanish-speaking Republicans to high positions in the administration. By election time there were no fewer than fifty Spanish-speaking civil servants, mostly Mexican-Americans, in top government positions. This was more than a new precedent; the Johnson administration had named only six Spanish-speaking office-holders and the Kennedy administration even fewer. And the White House had not failed to include a few Spanish-speaking officials among the President's "surrogate" campaigners, who took on George McGovern and the Democrats while the President stayed behind in Washington.

But the administration's "Chicano Strategy," as it came to be called, did not stop with appointments. The administration took advantage of the election year to pour an estimated $47 million into projects benefitting Spanish-speaking citizens, many of them funded on a one-year-only basis. At least $11.4 million went to projects which federal officials themselves conceded would not otherwise have qualified for funding and which would not be re-funded the next year. There were documents in the President's Cabinet Committee on Opportunities for Spanish-Speaking People (the administration's mouthpiece in dealing with the Spanish-speaking community), that directed more than $20 million to Texas and $17 million to California, these being the states with the heaviest concentration of Mexican-Americans.

In an election in which the incumbent often seemed to be opposed merely as a constitutional formality, one might ask why the President should be so concerned about the Mexican-American vote. But in mid-1971, when the administration unfolded its plan to woo the Chicanos, Mr. Nixon was anything but a cinch for reelection. That summer, beset by the Pentagon Papers, troubled by the continuing war in Southeast Asia and the failure of his economic policies, and threatened by the uproar over forced busing and a possible third-party bid by George Wallace, Nixon was neither a popular president nor a secure one. The Gallup and the Harris polls showed limited support for him, and political pundits were certain the country had entered an era of one-term presidents. By all indications, President Nixon would face another close election in 1972. And his record was winning one close race and losing another. Understandably, the election that had generated more second thoughts than any other for Mr. Nixon and his strategists was the 1960 contest. Several states could have gone the other way and given Mr. Nixon the Presidency eight years earlier. But the one state that he lost in both 1960 and 1968 — the state that offered the largest group of potential Nixon converts in 1972 — was Texas. In 1960, John F. Kennedy carried Texas by slightly more than 46,000 votes, but he won 85 percent of the Mexican-American vote. In 1968, Mr. Nixon, polling only 10 percent of the Mexican-American vote, lost Texas to Hubert H. Humphrey by fewer than 40,000 votes. GOP strategists figured that a shift as small as 5 percent in the Mexican-American votes would have carried the state's 26 electoral votes for the Republican ticket.

In another close election, the Mexican-American vote in Texas conceivably could become the balance of power. And President Nixon, constantly mindful of the minute, momentous gap between winning and losing, tried in 1972 to make certain that he had the balance of power of the Chicano vote.

It was election night 1972; President Nixon's reelection landslide had begun early, and already Democrats were dreaming of victory — next time — with Ted Kennedy. Mr. Nixon did not need the Mexican-American vote in Texas; he did not need Texas, for that matter. But as the early returns in statewide elections were aired on the three major networks, it became apparent that something strange was going on in

Texas. For generations, the state had gone Democratic, rearing such sons as Sam Rayburn, Lyndon Johnson, and John Connally. But Texas joined the Nixon landslide, even though it was one of the states where the Nixon coattails were least expected to be grabbed. The early results showed a Republican, State Senator Henry C. Grover, holding a slight edge over his Democratic opponent, millionaire Dolph Briscoe.

Grover was leading, but with only a plurality of the vote. It was obvious early in the evening that a third-party candidate, Ramsey Muñiz, was affecting the outcome. This young, articulate Mexican-American lawyer was running under the banner of La Raza Unida, itself a young, sometimes militant party that was the brainchild of the Chicano movement in the Southwest.

For the past several months, Muñiz had been crisscrossing the state, just like the other candidates. But unlike the other candidates, who were traveling with chartered jets and staffs to coordinate their campaigns, Muñiz needed small contributions even to drive his own car, with badly worn tires, from town to town; when he had to travel by air, he went alone in the coach cabin. Muñiz's campaign was disjointed. He met different faces at different stops, and often he didn't know who would meet him at his next destination or whether the speaking engagements had been set up. His crowds were always the same: mostly low-income Mexican-American men and women in the small South Texas towns, their aging faces wearing the problems of their past, along with some students and Chicano activists, and perhaps a handful of white-collar Mexican-Americans in the cities. He was the Chicano candidate in the race, to be sure, but it was harder to be certain how much of the Chicano constituency he represented.

One thing was certain, though: he was not like any other Chicano in major-league American politics. Muñiz was all at once pugnacious, fearless, compassionate, strong, antic, and driving. He was extraordinarily handsome—bronze complexion, longish sideburns, and straight, silky-looking brown hair—with one feature that was strikingly un-Chicano—captivating hazel eyes. A former football star who had given up a $12,000-a-year establishment position to run for governor, he had nothing but hope going for him—and the charisma that led a *New York Times* writer to describe him as a Chicano Robert Redford.

Muñiz ran on a liberal platform, calling for a corporate profits tax, decentralized regional governor's offices, upgrading of public education to equalize educational opportunity, and economic development of neglected areas of the state. All these measures were badly needed in Texas, but they were opposed by the same monied establishment that controlled Texas politics and the state government, the very people whom the Chicanos blamed for the plight of most of the state's 2.1 million Mexican-Americans. In addition, Muñiz was spouting rhetoric that for the first time in the history of Texas politics reflected the hopes and the frustrations of the masses of the disenfranchised Mexican-Americans in the state. In a speech at San Antonio, he told a crowd of several hundred in the city's westside *barrio:* "They've always told us about the American dream. We've had that American dream waved in front of our noses all our lives. But man, all we've had is a nightmare. I'm telling you that from now on, we're going to have that dream, and they're going to have the nightmare."

To an Austin crowd, he said: "We will determine the governor's race and any other race we enter down to the municipal level, and the presidential nominee who wants to carry Texas will have to deal directly with La Raza Unida. If the Chicano uses his voting strength wisely, he can determine who will sit in the White House from now until the country changes for the better or dies from its malignancy."

And to a group of Mexican-American students in El Paso, he said: "In our history books, we've had no one to relate to. You can relate to George Washington about as much as I can relate to the man on the moon. And when they talk about Columbus discovering America, they fail to point out that when he landed here, our ancestors were already here waiting for him. . . . All the things we're doing right now, we're not doing it for me. We're doing it for you. You are the future of our people. We're going to pave the streets for you, but you've got to help us and stay in school as long as you can. . . . Note that I didn't say one word about burning, marching, demonstrations, pickets, or boycotts. Those are reactions against an oppressive system. But the only way to correct the system is to become active in the process that determines and runs it."

This talk was heady stuff for the Chicano activists who had seen La Raza Unida organized as a regional party in South Texas only two years earlier but in 1972 made the party into the national political arm of the Chicano movement. La Raza Unida's Texas strategy was simple: to pull away from the Democrats enough traditional Democratic Mexican-American votes so as either to turn the tide for the Republicans as they hoped to do or to make the Democrats sweat a close victory. Except in a few liberal circles, however, the state's pols did not take La Raza Unida seriously. It was not until the final days of the campaign that Muñiz drew the attention of the other two candidates and of the media that had ignored him.

Finally, on election night, as the early returns showed a close gubernatorial race, the first stirrings of La Raza Unida's impact could be both felt and seen. Gradually, Briscoe was whittling away Grover's early lead until, late that night, the Democrat overtook him by a few percentage points and held on to win in the state's closest gubernatorial election since Reconstruction. But Muñiz held on to 6 percent of the vote, which otherwise undoubtedly would have gone Democratic, making Briscoe the first governor in seventy-eight years to be elected with less than a majority of the votes. Texas had a plurality governor, and La Raza Unida had made its impact.

It is particularly poignant that the Mexican-Americans entered the mainstream of American politics amid the hopes of the 1960s. There was a moment in the mid-1960s, when Lyndon Johnson had declared war on poverty and promised to banish it from the nation, when all the old problems on the American agenda—race and regionalism, poverty and public education, medical care and housing—seemed capable of resolution. The country was united. Blacks and whites joined hands and marched together. There were no riots, no rancor, no revolution, no dissenters. If this was not the Great Society President Johnson sought, at least it was a society offering hope and promise to the twenty-five million American poor, amid a growing affluence around them.

But by the end of the decade, the country was cleft in

two, more deeply divided than at any time since the Civil War. At home, there were riots and the beginnings of a revolution in the streets. Abroad, America was embroiled in the most unpopular war in her history.

Few groups were as patient as the seven million Mexican-Americans. If they ever felt that discrimination and injustice were unbearable, they needed only to look at the plight of the blacks, particularly in the South, to see that things could be worse. And if their hopes for a better life were ever stirred, the hopes climaxed in 1960 when, with cries of *"Viva Kennedy!"* the Mexican-Americans had rushed to support the presidential candidacy of John F. Kennedy, whom they felt partly responsible for electing. And when President Johnson pushed through the Congress civil rights and social legislation, aimed primarily at alleviating the plight of the blacks, the Mexican-Americans patiently awaited their turn in line, figuring that what would improve the lot of the blacks undoubtedly would also help the browns.

But the War on Poverty, much like the war in Vietnam, proved to be a disaster for the Johnson administration. While the ideal of eradicating poverty may be unattainable, the War on Poverty fell so short of the presidential rhetoric that ultimately the disillusionment of its supporters augmented the strength of its opponents. Outmaneuvered for the federal dollar by the blacks, the Chicanos turned their backs on the program and on a President whose first teaching job had been at a predominantly Mexican-American school in South Texas. Possibly if the Vietnam War had not drawn most of the nation's attention and protest, the Johnson domestic problems would have come under the scrutiny devoted to foreign affairs—to their profit.

So, amid the prosperity of the 1960s, the promise and hope aimed at the disenfranchised stirred their aspirations only to dash them down. Now there was an uncomfortable gap between what the Chicanos wanted and what they actually got. That gap amounted to classic conditions for revolution, in an era when revolutionary movements are unlikely to succeed. If the violence of the mid-1960s taught future revolutionaries anything, it was that violent revolution cannot succeed in urbanized America, where sophisticated communications and transportation systems can deliver national guard troops quickly and efficiently to take care of any disruption. The blacks and other new revolutionaries have had to take other routes, and gradually the Chicano revolt, too, has turned to politics. Through the political process, the Chicano movement is seeking to change the social and economic structure and ultimately to alter the political system itself.

In 1972 the different factions of the Chicano movement met for the first time for the lofty purpose of organizing a national political party—La Raza Unida. The immediate impact of such a party on American politics was questionable, but the symbolic message it was sending to America was indelible: if the 1960s had been the decade of the Black Revolution, then the 1970s would be the age of La Raza.

The Chicano movement actually came out of the mid-1960s when, in the wake of the black revolt and the new emphasis on social change, César Chávez launched a classic drive to organize the exploited farm workers in California. The Chávez movement became *la causa,* a controversial labor strike against the California table-grape growers that ultimately turned into a political issue. With organized labor lending support, the farm workers focused their attention on a consumer boycott that became the largest, most effective boycott in American labor history. In mid-1970, the Chávez forces finally won their grape victory. But this was only the first step in a movement to accomplish what had previously been impossible in the annals of American unionism: organizing the masses of farm workers in the country.

Even more significant, Chávez awakened the public consciousness, and he himself became a national figure and the hero of the country's Mexican-Americans, who themselves were aroused to support their cause. But the movement triggered in the California grapefields has taken on different guises, the most obvious of which is a militant stance like the black movement's. In California, the Brown Berets styled themselves after the Black Panthers; in Denver, Rodolfo (Corky) Gonzales began preaching a Chicano nationalism theme that has familiar rings of the old Black Power and Black Nationalism that dominated the rhetoric of the 1960s.

In northern New Mexico, militancy actually turned to violence in 1967, when Reies López Tijerina and his armed followers became involved in a shootout at the courthouse of the tiny town of Tierra Amarilla. Tijerina and the courthouse raid were immortalized within the movement; but the shoot-out, with all the charges and countercharges that arose from it, did not fulfill its goal of recovering the ancestral Spanish land grants.

In the 1970s the Chicano movement took its confronta-tion tactics out of the streets and into American politics. Evolving from the militant rhetoric of the Mexican-American Youth Organization (MAYO), La Raza Unida party was born in the South Texas town of Crystal City, where Mexican-Ameri-cans took over the schools and the city and immediately set about redirecting the priorities of the community. By 1974 La Raza Unida had become the cutting edge of the Chicano movement, with the forefront of the movement in Texas. The impact of La Raza Unida in its first statewide effort was greater than Texas politicians wanted to concede. The major effect was Ramsey Muñiz's role in making a close election even closer and eventually denying the winner a majority of the popular vote. But just as significant was the role the party played in writing the political obituary for former U.S. Sen-ator Ralph W. Yarborough, the onetime hero of the hetero-geneous liberal wing of the Texas Democratic party.

Along with Albert Gore of Tennessee, Yarborough was among the last of the old-time Southern populists to serve in the Senate and, like Gore, he became one of the "radic-lib" senators in 1970, at whom the Nixon administration planned to aim its mid-term campaign. Yarborough was an avowed liberal, the only statewide officeholder ever elected by Texas liberals; and he was anathema not only to the Nixon admin-istration but to the conservative wing, which, together with the Rayburn-Johnson-Connally regular Democrats, had con-trolled the state party for generations. But in 1957, Yarborough managed to edge past the moderate-conservative Democratic forces to win a special election to the U.S. Senate. He was reelected in 1958 and 1964, and eventually he became the voice of the state's liberals, Mexican-Americans, and blacks. In the Senate, Yarborough championed such causes as the 1966 minimum-wage expansion bill and the federal funding for bilingual education programs, but there was no break in the feud between him and the Connally forces within the state party. In fact, it was the disagreements within the Texas Democrats that forced President Kennedy to make his tragic trip to Texas in November 1963. Finally, the conservative-moderate forces won their struggle and in doing so, carried out the Nixon strategy of ridding the Senate of one senator with whom the administration had strong philosophical differences.

In the 1970 Democratic primary, Yarborough was beaten by a former South Texas congressman, Lloyd M. Bentsen, who had the support of the Democratic establishment, while Yarborough's liberal-Chicano-black coalition was disastrously splintered. Yarborough was hurt by a surprisingly low turnout among Mexican-American and black voters, the result of overconfidence and poor organization within his campaign. Also, some observers thought that La Raza was a factor in the low turnout—the party's organizers had urged Mexican-Americans to stay away from the polls.

By 1972, however, there could be no doubting the impact of La Raza Unida in defeating what liberals had hoped would be the resurrection of their champion. Yarborough, even at age sixty-eight, was a tireless campaigner with his eyes set on the senate seat held by the diminutive John G. Tower, who himself had won Lyndon Johnson's old senate seat in a special election in 1961 after Johnson became vice-president. Ironically, Tower himself won in 1961 and was re-elected in 1966 with the help of liberals who had deserted conservative Democratic candidates. In the back of their minds, liberals kept the possibility that someday a conservative Republican would be easier to defeat than a conservative Democrat. In 1972, the Texas liberals felt their time to strike had come, and Yarborough entered the Democratic primary against Dallas attorney Barefoot Sanders, a former White House aide to President Johnson who cultivated a Huckleberry Finn demeanor. Yarborough was counting heavily on the old liberal-labor-Chicano-black coalition that had elected him three times in the past and, with relaxed voter registration laws and the eighteen-year-old vote, he was figuring on an extremely heavy turnout in the primary.

At the same time, however, La Raza Unida was campaigning to get on the general election ballot. To do so, the party was required by the Texas election code to collect the notarized signatures of 22,358 eligible voters—2 percent of the votes cast in the previous gubernatorial election—who did not vote in either the Democratic or the Republican primaries. This was a long, tedious task, but the party eventually got voters who would have gone to the Democratic primary and, in all likelihood, would have voted for Yarborough. By late summer, La Raza Unida met the election code requirements and got on the ballot. In the process, Yarborough lost to Sanders in a runoff that probably ended his political career. In the primary, Yarborough came within a hair's breadth of winning the nomination, finishing just shy of a clear majority with 49.987 percent of the popular vote. He missed victory by 536 votes that conceivably could have come from any voter group. But this figure represents about 2 percent of the number of Chicanos who refused to vote and instead signed petitions to get La Raza Unida on the general election ballot.

Much like George Wallace, the Chicanos in 1972 sent the establishment a message of protest that went beyond politics. Their political disenfranchisement is only part of the overall plight of most of the country's millions of Mexican-Americans. Most of them live in the Southwest, and most of these are trapped in the *barrios* of the cities, where the years of discrimination and injustice have produced malnourished children, substandard housing, unpaved streets, outdoor privies, low wages, and high unemployment percentages. The end product is the great number of high school dropouts whose only promise is to continue the depressing cycle in which they live. Until the late 1960s, the Mexican-Americans' cries of injustice and discrimination at the hands of local law enforcement and education officials were usually dismissed. But in the early 1970s, the U.S. Commission on Civil Rights began releasing a series of reports documenting what the Chicanos had long known but officialdom had refused to acknowledge: that Mexican-Americans suffered discrimination in all phases of the administration of justice, from beatings by the Texas Rangers to elimination from grand juries; that Mexican-American students often were as segregated as blacks, received inferior schooling, and were denied the use of their mother language, even as a transition to English; and that the statistics on poor achievement by Mexican-American students were as bad, if not worse, than had been alleged.

Indeed, as Ted Kennedy put it, the Chicanos were "strangers in their own land." The Chicanos' ancestors were in the Southwest long before Plymouth Rock became a part of American history. The blending of the bloods of the Spanish conquistadores and the conquered Indians that created the present-day Mexican-American began in the early 1500s, a century before the settling of New England. Eventually, however, the Mexicans of the Southwest, much like the American Indians, became victims of another conquest, this time of the mid-nineteenth century U.S. philosophy of "manifest destiny," the taming of the West. A tragic war, which historians blame on the United States, resulted in Mexico's losing half her territory and signing a peace pact, the Treaty of Guadalupe Hidalgo, which the United States ignored through the years. Thousands of Mexicans resided in the territory won by the U.S., and although their rights were protected by the treaty, America's new "foreigners" soon found the new order exploiting and robbing them of their economic base, attempting to annihilate their culture and negating their mother tongue and identity. And more than a century later, Mexican-Americans were still facing the same troubles. In California, where the state constitution was penned in both English and Spanish and was signed by Spaniards and Anglos alike, there were documented reports of Mexican-American children being punished for speaking Spanish at school. In Texas, where Spanish settlers took a role in the revolt against Mexico and even died alongside the immortalized Anglo heroes at the Alamo, Mexican-Americans complained about harassment and beatings at the hands of law enforcement officials, particularly the Texas Rangers, themselves legendary in the state's history books.

As late as 1970, when the Census Bureau undertook the most extensive social and economic study ever made of Spanish-origin Americans, they found that these citizens earned only about 70 percent of the average American family's income, were more likely to be out of work, and had limited access to white-collar jobs. Only 25 percent of the men were in white-collar jobs, compared with 41 percent of men of all other origins, and the unemployment rate for the Spanish-origin worker was almost twice that for the remainder of the civilian population.

But until the Chicano movement began to awaken in the 1960s, the Mexican-Americans got little response when they protested their plight. Much as civil rights used to be construed as an issue for blacks and whites only, the "discovery" of hunger in America by Senators Robert F. Kennedy of New York, Joseph Clark of Pennsylvania, and George McGovern of South Dakota was thought to apply only to the blacks in the Deep South and the poor whites in Appalachia. The Chicanos had failed to arouse the feeling of guilt that the plight of the blacks had brought about. Because most of the Mexican-Americans lived in the Southwest, their problems were viewed by many in Washington and the East Coast, among whom support for the cause of the blacks had first blossomed, as a regional issue. The liberals failed to recognize that regional establishments existed in the Southwest, just like those in the South with a vested interest in keeping the blacks in their place. Finally César Chávez's farm labor movement opened the door for an outrage that had been pent up for years. In Chávez's footsteps came names like Tijerina, Corky Gonzales, and José Angel Gutiérrez, the founder of La Raza Unida party and among the brightest of all the leaders to emerge in the civil rights era.

In 1972 the Chicanos became a national concern. From being an almost forgotten minority group in the rash of school desegregation lawsuits, Mexican-Americans made themselves into an issue before the courts, where, in an affirmation of the obvious, the Chicanos were declared a "separate, identifiable minority." In the first part of the year, one among the growing number of skyjackers stood out—Ricardo Chavez-Ortiz, a Mexican national, who hijacked a jetliner from New Mexico to Los Angeles and then, as a condition for surrendering, went on television and radio to protest the mistreatment and injustices suffered by Mexican-Americans and other minorities in the country. But this was a presidential election year, and much of the new Chicano outrage had political overtones. The young Chicano activists rejected their own elected officials, heckled and shouted down even Ted Kennedy in front of a Mexican-American crowd in Los Angeles, and steadfastly refused to back the presidential candidacy of George McGovern, even though this crown prince of the "new politics" had opened up the Democratic party to

Mexican-Americans as never before and even though his shaky campaign promised to improve the lot of Mexican-Americans and the other downtrodden groups. But in a way that typified the drawbacks and mistakes in the campaign, McGovern, in spite of such pressing political issues as Watergate, ITT, and hidden GOP contributions, chose to single out La Raza Unida with an unsubstantiated charge of accepting $1 million from the Republicans in exchange for neutrality in the presidential race. The charge only alienated further an already alienated minority.

Meanwhile, the Republicans made an effort to attract and influence the Mexican-American vote in 1972, and by all indications they reaped some successes. The administration's appointments of Mexican-Americans and its pouring of funds into Spanish-speaking programs were only part of the strategy. Several documents coming from the Committee to Reelect the President hinted of a strategy to "sabotage" the non-GOP Mexican-American voters by influencing them either to support La Raza Unida or to stay away from the polls.

Obviously the Republicans could not expect to win over La Raza's radicals, but they wooed and won a group that can be described as Emerging Brown Middle America, the middle-class and upper-middle-class Mexican-Americans who have reaped the fruits of prosperity. Brown Middle America grew in numbers in the 1960s and the group continues to grow in the 1970s, as the first wave of Mexican-American college students has graduated and joined the ranks of Mexican-Americans who were already active in the business and professional worlds. Brown Middle Americans have moved into the suburbs, and like most everybody else in the new prosperity, they are more conservative than their parents, both economically and politically. They related well to the middle-class Mexican-Americans who were named to high positions in a Republican administration, and they felt threatened, too, by the "new politics" of the Democratic party. Thus, in their own way, the middle-class Mexican-Americans who broke their traditional Democratic ties to consider themselves "independents" if not Republicans, became a party to the Chicano revolt and, in their own right, part of the Chicano movement.

To say this, of course, is to point out that the Chicano

movement is deeply divided. La Raza Unida has divorced itself of its past ties to César Chávez, who represented the past links to the Democrats, and, likewise, the new Brown Middle Americans want nothing to do with the highly vocal young Chicanos, who can be irreverent as easily to brown authority as to white authority. Even within the cutting edge of the movement—La Raza Unida—there are divisions. The astute Chicano politicians who founded the party and slowly developed its power have to contend with Chicano nationalists, who seek a totally isolationary stance regardless of the political costs. The factionalization extends even to what the Mexican-Americans should call themselves. The young activists have cut through the hyphenated, multi-syllable clumsiness of such terms as "Spanish-speaking," "Spanish-American," "Spanish-surnamed," and "Mexican-American" and have taken on the name "Chicano" as a badge of identity. Older and middle-class Mexican-Americans shudder at the word, thinking it derogatory, even though they themselves can't agree on a single term.

Now that the Chicanos' moment on the stage has come, the country already bears the marks of tumult. It is an apocalyptic time, with Vietnam and its aftermath the fifth horseman whose trail threatens to overshadow and obscure the injustices and social problems at home. It is the fate of the Chicanos to revolt at a time when the old values are changing, when new forces are rising, when society and government are under severe challenge. It is their fate, too, to come forward when the cry for social justice no longer seems adequate to the moment. The Chicanos speak as American primitives, but they are leaving a legacy as American originals. They are both proud and profane, full of promise and imperfections. They have done more than their country realizes or appreciates, and they dream of accomplishing even more.

In that, the Chicanos, struggling to find their own identity and place in history, are like America herself.

2 CHICANO POLITICS: "REMEMBER THE ALAMO!"

The morning after the 1972 general election, his unsuccessful Texas gubernatorial bid already history, Ramsey Muñiz felt a compulsion to visit the Alamo, the old Spanish mission in the heart of San Antonio — the building that has come to symbolize Texas independence. It was at the Alamo in 1836 that the Mexican General Santa Anna massacred a small Texas force led by Davy Crockett and Jim Bowie and nearly wiped out the Texans' dream of independence. But several weeks after the massacre, Sam Houston regrouped the Texas army, and with Texans shouting the battle cry, "Remember the Alamo!" they defeated Santa Anna and the Mexican army of several thousand men.

Muñiz's visit to the Alamo the morning after the election had a symbolism of its own. As the gubernatorial candidate of the Chicano movement's La Raza Unida party, Muñiz had received slightly more than 6 percent of the state vote and had taken away enough traditional Democratic votes from Dolph Briscoe to make him the first plurality governor since the turn of the century. With Muñiz playing the "spoiler's" role, Republican State Senator Henry C. Grover had come agonizingly close to becoming Texas' first GOP governor since the 1870s.

Muñiz's strength, though it failed to siphon off enough Democratic votes to elect Grover, surprised most political observers in the state, who generally conceded that La Raza Unida had made an impact that could not easily be ignored.

"We said we would make a political impact and that we would be the balance of power in this state," Muñiz told a friend as they walked through the early morning dew on the manicured lawn of the Alamo grounds. "We've done that, but we've only started. You know, this is the first time I've ever come to this place. When I was growing up, I used to hear kids holler, 'Remember the Alamo! Remember the Alamo!' But it was always the white kids, never the Chicanos or the blacks. I look back now, and I understand. Those words have taken on a meaning of racial supremacy. They've continued to be a battle cry against the Mexican-American, but all that's over with. From now on, 'Remember the Alamo,' will be the political legacy of La Raza Unida."

Such has been the intoxicating rhetoric of La Raza Unida. Nowhere has the pitch of La Raza Unida movement reached the height it has in Texas. Muñiz led a ticket of five statewide candidates, about a dozen legislative candidates, and numerous candidates for county-level positions around the state. In terms of victories, however, La Raza Unida's success came only in South Texas, mainly in Zavala and LaSalle counties, where the party was already strong and where Mexican-Americans make up more than 90 percent of the population.

But it was against the overall political landscape of the state that La Raza Unida, despite its defeat in numbers, made its impact. In 1972, it became apparent that La Raza Unida was part of the broader movement away from the major parties. The Chicano political movement may exaggerate, but it certainly does not distort the mood of bitter disenchantment of American politics. A Gallup poll in early 1972 showed that 31 percent of the American electorate considered itself independent; in 1968, the figure was 27 percent; four years earlier, it was only 22 percent.

"We have to define what we mean by winning because there are ways of winning without actually getting your candidate elected," said Gutiérrez in sizing up his party's impact in

1972. "You can win by keeping someone from being elected, by being the balance of power and by making conditions exist to bring attention to the problem, no matter whether you're in the majority or in the smallest minority. The 'gringo' concept of winning only if you're elected excludes any voice by a minority."

Crucial to La Raza Unida's strategy in Texas was the idea of hurting the Democratic party enough to make it more responsive, or, better, of triggering a realignment of political powers in a state where Republican strength had been growing. In 1972 the rise of La Raza Unida, the growth of Republican power, and the Democrats' implication in a series of statehouse scandals all gave an indication that Texas politics was actually being realigned, although at a slower pace than La Raza Unida leaders wanted. During the home stretch of the campaign, the conservative Republican Grover told reporters that a strong Muñiz showing would have "considerable effect" on the state's two-party structure. "[La Raza Unida] will either become a permanent third party or may for a few years and then gradually be pulled into the Democratic party," he said. "The Democratic party [in Texas] would have to become more liberal to bring them in. And what's going to happen is that there won't be any room for conservative Democrats, and you'll find them coming over to the Republican party."

Whatever the impact, no party stands to lose as much as the Democrats, either by the defection of conservatives or by the loss of Chicano votes to La Raza Unida and the Republican party. The rise of La Raza Unida reflects the splintering going on within the old Roosevelt coalition that has been the backbone of the Democratic party. Mexican-Americans suddenly began to realize they had little to show for their long allegiance to the Democrats. Chicanos were discontented even with their own elected leadership. In October 1971, four Spanish-speaking congressmen and Senator Joseph M. Montoya of New Mexico sought to pull together a nationwide coalition of Spanish-speaking people to unify the different regions of the country and build up political strength for the 1972 election year. The congressmen expected 200 to show up for the Spanish-speaking political conference. But the crowd turned out to be closer to 2,000, and Senator Montoya and U.S. Representatives Edward R. Roybal, D-Calif., Manuel

Lujan, R-N.M., and Herman Badillo, D-N.Y., found themselves unwelcome at their own meeting: the grass-roots Chicanos and Puerto Ricans served notice they no longer could be
taken for granted by the Democrats.

The conference typified the new aggressiveness, to the
point of militancy, among the young Chicano activists. During
the U.S. senatorial campaign in California, Democrat John V.
Tunney was forced to flee from a campaign appearance in
Los Angeles when Chicano demonstrators, egged on by shouts
of "Get Tunney," surrounded him. Toward the end of his
campaign against Republican incumbent George Murphy,
Tunney, then a member of the House of Representatives,
appeared coatless to speak to a crowd of several hundred in a
parking lot. But he could hardly be heard as the demonstrators,
to the accompaniment of handclapping, kept chanting "Down
with Tunney" and "Chicano Power" and "*Raza, sí, Yanqui,
no.*" The disturbance forced Tunney to cut short his remarks,
and as he was leaving, he was surrounded by a crowd with one
of the Chicanos shouting into the microphone, "Get Tunney,
get Tunney!" A fight erupted, but Tunney and actor Henry
Fonda, who was campaigning with him, were whisked away,
even though Chicano youths jumped on the hood of the candidate's car and banged and kicked the sedan while the congressman was driven from the parking lot to a waiting heli-
copter several blocks away. Later, saying he felt his safety had
been "endangered" when he was jostled and heard the shouts,
Tunney said he was "convinced there is very little one can do
with them because they refuse to allow a dialog. . . . What it
demonstrates to me is that you've got this polarization in our
country, and you have a graphic example of radical anarchists
who despise 'our' institutions and who hate public officials
whom they consider to be symbols of our institutions."

And this wasn't a lone incident. In the 1972 presidential
campaign, only a week after La Raza Unida organized into a
national political party, a group of about two dozen Raza
Unida activists repeatedly heckled Senator Edward M.
Kennedy as he spoke to a predominantly Mexican-American
crowd of about 2,500 at a McGovern rally on the mall of East
Los Angeles College.

When Kennedy arrived at the college, he saw the group
of hecklers who were waving the flag of Mexico and hold-

ing up placards with such inscriptions as: "Kennedy and McGovern are carpetbaggers and political pimps," "What have we gained from the Democrats?" "Send the Irish back to Ireland," and "*Raza, sí*, Kennedy, no." Secret Service agents, sheriff's deputies, and campus police kept a watchful eye on the demonstrators, who later subjected California's senior U.S. senator, Alan Cranston, to the same treatment when he spoke briefly. But the shouting and heckling continued, and before beginning his speech, Kennedy, recognizing the apparent futility of halting the shouts, invited one of the activists to come up to the platform and talk to the crowd—which one of them did for nearly eight minutes. Kennedy himself introduced the Raza Unida representative, José Uribe, who spoke in Spanish; and as the crowd occasionally interrupted him with boos, Kennedy arose, stood behind Uribe, and motioned with his hands for the crowd to cut it out. Uribe told the audience that the only time politicians came to the Mexican-American community was when they wanted something and called those Mexican-Americans on the platform with Kennedy *vendidos*—sellouts. As Uribe left the platform, his group held up more signs; among them were two saying, "Ted Kennedy *fuera de mi tierra!*" ("Get out of my land!") and "Recall Kennedy and Rodino." (This was a reference to U.S. Representative Peter W. Rodino, Jr., a Democrat from New Jersey, chairman of the House immigration subcommittee, who had charged that illegal aliens were aggravating the national unemployment situation.)

Kennedy, who made no attempt to read from his prepared text, followed Uribe to the microphone, saying "we are a party made up of many different ideas and ideologies." But "Chicano Power" chants continued, and finally he asked with a smile: "Does La Raza believe in free speech?" The heckling still continued, but Kennedy ignored it and launched an extemporaneous speech praising the candidacy of George McGovern.

In his prepared speech, about the forgotten and broken promises of the Nixon administration, Kennedy decried the injustices against Mexican-Americans, including the killing two years earlier of *Los Angeles Times* columnist Ruben Salazar: "The cause of justice in America has not yet triumphed. It has not triumphed for Mexican-Americans. It has not triumphed for black Americans. It has not triumphed for poor Americans. So long as these Americans do not share equally in the benefits of law, the nation remains flawed, its promise unfulfilled. . . . When are the Republican administration and the White House going to start keeping those promises? I think that the people of La Raza demand an answer. When the oil companies want an answer, they come up to the White House and they get their answer. When corporate agriculture wants an answer, they make a telephone call and they get an answer. And when ITT wants an answer, they walk right in to the highest offices of this land, and they get their answer. I think twelve million Spanish-speaking Americans deserve an answer."

It is significant that the brother of President Kennedy and Robert Kennedy, both of whom had been revered and elevated to a kind of sainthood by Mexican-Americans, should be so harshly treated by even a small segment of that same minority group. For if anyone represented the unfulfilled hopes of the Chicanos during the past dozen years, it was the Kennedys, whose own tragedy had served only to magnify the despair and frustrations of the Chicanos and others who had attached their own aspirations to the promise the Kennedys extended.

But the heckling of Kennedy and La Raza's direct affront to Democratic leaders marks only one of the new directions in which the Mexican-Americans were heading. For decades the Mexican-American masses throughout the southwestern states were considered safely in the Democratic fold—just as they were in Texas. In California and Texas, Mexican-Americans have usually voted nine-to-one Democratic, with the Republicans making little effort to fight the Democrats for the Chicano vote. But despite their allegiance to the Democrats, the Mexican-Americans remain grossly underrepresented in the California Assembly, in the Texas Legislature, in Congress, on city councils and school boards, and, more amazingly, even in the city and county governments of the areas like South Texas where they compose 90 percent of the population. The only state that does not fit into this political pattern is New Mexico, with its unique political heritage in which Hispanos —as the Spanish-speaking in the state prefer to be called— have participated more fully in politics than the Spanish-speaking in any other state. Traditionally, the Hispanos have shared in the elective or appointive offices of New Mexico — usually there is one Spanish and one Anglo senator, with the governor and lieutenant-governor positions alternating between the two groups. New Mexico's Spanish-speaking population makes up nearly a third of the whole, and they were almost half of the state's population before New Mexico absorbed heavy immigration after World War II. And unlike the Mexican-American populations in the other southwestern states, most of New Mexico's Spanish-speaking are not recent immigrants from Mexico but instead descendants of the Spanish conquistadores and the Pueblo Indians.

But this is a sharp contrast to the politics of California, Texas, Colorado, and Arizona, where Mexican-Americans historically have been asked to vote the Democratic column but have received few observable gains. Finally change has begun. In the 1950s, the hopes and aspirations among Mexican-Americans that were stirred by military service in World War II began turning into frustration and dissatisfaction. In 1959, with a presidential election only a year away and finding themselves with little influence in Democratic politics, both nationally and in their home state of California, a couple of political activists — Bert Corona and Edward Quevedo — organized the Mexican-American Political Association (MAPA), which became the leading Mexican-American political group in the state and by the mid-1970s, claimed over sixty chapters. Although it later served as a group that sought out candidates, endorsed them, and offered voter education and registration assistance, MAPA's immediate impact in 1959 was as a catalyst for political activism. In Texas, Mexican-Americans in 1960 rallied behind the Viva Kennedy Clubs that were instrumental in giving John F. Kennedy a slim 46,000-vote victory and the state's twenty-five electoral votes. In the wake of the election, there came more political activism and new organizations. The Political Association of Spanish-Speaking Organizations (PASSO) grew out of the Viva Kennedy Clubs, with assistance from MAPA, the League of United Latin American Citizens, and other groups. In Arizona, the American Coordinating Council of Political Education (ACCPE) became the state's version of PASSO (which ultimately limited its activity to Texas).

The growth of these organizations coincided with the

election of Mexican-American leaders in the Southwest. In 1961, Henry B. Gonzalez won a special election and became Texas' first Mexican-American congressman. A year later, Los Angeles City Councilman Edward Roybal joined him in the House of Representatives. In 1964, Eligio (Kika) de la Garza made it three Mexican-Americans in the House, and Joseph Montoya was elected to the Senate. All of these men were Democrats, and in 1968 they were joined by a Republican, Manuel Lujan, who was elected by New Mexicans to the House.

The election of a Republican Mexican-American marked the beginning of the slow decline of the traditionally Democratic organizations such as PASSO and MAPA in their respective states. Sometime in the mid-1960s, amid a time of growing prosperity and the flood of Great Society social legislation, the thrust of the political activity triggered by MAPA and the Viva Kennedy Clubs lost its momentum. Perhaps, like other political activity at the time, these groups were neutralized by the consensus politics of President Johnson. And when the wave of protest exploded in the country, the traditional Mexican-American leadership was caught off guard. Much as the Vietnam protest was aimed at Lyndon Johnson, the accompanying rise of the Chicano movement took the established Mexican-American leadership as its target. This movement slowed down briefly in 1968 when, like many other protesters, a large segment of the Chicanos turned to one last glimmer of hope from the past: Robert Kennedy. In California, with César Chávez calling on the Mexican-American masses in the state to support his old friend, the Chicano vote assured the primary victory for Kennedy, who was gathering the momentum to stake a claim on the Democratic nomination.

Robert Kennedy's death, however, did as much as the unfulfilled promises of the past to foment the Chicanos' political revolt, both the rise of La Raza Unida among the young activists and the slow migration of middle-class Mexican-Americans to the Republican party. When John and Robert Kennedy died, more than one political pro has said, the Democratic party died for the Mexican-Americans.

In the late 1960s, Chicano activists throughout the Southwest began calling for an independent Chicano political party. Among the strongest advocates of political independence was

Rodolfo (Corky) Gonzales, the Denver activist who had parlayed a boxing career into an establishment position in local Democratic politics and then had thrown that back at the establishment and returned to *barrio* activism. Gonzales centered his movement around the Crusade for Justice, a Denver-based multi-service center, from which he organized the 1969 Chicano Youth Liberation Conference, itself a turning point in the history of the movement.

It was not until 1970, however, that the idea of an independent political party crystallized when José Angel Gutiérrez, a young doctoral candidate in political science at the University of Texas, founded La Raza Unida to capture control of Crystal City, his hometown, a dusty agricultural community of about 8,000 persons, almost all of them Mexican-American, situated in South Texas, 125 miles southwest of San Antonio. Within two years, La Raza Unida controlled all of Crystal City and much of the county government, making the town the Chicano political capital of the Southwest. La Raza evolved into a movement that whetted the appetites of other Chicanos, and by 1972 the organization was a statewide party in Texas, moving into national prominence. Here was a new, widespread Chicano political movement that was also a break with both the traditional Democratic ties of the past and the party's "new politics" of the future.

Short on finances, know-how, and organization, La Raza Unida was born more as a political protest than a political party. In Texas in 1972, Lyndon Johnson was in retirement on his ranch, John Connally had bolted the reformed Democratic party to announce his support for President Nixon's reelection, and a statehouse stock fraud scandal hung like an albatross around the necks of Texas Democrats. The rise of La Raza Unida was part of the electorate's disenchantment, in Texas and throughout the country. Liberals in the state looked to State Representative Frances (Sissy) Farenthold, who quickly emerged as one of the most prominent women in American politics.

Sissy Farenthold epitomized the changing times. A two-term legislator from Corpus Christi on the Gulf of Mexico, she had been a member of the "Dirty Thirty," a group of reform-minded legislators who sought to make state officials accountable for their roles in the state scandal involving legislation passed in exchange for quick-profit stock deals. With the odds heavily against her, she announced her gubernatorial candidacy and launched a crusading, often strident, campaign in which she supported a state corporate profits tax, regulation of utilities, abolition of the Texas Rangers, and reformation of the board of regents governing the University of Texas—all issues strongly opposed by the Texas monied establishment. With much of the McGovern coalition building up in the state behind her candidacy, and with support from such names as television actress Marlo Thomas, writer Gloria Steinem, and former U.S. Attorney General Ramsey Clark, Sissy became the giant-killer in Texas politics. In the Democratic primary she outpolled everyone except wealthy rancher Dolph Briscoe, upsetting the bid of Lieutenant Governor Ben Barnes, the golden-haired boy wonder of Texas politics who ran with the support of the old Democratic establishment—Lyndon Johnson had predicted a promising future for him in national politics. The runoff between Briscoe and Farenthold was anti-climactic; Sissy's effort was buried by the establishment machinery which united en masse behind Briscoe. But Farenthold was a symbol not only of reform but also of the whole gamut of women's rights issues. At the Democratic National Convention, she was nominated for the vice-presidency in opposition to Senator Thomas Eagleton, the personal choice of George McGovern, whom Farenthold had supported long before he was considered a serious contender for the presidential nomination. Sissy's role continued growing, and in early 1973 she was selected to head the Women's National Political Caucus.

To La Raza Unida, however, Sissy was anathema, and by all indications this was a mutual feeling, with both sides embittered by the failure of each to support the other. La Raza Unida's drive for a place on the ballot contributed to Ralph Yarborough's runoff loss to Barefoot Sanders, and some Farenthold strategists felt La Raza Unida also played a role in Sissy's defeat. Actually, La Raza Unida's 25,000 registered voters who did take part in the primary could not have changed the outcome, but Farenthold strategists argued that the young Chicanos could have provided invaluable manpower assistance and perhaps even have wooed the Mexican-American vote that went to Briscoe.

La Raza Unida activists shook their heads, and in the general election they tried to swing the liberal-Farenthold camp behind Ramsey Muñiz's campaign. Their argument was clear: how could Farenthold turn her back on a candidate whose platform was almost identical to her own and support an establishment candidate whom she herself had described as a "bowl of pabulum"? Although Muñiz received some support from Farenthold backers, Sissy refused to back La Raza Unida and, perhaps with her own political future in mind, worked for the entire Democratic party slate. And just as Farenthold supporters had been angered by La Raza Unida, the young Chicanos, with some justification, pointed an accusing finger at Sissy and white liberals who they said had confirmed their worst suspicion—that while the liberals expected, even demanded, the state's Mexican-Americans to support their candidates and causes, they were not necessarily prepared to back the Chicanos and la causa.

But even without Farenthold's support, Muñiz drew more than 200,000 votes—6.3 percent of the vote—while the difference between the Democratic and Republican candidates, Briscoe and Grover, was fewer than 100,000 votes in an election that drew 3.4 million Texans to the polls. The impact of La Raza Unida, however, went beyond the 200,000 votes that stripped the Democratic candidate of a majority mandate. The party's influence went to the heart of Texas politics, which for the last generation has had a strong influence on national affairs. It's certain that any major change in the politics of the state will have a significant impact in American politics, particularly since, in the aftermath of 1972, both the Republicans and Democrats chose Texans to head the parties' national committees.

While traditionally a Democratic state, Texas in recent years has grown more and more Republican although the GOP leaders move their party ahead at a snail-like pace. Although the GOP has failed to launch any major assault on legislative seats or on some of the higher state offices, there are statistics showing a slow but steady Republican trend, as conservative political analyst Kevin Phillips, author of *The Making of a New Majority*, predicted there would be in the late 1960s. In 1960, Kennedy carried the state with only a 46,000-vote margin, even with Lyndon Johnson on the ticket. Eight years later, a last-minute boost to Hubert Humphrey's campaign from John Connally barely beat out Richard Nixon, who in 1972 had no more trouble winning Texas than any other state. Further evidence of growing GOP clout is John G. Tower, one of the most conservative men in Congress, who is well entrenched in one of the state's U.S. senate seats. Surely it is significant that in 1972 Tower defeated Barefoot Sanders, a former presidential aide to Lyndon Johnson who ran with the full support of the Democratic establishment. In 1970, the Republicans came within 200,000 votes of unseating an incumbent Democratic governor, and in 1972 that difference was cut in half. Such tidings have panicked old-style Texas Democrats, desperately trying to keep their party in the mainstream of this conservative state. Their nightmare: a Texas where being a Democrat is somehow disreputable, not only in the country clubs and executive suites of Dallas and Houston but also in small-town cafes and churches. That nightmare recurred even more frequently with the uncertain political role of former Democratic Governor John B. Connally. In 1973, the same Texas Republican leaders who in 1970 cursed the alliance between President Nixon and their ancient foe were hoping for Connally's conversion to Republicanism and a Connally drive for the presidency in 1976. To them, Connally as Mr. Republican in Texas might suddenly uplift the party to majority status, and that could mean widespread Republican victories even in the Texas Legislature, already changing in party affiliation because of single-member legislative districts in the cities.

The independent Raza Unida makes the emergence of a strong, viable two-party system in the state an even greater possibility. Either way the state swings, there is sure to be an impact nationally, making La Raza Unida a double-edged threat. If the Chicano activists continue to withhold their support from the Democrats, there will be one more Republican state to go on splintering the old Democratic coalition; if the Chicanos are wooed back into the Democratic fold, the concessions they win will move the predominantly conservative Texas party a great deal closer to the moderate-liberal posture of the national Democratic structure. And in a close presidential race, La Raza Unida, which is considering a national ticket of its own in 1976, possibly could play just such a balance-of-power game and play in Texas, and possibly California, a Chicano version of the 1968 George Wallace strategy.

The concessions to the Chicano activists would have to be what the Chicano movement has been calling for since the late 1960s: a greater role in the political system and comprehensive, well-funded educational and economic programs for Texas' 2.1 million Mexican-Americans, almost a fifth of the state's population. But the Mexican-Americans, by and large, are in conflict with the state's establishment leaders, whose businesses depend on cheap labor and freedom from the burdens of a corporate profits tax, which would be essential to finance the costs of educational, training, health, and medical programs sought by the Chicanos.

These were the issues on which Ramsey Muñiz launched his quixotic campaign for the governorship. Early in the year, after Muñiz resigned his administrative position with the Model Cities program in Waco, La Raza Unida appeared to have little chance of making more than a token effort statewide. The party was not yet well established in the portions of South Texas that had been designated target areas; there was no money or organization outside a few South Texas counties; the Republicans already were making overtures to the Mexican-American vote; more than a dozen established Mexican-American leaders had turned down the offer to carry La Raza's mantle; and the party faced a major task in even getting on the general election ballot. It was only at the end of a fruitless hunt for a gubernatorial candidate that the party leaders turned to Muñiz, who wasted little time in accepting the offer.

Muñiz's campaign wound up surprising even the state leaders of La Raza Unida, who had privately set the modest goal of 70,000 votes for governor—roughly the number of votes required by state law to assure the party of a place on the statewide ballot for the next general election. The party leaders neither expected nor particularly wanted a full-time gubernatorial candidate, but that is what they got in Muñiz, the product of a poverty-ridden family from Corpus Christi, Texas, who seemed to thrive on uphill struggles. As a youngster, he had a speech impediment—a pronounced stutter—that went unrecognized and untreated until he was in junior high school. His father, a mechanic, had a fifth-grade education; his mother made it through the sixth grade. Muñiz spoke only Spanish until he began school, and even then he spoke English only while in class. The cornerstone of Muñiz's struggle out of poverty was athletics, long the great equalizer for both Chicanos and blacks. In 1960 Muñiz was a captain of the Corpus Christi Miller High football team that won the state championship, and that victory inevitably led to a football scholarship to Baylor University in Waco. Despite being plagued by a series of knee injuries that required several operations, Muñiz lettered three seasons on the Baylor varsity. Later, when both high school and college coaches recalled Muñiz as an athlete, they dwelled on his dedication and determination. In his senior year, he recovered from an early-season knee operation in six weeks and finished the year as a starter; the normal recovery time for such an operation is an entire season. In the mid-1960s, Muñiz entered law school, and there he began the metamorphosis that turned him on to the movement.

"When I was an athlete, a starter, a letterman, everything was going fine," he later recalled. "I was accepted for the most part. People I didn't know came up and said, 'Hi, Ramsey,' and started talking to me. But the year I entered law school, I wasn't an athlete any longer, and the doors that had once been opened were closed. When other students talked to me, I wanted to talk about the law and politics. They wanted to talk about Mexican food and Mexican whorehouses in the border towns. Before I entered law school, I was accepted as an athlete, and it would have been easy for me to assimilate to the point that I could lose sight of my past. But, man, I soon learned you can't be an Anglo when you're not. It's not that I lost my identity, but I was abruptly awakened to it when I started looking around and seeing that the rest of my people weren't getting the same opportunities I had. Man, our people are hurtin' bad, real bad."

In his campaign, Muñiz stirred up Texas politics so much that even his own party leaders, whose popularity and leadership he rivaled, eventually came to fear him. He was unlike any other Mexican-American candidate Texas had seen. Often campaigning alone, Muñiz took his bid throughout Texas, claiming to have gone into small towns in South Texas never before visited by a politician. His rallies often became

Mexican fiestas, with tacos and tamales sold to raise money and with the crowds usually going into frenzied applause and cheers: *"Viva Ramsey! Viva La Raza!"* He drew more reaction from Mexican-Americans in Texas than any other Chicano movement leader—and that apparently did not set well with some Chicano leaders—and he developed his own faithful both within and outside La Raza Unida.

Muñiz sought to build a populist coalition of Chicanos, blacks, liberals, students, and intellectuals—the kind of grouping that has been called a "new majority." Muñiz distributed his campaign literature in the black ghettos of Texas cities, describing the party as a broad-based organization and calling it "The United People's Party" in an attempt to reduce the nationalistic tones that La Raza Unida seemed to conjure in some quarters. He made a personal appeal to the leaders of the Southern Christian Leadership Conference, holding its 1972 national convention in Dallas, and he received a public endorsement from none other than SCLC President Ralph David Abernathy, who said of Muñiz: "He's not black, but he's almost black. He's brown." Muñiz also received the endorsements of several black activists, including a black Democratic legislative candidate from Houston who went on to win election to the Texas House of Representatives. Running on what was basically a liberal Democratic platform, Muñiz also drew the support of college students; and in the home stretch of the campaign, the student body presidents of a dozen universities and colleges in the state, including the University of Texas, publicly endorsed Muñiz, whose campaign was helped by the liberals' disenchantment with Dolph Briscoe. Considered a moderate-to-conservative Democrat, Briscoe was a lifeless campaigner with a reputation for vacillating. He had performed poorly at the Democratic National Convention where in the span of a few minutes, he switched his support from Senator Henry C. Jackson to Governor George Wallace to Senator George McGovern. In August, a month after the convention, the *Texas Observer,* an influential bi-weekly, described Muñiz as "a long-long-odds candidate, not a hopeless splinter candidate."

Muñiz's campaign became without doubt the most lively focal point in the gubernatorial race. His appeal was emotional, calling on the public's sense of justice. Often when he spoke he mixed that appeal with wry asides in Spanish and a heavy sprinkling of "hells" and "damns" that made for stunningly funny results. Often, too, there was a muttered dig at the establishment. Briscoe, a wealthy cattle rancher, became known as *la vaca* (the cow) in Muñiz's diatribes: "The only difference between *la vaca* and Hank Grover is that *la vaca* wears glasses." Occasionally, Muñiz did an imitation of a Texas-Anglo accent that came off as a drawl-twang with Spanish rhythm. Before an appearance on a Texas version of "Meet the Press," Muñiz boned up on the issues and spent long hours preparing, only to recount later in a tone of disgusted amusement: "All they asked me was if I was serious. If I really thought I was qualified. Compared to Briscoe and Grover?"

Muñiz's driving campaign was in stark contrast to his two major opponents'. Briscoe sidestepped the issues and refused to appear on television interview programs with other candidates. Meanwhile, Grover, whose strength was vastly underrated by most political observers, was generally seen as a right-wing extremist who throughout most of the campaign was at odds with other segments of the Republican party. But it was not until the final weeks of the campaign that Muñiz finally began drawing the serious attention of the candidates and the media, which in Texas is mostly an adjunct to the conservative establishment. In El Paso, Muñiz publicly challenged Grover to a debate. But Grover walked away and hurriedly cancelled a speaking engagement at the University of Texas at El Paso, where this confrontation took place. Two days later in Houston, Muñiz again shook up the political scene when he issued an unsubstantiated charge that Briscoe had undergone electric shock therapy for "severe depression" twice during the previous eighteen months. There were rumors earlier in the campaign, but these had gone unconfirmed, despite extensive research by several investigative reporters. Coming only days before the election, Muñiz's baseless charge had an uncertain effect on the campaign, although it tainted his image as a crusading Chicano knight and perhaps created a sympathy backlash in Briscoe's favor.

But even late in the campaign, many people regarded Muñiz as a splinter candidate, the Chicano candidate, the radical candidate. In reality, Muñiz was more a hard-line liberal whose own experience with poverty and discrimination gave him a measure of princely contempt for some of his Chicano activists who might have been more concerned with Chicano power than with basic issues like health and medical care. "When I was a freshman at Baylor," Muñiz recalled in one interview, remembering a sad time in his life, "they finally called me home. My mother had not wanted to tell me. She wanted me to continue my education. So I didn't know it was that serious until I got home. She didn't get adequate medical care. We didn't have the money to provide the type of medical care she needed. When I got home, I tried to get her admitted to a hospital and at first they wouldn't let her in because we didn't have enough money. They finally let her into a ward, something, where they had thirteen beds in a room. I know, it was called the county ward. We had to place her in the county ward. It was just too late. If it had been now, something could have been done. I don't think they had the programs then for poor people. This was '63 we're talking about, and the OEO didn't come in until '64. Even if they did have programs to help then, we didn't know it. We never talked about welfare in our house. My father sold everything we had. He sold the house, the car, everything. When she died, we had nothing."

Hilda Muñiz died of cancer, without medical care until the final two weeks of her life, but her plight was all too typical of the health problems in the Mexican-American *barrios* in Texas and the Southwest. For the Chicanos, medical care cannot be considered apart from the crushing numbness of the *barrio* life, where racism in the form of malnutrition and poor prenatal care takes its toll early. Health statistics for the Southwest show that brown fetuses are aborted or born dead more often than white ones; more of them are thrust forth prematurely, at higher risk of damage to the delicate mechanisms of the brain. Once the child is born, malnutrition, infection, and inadequate health care exact their price in stunting of ultimate stature and in maldevelopment of the central nervous system. Before a small child learns he is Mexican-American, he has experienced what it is to be Mexican-American. He is two and a half times more likely than other American children to live in dilapidated housing units and three times more likely to be grossly overcrowded than whites who pay the same rent. Since his parents have had less education, his home fewer books, his community fewer educational opportunities, and his parents less know-how in preparing him for school, the Mexican-American child's development quotient, which at one year was indistinguishable from that of his Anglo counterpart, will have fallen well behind by the time he is three, and still farther behind when he starts bravely off to school at six.

It is a cycle of deprivation that begins with the lack of proper health care during pregnancy. Nutritional surveys have found alarming rates of malnutrition in some poverty areas, with a grim chain of ill-nourished mothers giving birth to ill-nourished children with a high risk of mental retardation. Babies inadequately nourished in the womb and ill-fed after birth are likely to have impaired behavior and learning ability. An infant's brain attains 80 percent of the adult weight by the time he is three, when the body weight is only about 20 percent of that at maturity.

The devastating impact of poor nutrition on Mexican-American children was strikingly documented in the ten-state National Nutrition Survey ordered by Congress in 1967, but the report was not released until 1971 after the Nixon administration was accused by Senate critics of suppressing it because it identified fifteen million malnourished Americans, an increase of five million over earlier estimates. In Texas, the survey found a 30 percent retardation among Mexican-American children between infancy and six years of age, meaning that children who were five years old actually had the skeletal maturation of only 3.9 years. "Growth retardation among the poor in the United States," U.S. Senator Ernest Hollings of South Carolina said on the Senate floor, "is little different from that of problem areas in Africa, Asia, and Latin America. . . . The survey has proof of growth retardation, with the highest concentrations among Mexican-American children in Texas."

The plight of a large segment of Mexican-Americans in Texas left no question of the wealth of issues, particularly the Chicano civil rights issues, at Muñiz's fingertips during the campaign, but there could equally be no question of the poor political organization supporting him. Outside the few South Texas counties where La Raza Unida first blossomed to power, the party could realistically count on few communities where Chicano activists had formed any type of useful political structure. In most cities and towns outside South Texas, La Raza Unida's party workers quickly surfaced whenever Muñiz showed up to campaign, but they just as quickly faded away when he departed. Often all that was accomplished was a well-attended side-show performance that left Muñiz badly miscalculating his own strength. At one point early in his campaign, he figured that 200,000 votes, plus a place on the general election ballot, would be moral victories; by the end of the campaign, his confidence bolstered by the crowds he was drawing, Muñiz tripled the number of votes he expected to get. In most instances, though, the numbers in the crowds were not representative of his supporters; instead, they constituted just about all of his strength in that locale. Short on political experience, La Raza Unida party workers often did nothing more than work with other supporters, completely neglecting the long, tedious work involved in building a local organization—the conversion of sympathizers into supporters, supporters into workers, and workers into astute politicians concerned with broadening the base of the party.

Despite the potential of drawing blacks, disenchanted liberals, and a large section of the Mexican-American vote, La Raza Unida managed to barely touch a cross-section of those groups. The final election results showed Briscoe with 1,633,493 votes, or 47.9 percent of the vote; Grover with 1,533,986 votes, 45 percent; and Muñiz with 214,118 votes, 6.28 percent and approximately ten times the votes drawn by the Socialist Workers candidate. Within La Raza Unida's circles came the realization that its campaign, while long on rhetoric, had been short on efforts to crystallize the potential support in the black communities, in the liberal camp, and among middle-class Mexican-Americans—voter groups whose disenchantment conceivably could have been better tapped with the work of a coordinated political organization behind Muñiz's campaign.

As limited as they were, the results were an unexpected jolt to most political observers, who gave La Raza Unida little chance of making significant impact and who were keenly aware of the great obstacles that confront all third-party movements. Muñiz's 200,000 votes only underscored the Mexican-

Americans' frustration with the Democratic party. In addition, the impact of Muñiz's campaign along with the birth of La Raza Unida took the young Chicanos out of the cocoon of Chicano politics and into the real world — American politics — where compromise and backroom deals often are the only ways through tight passages and where right does not necessarily carry might.

In Texas, the Chicanos did what the Spanish-speaking people in other parts of the Southwest have failed to accomplish. César Chávez has not dared challenge the California political establishment as he has the state's powerful growers. Reies López Tijerina tried such a challenge without success in New Mexico. In Colorado, a third-party movement led by Corky Gonzales has been underway for several years but has yet to make a significant impact. La Raza Unida has become a special concern in Texas because the defection of a large segment of the state's largest minority group from the main struggle for control of Texas threatens to leave the liberal coalition at the mercy of the conservative establishment and the emerging Republican party. In the future, there is reason for concern over the rise of La Raza Unida in California, where the Mexican-American community has been systematically short-changed over the years. They lose every legislative reapportionment battle, even those controlled by their erstwhile friends in the Democratic party. They watch as the major funding of social programs pours into the black community, and it is this that caused Martin Castillo, a Los Angeles attorney, to abandon the Democrats for Nixon's campaign in 1968 and later to become the Nixon administration's leading Chicano for a period.

La Raza Unida is a culmination of the political activism among Mexican-Americans that began taking shape in the late 1950s. Those early activists sought political recognition and independence, and the ultimate end, short of a violent assault on the political system, could only be an independent party. Though perhaps not entirely representative of the country's Mexican-Americans, La Raza Unida reflects their hopes and their despair. Outside the traditional political system, La Raza Unida leaders are free to criticize, harass, condemn, ridicule, and curse the political establishment without the fear of ostracism that a Democrat or Republican would face if he were to paint as candidly the bleak picture of the Chicanos' past and to seek radical change as aggressively. José Angel Gutiérrez has accused the "gringo" of having "divided us, raped us, robbed us, repressed us," but the advent of La Raza Unida is a turning of the tables.

By all indications, the Chicanoizing of American politics has only begun, and the continuing problems of discrimination, inequality, and injustice in the *barrios* of the Southwest are surely portents of further activism. As with other problems facing urban America today, nobody knows where the next ten years will lead the Mexican-Americans, to say nothing of the longer perspective. Certainly no one should imagine that there will soon emerge the dream of the Chicanos — large-scale programs aimed at embracing and correcting the problems that have developed over more than a century. But neither is the future likely to be characterized by the present social, political, economic, and legal forces that have oppressed much of the Mexican-American population. The only sure thing is that there will be cracks in the system. These augur even more of the eternal pulling down and rebuilding that has been the recurrent feature of the American political system.

3 LA RAZA AND AMERICAN JUSTICE

In the late summer of 1972, just two months before the nation opted for "four more years," the Chicano leaders came together in El Paso to organize La Raza Unida into a national political party and to determine its future. But life is more crucial than politics, and the first official utterance concerned the fatal shooting of a Colorado party leader, slain by an Anglo under highly questionable circumstances while en route to the convention.

Ricardo Falcon, a twenty-seven-year-old activist from Fort Lupton, Colorado, became the Raza Unida party's first martyr, and his death triggered a wave of new protests in the Southwest. Falcon's name joined the litany of fallen Chicanos evoked by other young activists and by politicians such as Senator Edward Kennedy. In an era when law and order are a national concern, Falcon's death and the law's handling of his case served only to confirm the bleak picture of inequality and unfair treatment of Mexican-Americans by institutions responsible for the administration of justice. The Raza Unida leaders described Falcon's death as a "wanton, racist murder . . . another dark day in the history of white America" and sent telegrams to numerous federal officials, including President Nixon, asking for a federal investigation. Democratic presidential nominee George S. McGovern also asked for an investigation and termed the killing an "act of insanity," although he later retracted those words after La Raza Unida refused to endorse his candidacy.

If Falcon had been Anglo, the killing would have generated little interest. But Falcon's death, in conservative southern New Mexico at the time of La Raza Unida's national convention, took on racial overtones.

According to authorities who investigated the killing, Falcon was shot twice during an argument with a service station owner in Orogrande, New Mexico, a village of about seventy people some thirty-five miles south of Alamogordo, where Falcon's car overheated and was forced off the highway. While having the car serviced, Falcon and the station owner, Perry Brunson, got involved in an argument that led to a fight, and Brunson pulled a weapon and fired. Later Brunson was charged with manslaughter and released on his own recognizance — which infuriated the Chicanos, who felt both the charge and the failure to require bail had been unjust.

"No Chicano, black, or minority group person in [New Mexico] or in any other state in the Southwest arrested on these kind of charges could have walked out of jail on his own personal recognizance," Corky Gonzales, the head of the Crusade for Justice in Denver, told a press conference the first day of the convention in El Paso. On the same day, Priscilla Falcon told newsmen that she and a handful of Colorado Chicanos had returned to the Orogrande-Alamogordo area to check on the progress of the investigation but had been repeatedly rebuffed by "discourteous, insensitive and unfeeling" officials there.

Falcon was one of La Raza Unida's most active organizers in Colorado, where he had a long career of social and political activism. At one time an official of the United Mexican-American Student (UMAS) organization at the University of Colorado in Boulder, he was deeply involved in recruiting Mexican-American students for the school and was responsible also for several demonstrations and marches on the administration building. Falcon was considered a militant and radical by the university's president, Frederick Thieme, and he was finally expelled and forbidden by a restraining order from setting foot on any property owned by the university. Falcon was to have been a Raza Unida Colorado legislative candidate in the 1972 November election, but it is likely that his tragic death made a much more significant impact than his candidacy would have done. In Denver, the Chicanos held several rallies and a protest march to the statehouse to honor Falcon and to display the Chicano discontent. Several young supporters carried his body, in a plain brown casket, for miles in a funeral procession that drew more than 1,000 people representing every major Mexican-American organization in the Southwest.

An Otero County grand jury indicted Brunson on a manslaughter charge, and when his trial began in December, about fifty Chicanos marched the thirty-five miles from the scene of Falcon's death in Orogrande to a courthouse in Alamogordo where the trial was to be held. Outside the courtroom the number of Chicano activists quickly multiplied, and most of them never did get seats. On December 7, three days after the trial began, Brunson, who had pleaded self-defense, was acquitted. The decision left the Chicanos even more embittered and frustrated than they were before.

"The decision of the district court in Alamogordo was not one which could be called due process, but rather it was a whitewash," said Juan José Pena, the New Mexico state chairman of La Raza Unida, after the acquittal. "It would seem that the jury took no note of the testimony which was given by the witnesses who saw Falcon shot. How can it be self-defense when [the man] who was shot was unarmed and in a strange territory? If the gun had not been produced [by Brunson], it is more than likely that the whole affair would have been no more than an altercation. On that basis, it was Ricardo Falcon who was defending his life, not Perry Brunson. We of the *partido* de La Raza Unida cannot but sympathize with the frustrations of our brothers from Colorado for the shameful way in which a part of our state treated those guests who had come so far only to see justice miscarried."

At the same time that La Raza Unida was organizing into a national party, a group of Mexican-American attorneys and law enforcement and court officials met in Phoenix at the first National Conference on the Administration of Justice and the Mexican-American, and they established the Chicano Institute of Law and Justice. As its first "watchdog" case, the institute selected the Falcon shooting and undertook its own investigation of the case. Even more significant, for the first time a group of middle-class Mexican-Americans was serving notice on the American legal and judicial systems to change their ways.

"The country had better shape up or the Chicano will find ways to make changes in the lily-white system of justice," said José H. Rojo, deputy director of the Houston Legal Foundation and one of the driving forces behind the institute, at the three-day Phoenix conference of 300 Mexican-Americans from throughout the Southwest.

The warning was a long time in coming. The Falcon case is only a recent incident in a long history of discrimination and injustice for Mexican-Americans at the hands of American justice. The history begins with the entry of Anglo-Americans into the Southwest, and it proceeds through more than a century of racial hostility. The plight of the Mexican-American is living proof of Anglo conquest of the area, even though the Spanish heritage there is older than the American union.

Until 1821, when Mexico gained its independence, what is now the American Southwest was part of a Spanish colony with Spanish culture. As early as 1538, the Spanish set up a printing press in Mexico City; by 1551, there was a university in Mexico City; and by 1609, the Spanish had left a series of missions along the California coast, established Santa Fe, and ranged as far north as Kansas. But there was little cohesion among the Spanish colonies in North America, where royal power was represented by the Viceroy in Mexico City. In contrast to the British, who usually emigrated as families, or even as communities, the Spaniards seldom brought wives or families to the New World and instead married Indian women, creating a fusion of races known as the *mestizo,* the ethnic wellspring of the Mexican-American.

Not until the early nineteenth century, and then only in Texas, did immigrants from the United States come to the territory under Mexican sovereignty. The newly independent Mexican government offered grants of farm and grazing land to encourage American settlers. Yet by 1834, the English-speaking population of Texas probably did not exceed 18,000.

When the first Anglo-Americans arrived in the Southwest, the Mexicans taught them to survive in the desert, to irrigate and cultivate the land, to raise cattle, to use the horse, the lariat, and the western saddle. They learned a new vocabulary—bronco, stampede, arroyo, mesa, savvy, cowboy—and acquired an architecture suited to the climate and the land.

Ironically, it was the immigration the Mexicans encouraged that was their undoing. As the American population grew, so did problems between the Mexican and American governments. When a new Mexican constitution in 1835 swept away many local rights, the Americans joined some Mexicans in revolting and proclaiming the Republic of Texas. In 1845, Texas became the twenty-eighth state of the United States, and forces started in motion that ultimately led to war between Mexico and the U.S. Hostilities ended after the Americans occupied Mexico City in 1847, and the Treaty of Guadalupe Hidalgo was signed in 1848. Except for the territory later acquired through the Gadsden Purchase of 1853, all Mexican territory north of the Rio Grande, which embraced all or parts of the present states of California, Texas, New Mexico, Arizona, Colorado, Utah, and Nevada, was lost to the United States. Mexican citizens residing in the area were given the choice of returning to Mexico under no penalty or tax, or of remaining and becoming American citizens automatically after one year following the ratification of the treaty. Property rights were to be respected and protected during the interim period, and all rights of citizenship were conferred upon those who elected to stay. The majority of Mexicans north of the Rio Grande chose American citizenship, even though Mexico offered resettlement and land grants. Constitutional guarantees of their rights as U.S. citizens, continuing political instability in Mexico, and a 300-year history of settlement in the territory were the major factors that led Mexicans to renounce their original citizenship.

Soon after the Mexican War, the Anglo-Americans swept westward to the Pacific, and the growth of cattle and cotton empires in Texas, along with the discovery of gold in California, moved Anglo-Saxons into the Southwest at such a rate that the Mexican-Americans were quickly outnumbered. Only New Mexico maintained a majority of Mexican-Americans after becoming a U.S. territory. The slower pace of American settlement there is due in part to the extraordinary hostility of Indian tribes there. Also, New Mexico was thought to offer few economic opportunities. The few Anglos who settled in the territory generally stayed in the urban areas in the southern half, intermarried with the Mexicans at the upper levels of society, and made a pleasant and profitable accommodation with their new neighbors.

In Texas, however, hostility toward Mexicans was born in the struggle for Texas' independence and the Mexican War, and it continued long after the Treaty of Guadalupe Hidalgo was ratified. The entire area between the Nueces River and the Rio Grande saw countless border raids by both Mexicans and Texans. An imported slave culture influenced Anglo attitudes; although Mexicans were not considered as low a category as Negroes, they were regarded as racially inferior to Anglo-Americans.

Meanwhile, to California, as to other parts of the Southwest, came Anglo-Saxon banking, land, and business practices that were foreign to traditional Spanish ways. Ancient land titles dating from the sixteenth century were difficult to validate, and the American system of land taxation, which was based on an assessed value of the land rather than the value of the produce of the land, all but stripped the original Californians of their lands. Drought and the mining industry helped to destroy the great ranching empires, and by the 1860s, five-sixths of the land in Southern California was reported delinquent in tax payments. More than 40 percent of the land owned by the once wealthy and influential Mexican families was sold for as little as twenty-five cents an acre. With the decline of economic influence, Mexican-American political power also waned.

In the early part of the twentieth century, the number of Mexican-Americans in the Southwest grew rapidly with several waves of emigrants from Mexico. Eventually more than a million left Mexico because of the political instability during the 1910–1920 revolution. Also, the United States has never had an immigration quota for Mexico. In addition, the rise of cotton cultivation in Texas, the growth of mining in Arizona and agriculture in Colorado, and the rapid expansion of the citrus and vegetable industries in California all created enormous demands for cheap labor which the Anglo

population could not or would not supply. Manpower short-
ages in two world wars redoubled these demands, and Mexican immigrant laborers became the principal work force for
California agriculture.

Ultimately what developed was a lower economic status
for Mexican-Americans. Along with darker skin and a foreign
language, the Mexicans' poverty reinforced the Anglo idea of
racial inferiority. The prejudice led to separate schools for
Mexican-Americans in some Texas communities and to other
forms of discrimination. As late as 1943, the Mexican government refused to permit Mexican laborers to work in Texas
because of discriminatory practices against Mexican nationals
and Mexican-Americans. This position led the governor of
Texas to establish a Good Neighbor Commission, and caused
the state legislature to adopt a resolution which, without
naming Mexican-Americans, recognized them as Caucasians
and entitled them to enjoyment of "white only" public ac-
commodations. But that resolution did not end the hostilities
that had built up over the years, and in 1943 Mexican-American
relations with the majority community were jarred by the
notorious "zoot suit riots" in Los Angeles. Anglo sailors
claimed to have been attacked by a gang of Mexican-American
youths dressed in a foppish style of the time—"zoot suits,"
with padded shoulders, wide lapels, and pegged pants. In
retaliation, about 200 sailors, joined by other servicemen and
civilians, roamed the streets of the Los Angeles *barrio* attacking Mexican-Americans.

In the generation that followed the "zoot suit" riots and
the acknowledgement in Texas of Mexican-Americans as
"whites," the Mexican-Americans' struggle for parity and the
continuing hostilities were overshadowed by the dawning of
the black civil rights movement. But today, the Chicano civil
rights issue still confronts the Southwest, and not the least
of the problems is the discrimination against Mexican-Americans in the administration of justice.

In 1970, the U.S. Commission on Civil Rights issued an
unprecedented report documenting widespread evidence
that Mexican-Americans are denied equal protection of the
laws by law enforcement agencies and in the administration
of justice in all five southwestern states. The commission
found that "Mexican-American citizens are subject to unduly

harsh treatment by law enforcement officers, that they are often arrested on insufficient grounds, receive physical and verbal abuse and penalties which are disproportionately severe. We have found them to be deprived of proper use of bail and adequate representation by counsel. They are substantially underrepresented on grand and petit juries and excluded from full participation in law enforcement agencies, especially in supervisory positions." There were eighteen recommendations for corrective action on both the federal and state levels. Three years after the report was issued, little action had been taken on the recommendations by either the federal or state governments.

Even when the law is on the side of the Chicanos, getting fair treatment is a slow, frustrating process. For example, in mid-1972 a three-judge federal court declared five Texas laws unconstitutional in connection with a farm workers organizing case in the Rio Grande Valley. This decision, though, came after four and a half years of deliberation, and the appeals procedure threatened to drag a final settlement in the case into the mid-1970s, almost a decade after efforts to organize farm workers between June, 1966, and June, 1967, triggered the original lawsuit. The federal panel threw out the Texas penal laws dealing with unlawful assembly, breach of the peace, and abusive language along with civil statutes regulating the number of pickets and secondary strikes or boycotts. All five laws effectively stifled the United Farm Workers organizing drive in South Texas, one of the biggest disappointments of César Chávez's farm labor movement.

The significance of the lawsuit and the decision, should it be upheld, is twofold. First, it would lift injunctions issued by a state district court that prohibited picketing and strikes, thus untying the farm labor movement's hands to launch a labor organizing drive using much the same strategies and weapons — the secondary boycotts and harvest-time strikes — that proved successful in organizing the union in California. Second, and just as important, the decision would deal a severe blow to the controversial Texas Rangers, the famous law enforcement organization that has, deservingly or not, earned an international reputation similar to that of the FBI, Scotland Yard, and the Royal Canadian Mounted Police.

The federal panel ruled that the Rangers, who were

among the defendants in the suit filed by six individuals and the UFW, had sided with the growers against the union by selectively enforcing the law, and it cited several instances of unprovoked violence by Rangers and other law enforcement officials. "The unjustified conduct of the defendants had the effect of putting those in sympathy with the strike in fear of expressing their protected First Amendment rights with regard to free speech and lawful assembly," the opinion said.

There was a stream of incidents behind the opinion. On October 24, 1966, Domingo Arredondo, the union president in Starr County, shouted "*Viva la huelga,*" while he was under arrest in the courthouse. In response, he was struck, pushed, and threatened with a gun at his forehead. On January 26, 1967, five union members were arrested while trying to recruit new members, and that night two leaders of a prayer vigil were arrested for unlawful assembly. On May 26, 1967, the Reverend Edgar Krueger of the Texas Council of Churches and union member Magdaleno Dimas were arrested by Rangers and held within inches of a passing freight train. On June 2, 1967, Dimas and two union staff members were arrested in his home by Rangers wielding sawed-off shotguns. All three were arrested and beaten. Dimas—sought for shouting "*Viva la huelga*" in the packing shed of one of the grower firms—was beaten so severely that he suffered a concussion and was listed in serious condition in a local hospital, where Dr. Ramiro Casso, a physician from McAllen, described it as "the worst beating I have ever seen law enforcement officers administer." Ranger Captain A. Y. Allee, who admitted beating Dimas, said: "I used what force was necessary to make the arrest."

In the aftermath of the Rangers' intervention, demands that the force be abolished came from the U.S. Civil Rights Commission, the Texas AFL-CIO, the Political Association of Spanish-Speaking Organizations (PASSO), and other groups. In 1972, on the eve of the Rangers' 150th birthday, they became a political issue in Texas, with Sissy Farenthold advocating that the Rangers be disbanded or withdrawn from South Texas. Cries of "abolish the Rangers," however, are nothing new; they have echoed intermittently since 1823 when Stephen F. Austin created the Rangers' predecessors as a frontier force to protect his colonists from the Indians.

The Rangers were later used to keep the Mexicans and Mexican-Americans near the border and in South Texas in line, and in 1902 the late Vice-President John Nance Garner—when he was a state legislator from Uvalde in South Texas—proposed that the Rangers be removed from South Texas. Since then, half a dozen bills have been introduced in the Texas Legislature to disband or curb the Rangers, but none has come close to passing.

The Rangers' badges are made specially for them out of Mexican pesos by a Fort Worth jeweler, and the Rangers surely symbolize the oppression Mexican-Americans suffer at the hands of the law. Former State Senator Joe Bernal, director of the Commission for Mexican-American Affairs in San Antonio, has repeatedly described the Rangers as "the Mexican-Americans' Ku Klux Klan," and in the history of the organization only a handful of Mexican-Americans have ever been asked to join. There is a line Mexican-Americans in South Texas sometimes quote: "Every *rinque* [Ranger] has some Mexican blood—he has it on his boots."

But the Texas Rangers are only a small part of the state's long history of maladministering justice. Mexican-Americans in South Texas still tell stories of wholesale killings in the late 1800s and early 1900s that rival the lynchings of blacks in the South during the same period. The stories might easily be discounted if it were not for published accounts sometimes boasting of stealing cattle, raiding villages, killing Mexicans, and then bragging about these exploits in saloons. Rarely was anything done by the law. The attitude there was typified by the legendary Judge Roy Bean, known as "The Law West of the Pecos," who is supposed to have claimed that frontier justice had "no law against killing a Mexican." In 1921, the *New York Times* commented editorially that "the killing of Mexicans without provocation is so common as to pass unnoticed," and fifty years later this is still a valid observation on the plight of Mexican-Americans at the hands of American justice in the Southwest.

It is curious to note that the most extensive manhunt in the history of the city of Dallas did not occur in 1963 after the Kennedy assassination. Instead, it came more than seven years later, in 1971, when law enforcement officers sought what Dallas newspapers described as the "mad-dog killers" of three sheriffs' deputies. The two killers were Mexicans who had lived in the predominantly Mexican-American west side of the city, and the manhunt that spread throughout the state eventually led back to Dallas, where Mexican-Americans from the west side were subjected to unlawful searches and arrests in the wave of the fervent trackdown. With the aid of informants, law enforcement officials traced the suspects to an apartment house where they were apprehended peacefully but not before the officers had mistakenly stormed into the home of Tómas Rodriguez in the middle of the night and left both Rodriguez and his wife seriously wounded in an exchange of gunfire. Rodriguez, who understood very little English, pulled a gun and returned shots at the intruders, later saying he had been afraid and had reacted to what he thought to be a threat on his home. Law officers, who admitted not announcing the reason for their presence before entering the apartment, later said they had broken into the apartment when they heard movements within and feared any delay would pose a threat to their safety or allow the suspects to escape. Although the federal courts refused to give Rodriguez damages for the mistaken break-in, which left him without the full use of an arm, these killings and their aftermath—which one Dallas paper described as "Four Dark Days in Dallas"— resulted in several lawsuits against lawmen. One was filed by Celso Cantu, a twenty-four-year-old Mexican-American who spent eight days in the Dallas County jail without bond and legal counsel and without being allowed visitors or the use of a telephone. He was arrested on suspicion of murdering the deputies. When he was finally released, with no charges ever having been filed against him, the two men who later were convicted of the three murders had been in custody almost four days.

Only a year earlier, in 1970, something happened in the mildewy South Texas farm town of Mathis, whose population is about two-thirds Mexican-American, suggesting that the injustices of the law against Mexican-Americans also extend to non-Chicanos sympathetic to Mexican-Americans, particularly if they are involved in trying to improve the conditions in South Texas. In Mathis, for a long time there had been no doctor who regularly treated the Mexican-American poor. Then Fred Logan, Jr., arrived on the scene in 1966; the last doctor to try the town had been driven out by the local Anglos. Logan, however, was an exuberant osteopath who wore a floppy hat, smoked corkscrew cigars, and refused to be bothered by the Anglos' disapproval of his interest in the poor. With his wife and two children housed twenty miles away in Corpus Christi for safety, the twenty-seven-year-old Logan established a storefront medical practice for the community's 4,500 Mexican-Americans. "They almost never could pay," his wife, Carrol, later recalled. "Once, right after he started, I discovered he hadn't billed anyone for weeks, and I just gave him hell because we were nearly starving. But he just smiled and said we were pretty lucky to have as much as we had."

Logan was a lively maverick in other ways as well, dressing up in a mod pinstripe suit that along with a healthy growth of beard set him apart from the Anglos in Mathis. He regularly attended Mexican-American fiestas and celebrations, and often, to the fury of the whites in Mathis and to the undisguised amusement of the Mexican-Americans, he rode his motorcycle into town decked in caricature Anglo "hick" gear: going shirtless in bib overalls with a straw hat and boots. Within a year, Logan scraped together the money for a modern clinic, and soon he was seeing about sixty patients a day. Then, in mid-1970, the Department of Health, Education and Welfare offered the area $167,000 for a migrant-workers' clinic. After white medical groups in the area turned down the offer, claiming there was no need for such a program, HEW officials approached Logan, who quickly accepted.

About a month later, after he had wrapped up his work at the clinic for the day, Logan rode his motorcycle out to a steak house six miles from town to drink with three Mexican-American friends. A few hours later, when he was drunk, Logan walked outside the restaurant and fired some blanks from a pistol into the air, causing someone to call the police. Within fifteen minutes, Deputy Sheriff Erick Bauch, who was particularly disliked by the Mexican-Americans, drove up, took custody of both the gun and Logan, and went off into the night. Six minutes later, the deputy sheriff put in a call for an ambulance. Logan, with two bullets from Bauch's .357 Magnum in his chest, was dead when the ambulance arrived on the scene.

The official police report asserted that Logan, while trying to escape, attacked Bauch and eventually forced Bauch to shoot him in self-defense. Bauch, however, never explained why, though he was larger than Logan, he could not subdue a drunken man rather than shoot him. The angry Mexican-Americans were made even angrier when they learned that Bauch's patrol car had been suddenly dispatched about 200 miles away on "sheriff's business" before anyone could look at it. The Mathis City Council, which is controlled by the Mexican-American community, called for Bauch to resign along with his immediate superior, Sheriff Wayne Hitt, and they renamed the main street of Mathis "Fred Logan Avenue." In an official resolution the council said Logan's death "suggests the possibility of political murder." The Mayor, Winston F. Botte, a civil engineer who was harassed both personally and professionally by the town's Anglos for his sympathy for the Mexican-Americans, said: "I've heard Anglos say of Logan, 'We ought to kill that s.o.b.' "

It rained the day they buried Logan, but almost a thousand Mexican-Americans withstood the summer downpour. They followed Logan's coffin down the muddy, unpaved *barrio* streets to the Mexican-American cemetery, where, with Chicano activists flying banners proclaiming him a fallen hero and martyr, Logan, thirty-one years old at the time of his death, became the first Anglo ever laid to rest in Mathis' Mexican-American graveyard.

This litany of incidents seems endless, and it is surprising that the outcries of the 1960s took so long to surface. The vocal discontent finally erupted only when the Mexican-Americans gained new awareness from the example of the civil rights movement.

In California, there was an incest case involving a Mexican-American youth and his younger sister that went before a state court in San Jose, whose Mexican-American community is the largest of any city in northern California. The case would have been nothing more than a family tragedy if Judge Gerald S. Chargin had not told the youth: "I don't know why your parents haven't been able to teach you anything or train you. Mexican people after thirteen years of age believe it's perfectly all right to go out and act like an animal. . . . We ought to send you out of this country—send you back to Mexico. You are lower than animals and haven't the right to live in organized society—just miserable lousy, rotten people . . . maybe Hitler was right, the animals of our society probably ought to be destroyed because they have no right to live among human beings."

The youth's attorney quickly interjected: "The court is indicting the whole Mexican group . . . what appalls me is that the court is saying that Hitler was right in genocide."

"What are we going to do with the mad dogs of our society?" Judge Chargin shot back. "Either we have to kill them or send them to an institution or place them out of the hands of good people because that is the theory—one of the theories of punishment is if they want to act like mad dogs, then we have to separate them from our society."

Presented to the *Los Angeles Times'* readership by columnist Ruben Salazar, the court transcript triggered a storm of anger and protest from Mexican-Americans, who demanded that Judge Chargin be removed from the bench. Ultimately, State Assemblyman Alex P. Garcia introduced a bill in the California Legislature seeking to impeach Chargin, but the resolution died without support.

The outcry here, however, was mild compared to the deep resentment for law enforcement symbols among Chicanos in Denver, where confrontation upon confrontation has built a bitter, openly hostile situation. In early 1973, the situation finally erupted into violence leaving one person dead from police gunfire, nineteen others wounded, and an apartment house in ruins from a bomb explosion. Much like the shootouts between police and blacks, this gun battle in the Denver *barrio* on March 17, 1973, signalled an uneasy warning that the Chicano movement might well follow in the footsteps of black militants who had resorted to urban guerrilla violence. In their search of the alleged snipers' apartment, the authorities uncovered a cache of weapons, including more than thirty high-powered rifles, many with telescopes, sawed-off shotguns, pistols, including .44-caliber magnums, and hundreds of rounds of ammunition.

It was more than coincidence that the dead man, Luis A. Martinez, twenty, was active in the Colorado Raza Unida party and a co-director of the Crusade for Justice, in a city where the 68,790 Mexican-Americans, 13 percent of the population, make up the largest minority group. In Denver, the number of Mexican-Americans living in the slums has been rapidly increasing, while the proportion of blacks in the same environment has been decreasing. Education further underscores the difference. By nearly every measure — achievement test scores, percentage of parents on welfare, neighborhood property values and rentals — the city's worst schools tend to be Mexican-American, and the dropout rate for Mexican-American students is 80 percent, twice the rate for black students.

Since the 1960s, when Corky Gonzales organized the Crusade for Justice, Mexican-American activists in Denver have kept up a steady protest against the police for brutality in a series of confrontations. Much of the Chicanos' bitterness stems from the frustrations of having no voice on the thirteen-member Denver City Council, while the city's blacks, who comprise a smaller percentage of the population than the Mexican-Americans, had two representatives in 1973. And nothing exacerbates that bitterness and frustration like the city's police force — as in most cities, the Mexican-American community's only direct contact with the system in which they have no elected voice.

The Denver Chicanos weren't surprised when, shortly after midnight on March 17, 1973, a police car moved in and parked conspicuously across from the Crusade for Justice headquarters. One of the group, Luis Martinez, did not hesitate in approaching the car, which had a police officer and a patrolwoman inside, to find out what they were doing. Martinez persisted in quizzing the officers, who finally ordered him into the car, informing him he had violated a jaywalking ordinance, and demanded his identification. Patrolman Stephen Snyder dispersed a small crowd that had begun gathering near the car, when suddenly Martinez bolted from the car, pursued by Snyder. When Patrolwoman Carol Hogue found Snyder moments later, he was bleeding from two wounds, and he told her he had just shot the suspect. Sniper fire broke out and continued periodically for the next two hours as more than sixty policemen moved into the area. Police returned the fire, aiming into an apartment building next to the Crusade for Justice headquarters, and the gunfire finally ended shortly after an explosion tore the side out of the apartment building where police estimated more than twenty sticks of dynamite exploded. Martinez's body later was found near a nearby medical center, and among the persons injured were twelve Denver policemen. Thirty-six persons, all of them Mexican-Americans, were arrested, and six of them were held for assault in connection with the sniper fire.

The gun battle only alienated the Denver Mexican-American community further, bringing a charge from Corky Gonzales that the Crusade for Justice was sure "there was a carried-out plot — a conspiracy" on the part of the police which led to the shooting and the explosion. A National Lawyers Guild attorney representing the Crusade accused the police of committing "mass violations of civil rights" in making the arrests, and two days after the shootout a United States attorney called on the FBI to conduct an investigation of the allegations of police brutality and summary punishment.

Against the landscape of the Chicano civil rights movement, the Denver shootout leaves little doubt as to the mounting frustration within some segments of the Mexican-American community, a frustration that would seem to augur not less but more turmoil in the cities of the Southwest. Justly or not, police and other law enforcement officials are being blamed not only for the inequities of the law today but also for the discrimination in the administration of justice for the last century and a half. As the Civil Rights Commission pointed out in its report *Mexican-Americans and the Administration of Justice in the Southwest,* the Chicanos have come to represent the forces seeking change in the country. "The commission recognizes that individual law enforcement officers and court officers have made positive efforts to improve the administration of justice in their communities. The fact, however, that Mexican-Americans see justice being administered unevenly throughout the Southwest tends to weaken their confidence in an otherwise fair system. In addition, the absence of impartial tribunals in which claims of mistreatment can be litigated to a conclusion accepted by all sides tends to breed further distrust and cynicism. . . . The police and the courts cannot resolve the problems of poverty and of alienation which play a large part in the incidence of crime which they attempt to control; and the police and the courts often treat legitimate demands for reform with hostility because society as a whole refuses to see them as justified."

While Chicano activists have reacted with direct confrontations in the streets and the parks, other Mexican-Americans have chosen the slower route of confronting the legal system itself. In 1968, a group of Mexican-American lawyers organized a program similar to the NAACP Legal Defense Fund, long a leader in civil rights litigation. With $2.2 million for an eight-year period from the Ford Foundation, the Mexican-American Legal Defense and Education Fund (MALDEF) quickly moved to the forefront of the struggle for Mexican-American legal rights. By the early 1970s, MALDEF was actively involved in several hundred cases and complaints covering the whole range of civil rights litigation, from police brutality complaints to public school desegregation lawsuits. MALDEF officials themselves have called the organization the "legal arm" of the Chicano movement in the Southwest.

There is no question that the Chicano movement—the active and militant response of Mexican-Americans to their plight in American society—has focused attention on the discrimination suffered by Mexican-Americans in the administration of justice. The long-standing national myopia about the injustices inflicted on the Mexican-Americans in the Southwest has been exposed for what it is. This unwillingness to see involved the federal government, which buried the shocking problems of Mexican-Americans behind other priorities; the press, which ignored the double standard of justice under which Mexican-Americans have been mistreated; the Mexican-American community itself, which suffered most but until recently feared to make an outcry against lawlessness; the sociologists and humanitarians who saw what was happening but failed to make themselves heard outside the academy; and the officials at all levels, who hoped if nothing were said, the problem would go away.

Rather than go away, though, it got worse—and while the nation as a whole continued to whistle and not look back, the Chicanos have guaranteed that injustice against Mexican-Americans will never again be simply ignored. Armed with such ammunition as the Falcon killing in New Mexico, the shooting death of *Los Angeles Times* columnist Ruben Salazar, and federal reports documenting the injustices, activist

Chicanos and concerned middle-class Mexican-Americans are talking about and demanding "law and order" for their people.

Meanwhile, there is no sign that the inequalities of the law will immediately disappear. Lawlessness will be with society forever, carried along on its own tide of pride, prejudice, and misunderstanding. This generation of Chicanos may end up being distinguished from other generations of Mexican-Americans only by its outcry, and by its marriage to the world of protest, which has aroused America's conscience to the problems and inequities in the country. In that sense, there is hope for Mexican-Americans and American justice, though the history of the two is good reason to be wary of the issue fading again into the past.

4 EDUCATION: THE EQUAL OPPORTUNITY MYTH

Demetrio P. Rodriguez, a middle-aged Mexican-American with an eighth-grade education, lives in one of the poorest sections of San Antonio, where two of his four children attend school in a school district that, next to Watts, is the poorest in the country. Edgewood, as the area is called, is crisscrossed by dusty, sometimes uncharted streets lined with small dilapidated frame houses. The average annual family income in Edgewood is about $4,000—below the federally established poverty guidelines. Rodriguez, a sheet-metal worker, is one of the leading citizens of the community, and his is a classic case of a parent who wants a better life for his offspring.

"All my kids are going to grow up to speak good English—not like me," he boasted to one interviewer in his own self-conscious manner. "You know, I took the high school certificate test twice and flunked it both times. It's the grammar and punctuation that get me. I got a chance to go to night school, cheap, but I'm so wrapped up in these different groups now I don't have time."

Short, stocky, and with a few streaks of graying hair, Rodriguez does not fall into the mold of the typical Chicano activist. But his community knows how active he is: he belongs to the San Antonio Neighborhood Youth Organization (SANYO): he's a board member of the Bexar County Migrant Farm Workers Association and a member of the Bexar County Civic Action Committee; and he has been president of the Nathan Hale Community Action Council. Most important, Demetrio P. Rodriguez became in the 1970s one of the most celebrated figures in American education. He represents the Mexican-Americans and other disadvantaged groups who want to secure a better education for their children in school districts like Edgewood, where there are low property values and low taxes.

In most states, school financing relies on local property taxes, with the result that poor districts have less money to spend on their school systems. In the Edgewood district of San Antonio, the state and local property tax allocated for each pupil in 1971 was $356, whereas the Alamo Heights district in an affluent part of the city had per-pupil allocations of $594. The Edgewood school system, which has 95 percent Mexican-American enrollment, had an average of $5,429 taxable property behind each student compared with $45,095 in Alamo Heights. As Rodriguez saw it, the result was an inferior education for children in impoverished areas and a denial of the low-income children's constitutional rights.

Rodriguez became the principal plaintiff in a class-action lawsuit challenging the state's property-tax method of financing public education. The suit was part of a national movement to achieve education reform through judicial action, and in late 1971 a three-judge federal district court in Texas struck down the state system and ordered that schools be financed according to the wealth of the state as a whole rather than its subdivisions. There were fifty similar suits in thirty states, but the Rodriguez case was the first to be tested in the Supreme Court.

In early 1973, however, the Supreme Court dealt Rodriguez a crushing blow with a 5-to-4 vote rejecting the challenge to the traditional system, maintaining that the states could allow spending to vary among rich and poor school districts even when this results in wide disparities in the quality of education. The decision, chargeable to President Nixon's four appointees to the Court, plus the swing vote of

Justice Potter Stewart, disallowed the claim that school funding patterns violate the Fourteenth Amendment's guarantee
of equal protection under the law. In effect, the Court held that
education, despite its "vital role" in American life, is not a
fundamental constitutional right.

"The poor people have lost again," Rodriguez said de-
jectedly. He agreed with other educational reformers, who
likened the ruling to the 1898 Supreme Court decision establishing the "separate but equal" doctrine in racial matters.
And it was not until 1954 that the Supreme Court struck down
that ruling.

But despite the Court's reversal of the lower court ruling,
the Rodriguez case focused unprecedented attention nationwide on both the plight of the poor in public school financing
and the special difficulties of Mexican-Americans in the
Southwest. The Supreme Court itself emphasized that it was
not "placing its judicial imprimatur on the status quo. The
need is apparent for reform in tax systems which may well
have relied too long and too heavily on the local property
tax," and left the task of reform to the legislatures. Meanwhile, in a dissenting opinion, Justices Thurgood Marshall
and William O. Douglas called the ruling "a retreat from our
historic commitment to equality of educational opportunity
and . . . unsupportable acquiescence in a system which de-
prives children in their earliest years of the chance to reach
their full potential as citizens."

It is significant that the case involved a Mexican-American as the principal plaintiff because, as was documented by
federal reports, the public school systems of the Southwest
have provided substandard education for minority students.
"An educational system that is inadequate for the minority
child is a costly system for our country," the U.S. Civil Rights
Commission said in late 1971 in one of a series of special reports on Mexican-American education. "The ultimate test of
a school system's effectiveness is the performance of its students. Under that test, our schools are failing."

In addition, the commission found that by the eighth
grade, 9 percent of the Mexican-American students have already left school and that 40 percent of all Mexican-Americans
drop out of school before graduation; Mexican-American high
school graduates actually have something closer to a tenth-

grade education obtained over a twelve-year, or a thirteen-
or fourteen-year, period. Out of every one hundred Mexican-
Americans who enter the first grade, sixty will graduate from
high school, twenty-three will enter college and only about
five will graduate. Further, Mexican-Americans are almost
three times as likely to repeat the first grade as Anglos and
almost twice as likely as blacks. And from 50 to 70 percent of
Mexican-American students in the fourth, eighth, and twelfth
grades read below grade level, compared to 25 to 34 percent
for Anglos.

The list of deficiencies and problems seems endless, but
always it comes back to two central issues: language and
culture. The Civil Rights Commission's series of reports
documented that, even in the 1970s, Mexican-American school
children in the Southwest are still being "penalized and
degraded" for the difference of their language and culture.
The commission found indications of "evident exclusion" in
schools, and Bishop Patricio Flores of San Antonio, the nation's first Mexican-American Roman Catholic bishop and
head of the commission's Texas advisory committee, blamed
the cultural disparity as the "root of the massive educational
problem in the Southwest."

Though he himself was a product of a poor English-language background, Bishop Flores was luckier than most of
the other Mexican-American youngsters he grew up with. "The
teachers would call you a 'stupid jackass' and things like that,"
he recalled in one interview. "Then there was the attitude that
these kids were retarded because they couldn't capture anything in school. But they couldn't capture anything in a language they didn't understand."

Apparently the language gap is a problem that must be
experienced to be fully understood and felt. For instance, it
was only after he got first-hand experience of the language
barrier that Senator John V. Tunney, whose California constituency includes the largest number of Mexican-Americans
in any state, really learned about the difficulties facing young
Mexican-Americans. In the 1960s, shortly after winning election to the House of Representatives, the Tunneys attempted
to enroll their son, Teddy, in a nursery school in Washington,
D.C. Teddy had to undergo a series of IQ and other admis-
sions tests, and he failed them.

"I don't think I'll ever forget the afternoon when Mieke [Tunney's wife] told me," Tunney recalled. "The teacher had tried to be kind, but what she had to say could not be said kindly. 'I'm afraid your son isn't up to our standards,' she said. 'He's weak in vocabulary, and he's slow to respond to questions.' My son? I was shocked, incredulous. This is the kind of news no father can accept easily even if it is true, but I was certain that it was not true. I know this bright and happy little boy, and I knew he was not slow.

"Then why weren't his IQ test results better? I tried to analyze the problem as he and I walked around Washington that afternoon, but wasn't getting anywhere. Then abruptly, Teddy solved the puzzle for me. He suddenly grasped my hand and said, *'Papa kijk! De brug!'* He was speaking Dutch: 'Daddy, look! The bridge!' This was not surprising. Mieke is Dutch, and she had recently taken Teddy on a six-week trip to the Netherlands to visit his grandparents. For a long while before the trip, to prepare him, she had spoken Dutch with him.

"Now I began to see what the problem was. Mieke and I had assumed he was learning English as well as Dutch: learning it from me, from playmates, from our friends. We were wrong. His three-year-old brain was apparently doing much or most of its thinking in Dutch. Confronted with an intelligence test in which all the symbols of thought were expressed in English, he had been defeated."

After discovering the problem, the Tunneys started their son on a crash English program that ultimately solved the language problem. In a speech to the 1972 Convention of Teachers of English to Speakers of Other Languages, Senator Tunney recalled the personal experience and publicly committed himself to pushing racial and cultural pluralism in the schools.

"Many of us — in government as well as in education — fail to recognize what our society has done to the cultural identity of our minorities," he said. "From the beginning of the educational process in this country, it has been the goal of our school system to homogenize its pupils, to serve the tradition of America as the great melting pot. It has long been thought that given enough time and pressure, all students would emerge from our schools with similar goals. At least, this is what was supposed to have happened. In fact, it has not happened. Many of America's students leave the schools totally unprepared for life in America. And because the schools have failed totally to meet their specific learning needs, these students have not been able to survive socially or economically in this country. Ironically, preserving and encouraging the student's inherited culture helps him deal with the alien culture outside the home.

"With our preoccupation with the melting pot, we have forgotten the value of cultural pluralism—to all Americans, whether Indian, Puerto Rican, Oriental, Chicano, black, or eighth-generation Anglo Saxon. . . . Obviously, the non-English speaking student is one who has failed to blend into the American mainstream. He has instead been an exile in his own land. America has punished him for cherishing his language and his culture. And because he is different, because he speaks little or no English, he has been excluded from participating in the advantages of American life. But he has not been the only loser. America, too, has lost."

The differences in language and culture perhaps help explain the findings made by the Civil Rights Commission in their study, the most comprehensive ever made of the education of Mexican-Americans in the southwestern states. Reports by the commission, a nonpartisan federal agency, documented a pattern of ethnic isolation among Spanish-speaking students in the Southwest, the schools' failure to respond to their cultural and linguistic differences, and the limited funds available to Mexican-American schools compared to Anglo school districts.

The commission found that Anglo students receive more positive teacher attention than Mexican-American pupils in the schools in the Southwest, concluding that the neglect of Mexican-American youngsters is "likely to hinder seriously the educational opportunities and achievement of Chicano pupils." According to the commission, teachers praise Anglo students 36 percent more often; they use Anglo students' ideas 40 percent more often; they "respond positively" to Anglo students 40 percent more often; and they direct questions to Anglo students 20 percent more often than to Mexican-American youngsters.

Throughout the country's history, the public educational

system has been a major element in enabling children of various ethnic backgrounds to grow and develop into full participants in American life. During the great waves of immigration in the late nineteenth and early twentieth centuries, we turned to the schools as the principal instrument to assimilate the millions of children of diverse nationalities and cultures into the American mainstream. By and large, the schools succeeded in accomplishing this task.

But the schools in the Southwest have failed to carry out this traditional role with the Mexican-Americans, that area's largest minority group. Of course, there are many reasons why they have failed. Most important, the history of the Southwest points up the differences between Mexican-Americans and other ethnic groups in America.

This group is not like the others, largely the descendants of immigrants who crossed the oceans to come to this country, cutting their ties to their homelands as they sought a new way of life. The earliest Mexican-Americans did not come to the United States at all — it came to them. They entered American society as a conquered people after the war with Mexico in 1848 and the acquisition of the Southwest by the United States. Furthermore, most Mexican-Americans who have crossed the international border since then have entered a society little different from the culture they left behind on the other side of the border.

For obvious geographical reasons, Mexican-Americans have maintained close relations with Mexico. In contrast to the European immigrant, most Mexican-Americans continued to follow a life-style similar to what they had always known. Also many Mexican-Americans exhibit the physical characteristics of the indigenous Indian population, and this sets them apart from the rest of society. In fact, some Anglos have always regarded Mexican-Americans as a separate racial group.

The dominance of Anglo culture is felt most strongly in the schools. The curriculum is chosen by Anglos, and not surprisingly, it reflects Anglo culture. Of course the language of instruction is English. In many instances, when Mexican-American pupils use Spanish in school they are punished because the schools are trying to enforce cultural exclusion.

As a result, the conflict of cultures in schools in the Southwest has continued. This cultural chauvinism has slowed down the learning process for Mexican-American students.

The Civil Rights Commission's reports and all the other recent studies on education make one point clear: no other institution in America draws more scrutiny or is subject to more criticism than the school. "Our schools are failing our children," the 1972 Democratic platform, asserted, and many people, from politicians to *barrio* teachers, would agree. And if the schools have failed, then it follows that Mexican-American children, at once the poorest and the least mobile, have suffered the most devastating consequences.

In 1968, Congress took a big step to help the Spanish-speaking student by passing the Bilingual Education Act. But what appeared to be a tremendous boost turned out to be a hollow victory. In the first year of the program, while the act's enthusiastic supporters were still celebrating their triumph, not one cent was appropriated for bilingual education—even though $15 million had been authorized.

This balking on appropriations shows a lack of commitment on the part of the federal government under the Nixon administration to the educational problems of Spanish-speaking students. In his first budget, President Nixon requested one-sixth of what Congress had authorized for bilingual education, proposing a bare $5 million. That year Congress ultimately appropriated $7.5 million—enough money to fund adequate programs for less than one percent of the three million children who needed the programs. The next year, the President recommended one-quarter of what Congress authorized. Congress doubled the amount, but the President responded by vetoing the education bill. In 1971, the administration proposed slicing the bilingual program in half. Again, in an amendment cosponsored by Senator Edward Kennedy, Congress doubled that amount, hiking it to a level of $25 million. President Nixon vetoed the bill again, but Congress managed to pass the measure over his veto.

At the midway mark of President Nixon's first term, Vice-President Spiro T. Agnew announced the formation of a new national organization to promote business development among the Spanish-speaking. The National Economic Development Association, or NEDA, was hailed by the vice-president for ensuring that "Americans of Hispanic descent get a fair chance at the starting line."

But in the *barrios* the Chicanos restyled the widely publicized NEDA, "NADA," which in Spanish spells "nothing." Why such a rude put-down for an organization that undoubtedly would help some worthy, energetic Spanish-speaking entrepreneurs? The answer, of course, is that NEDA, for all its good intentions, would be sure to help only those who had already made it—men and women already in business or ready to go into business. This was hardly the "starting line" for the Mexican-American in the Southwest.

On the very day that Agnew stood in the spotlight on NEDA's account, the U.S. Senate Select Committee on Equal Education Opportunity wound up a two-day hearing on minority educational problems. But the vice-president and NEDA got the lion's share of publicity. Complained Senator Walter Mondale, chairman of the committee: "We found that the best way to get television cameras out of this room and reporters to leave is to hold a hearing on Mexican-American education. There doesn't seem to be any interest. Yet this is the second-largest minority in America."

Mario Obledo, director of the Mexican-American Legal Defense and Education Fund (MALDEF), told the senators that it was a "tragedy" for federal and state governments to ignore the educational problems of Mexican-Americans. "How do you bring this to the attention of the American public?" asked Obledo. "Does it require some overt act of violence to bring it forth, or can it be handled in a manner that is conducive with the American way of life?" The Reverend Henry J. Casso, an educational consultant with MALDEF, asked Senator Mondale: "How long would you and I continue to do business with a lawyer who lost eight out of ten cases; a doctor who lost eight of every ten of his patients? Being a religionist, what would my bishop do if I lost eight of ten parishioners? Yet the institutions, including government, have remained mute to see eight out of every ten Mexican-American children drop out, kicked out, and pushed out of the educational institutions of this country. No one has asked an accounting for the vast sums of public money that have been wasted. But the young are demanding an accounting and I stand with them."

For years Congress has heard that inadequate education early on correlates with underemployment, unemployment, and poverty later in life. It's less well known how costly rectifying an inadequate education in later life can be. A survey of the Los Angeles Unified School District showed a total adult education budget for 1971 of more than $30 million. According to a school district spokesman, the adult education budget hits this big figure simply because over 50 percent of the adult population lacks a high school diploma or a salable job skill. Failure to educate a man in his youth is no saving to society when one city has to spend over $5 million *more* than the entire 1971 bilingual appropriation in order to cope with the problem of inadequate education among its adults. Clearly, one of the real problems with cheap education is that the taxpayer never stops paying for it.

The matter of cost is part of an endless cycle that ultimately winds up back on the issue of school financing and the Rodriguez case. The initial reaction to the decision was bleak disappointment. But as time passed, with reflection, people came to see that, as a practical matter, the Rodriguez case was not a death knell for school finance reform. Actually, the long-range impact on the course of education litigation could be more wide sweeping than anyone suspected at first.

"The problem with *Rodriguez* is not so much that we lost in getting the Supreme Court to order changes in school financing," said Stephen Browning, director of the school finance project of the Lawyers Committee for Civil Rights Under Law. "I think those changes will come eventually through the legislative process. I worry a lot more about the effect the Court's holding will have on other kinds of education reform totally unrelated to finance."

This anxiety, shared by other attorneys specializing in education law, is the Court's pronouncement that education, because it is not mentioned in the Constitution, does not qualify as a "fundamental interest." To a non-lawyer, questions of whether or not something is a "fundamental interest" may seem hopelessly arcane. But the concept is simple and, in practice, very important, for on it depends the way the courts will scrutinize state laws that discriminate between people.

The Supreme Court has devised two different standards for reviewing legislation challenged under the equal-protection clause. In run-of-the-mill cases concerning state regulation of business and labor, the Court applies what is described as "restrained review," or the "rational basis" test. The justices assume that the law in question is valid, and they sustain it as long as they can find a rational relationship between the classification established by the statute and a legitimate objective. But a much stricter standard is followed when a law either affects certain "fundamental interests" or is "inherently suspect." There is no presumption of validity, and rationality is not a sufficient justification. Instead, it is up to attorneys for the state to prove that the statutory classification is necessary for the achievement of a "compelling state interest." In addition, the state must also show that the law is so carefully drafted that it exactly fulfills the purpose it was designed to accomplish and that the same objective cannot be achieved by a method less burdensome to those affected by the law.

In the Rodriguez case, the lower court identified both a "fundamental interest" and a "suspect classification." As a result, the court had no difficulty deciding that the stricter equal protection tests should be applied. Education, they deemed a fundamental interest. Because the property tax system in Texas resulted in school expenditures that varied with the financial resources of each school district, the court decided that this was discrimination based on wealth. It considered this factor suspicious enough to qualify as a "suspect classification," even though the Supreme Court had never positively designated wealth as a "suspect classification." Then the lower court, invoking the strict test, found that the state had no compelling interest in maintaining a system that doomed children in poor districts to twelve years of badly equipped classrooms with poorly paid, half-educated teachers.

But the Supreme Court was not similarly moved. The Court was sensitive to the law reviews' long-standing criticism of its haphazard, subjective approach to equal protection and its tendency to invoke strict scrutiny whenever individual justices were outraged by a particular state law; and the majority decided this time to be precise. In an opinion written by Justice Lewis F. Powell, Jr. (in which conservatives William H. Rehnquist, Chief Justice Warren E. Burger, Harry A. Blackmun, and Potter Stewart concurred), the Court said strict scrutiny was unwarranted because the Texas law did not affect a "fundamental interest" and was not based on a "suspect classification." In the discussion of wealth as a "suspect classification," the Court dwelt on the absence of a definable class of poor people affected by the law. Previous Supreme Court rulings, particularly the ones striking down poll taxes and candidate filing fees and requiring the states to provide trial transcripts and attorneys for impoverished criminal defendants, were inapplicable here. In those cases, poverty inevitably meant an absolute deprivation of some important right, according to Justice Powell. Where education was concerned the case was different, for even the poorest children in Texas were receiving some education and could claim at most only a relative deprivation.

Although it was by far the most important education litigation involving Mexican-Americans, the Rodriguez case showed the growing prominence of Mexican-Americans in lawsuits seeking educational reform. In school desegregation cases in the Southwest, the Mexican-Americans suddenly became an important third element in the movement to rid public schools of old inequities.

The Southwest has a long history of isolating the Mexican-Americans from the rest of society. There was never a formal statute, but segregation of Mexican-American students was widespread. In California school segregation of Mexican-Americans was implied by the law. Under a statute enacted in 1885 and amended in 1893, it was possible to segregate Indians and Mongolians in California public schools; to many Anglo administrators, this category included Mexican-Americans.

In Texas, the segregation of Mexican-Americans from the Anglo world has been even more deliberate. In the early 1930s in Corpus Christi, restrictive covenants in deeds prohibited the sale of property to Mexican-Americans in the Anglo sections of the city. Most Mexican-Americans in this part of the state could find only manual labor in the cotton fields. They were sure to get unequal service in restaurants and stores. Anglo employes in a drugstore in Seguin, Texas, offered different kinds of service to Anglo, Negro, and Mexican-American customers. As one Anglo clerk put it: "We serve Mexicans at the fountain but not at the tables. We have got to make some distinctions between them and the white people. The Negroes we serve only cones." In Arizona, too, the Anglo community has long viewed itself as racially and economically superior to the Mexican-American. In the 1930s, an Arizona newspaper referred to the situation thus: " . . . the Arizona Mexicans have been segregated from the more fortunate Arizonans, both as strangers belonging to an alien race of conquered Indians, and as persons whose enforced status in the lowest economic levels make them less admirable than other people."

School segregation closely parallels socio-economic segregation. In Corpus Christi and surrounding Nueces County in the 1930s, the school officials gave two kinds of reason for segregation: association was considered undesirable from the Anglo's viewpoint, and separation was to the advantage of the Mexican-American. A Nueces County school board member, a farmer, declared, "I don't believe in mixing. They are filthy and lousy—not all, but most of them." And another school official explained, "We segregate for the same reason that southerners [sic] segregate the Negro. They are an inferior race, that is all."

In other areas of the Southwest, the separation was justified on the grounds that Mexican-Americans were the ones who benefited from the practices. Mexican-American children were isolated until they had overcome their "English-language handicap" and had become "adjusted." Pre-World War II data suggest that the Anglo-controlled school boards were simply carrying out the will of the majority society. As a result, school board members consciously and purposely established district boundaries that helped achieve the segregation of Mexican-Americans from Anglos.

Black and white pupils were separated by law in Texas, and although Mexican-American children were legally classified as whites, the school boards' policy and practice generally separated them, too, from Anglo children. Even though Texas has a compulsory school attendance law, the usual board policy is not to enforce it on Mexican-American children, particularly when doing so would mean that large numbers of them might go to schools with Anglos. In California, the segregation policy was even more subtle. Some California school boards required ethnic students to register in given schools. Other boards drew zone boundaries to keep the ethnics in their own homogeneous areas. Still other boards simply used a policy of transferring students from zone to zone.

One of the effects of the economic and social changes brought on by World War II was that the Mexican-Americans increased their demands for a better education. Those demands first reached a judicial forum in 1945, in a federal court in Orange County, California. In *Mendez* et al. v. *Westminster School District of Orange County* et al., some Mexican-American parents initiated legal action against four Orange County elementary school districts. The parents maintained that the school officials kept their children separate by "regulation, custom, and usage" solely because they were of Latin descent. Further, they claimed that the school officials were blocking due process and equal protection of the law, guaranteed under the Fifth and Fourteenth Amendments. The court cited the evils of segregation and the merits of commingling of the entire student body; it ruled in favor of the plaintiffs and enjoined the school districts from segregating. When the decision was appealed in 1947, a higher court upheld it.

In 1948, another important case came up in Texas. In *Delgado* v. *The Bastrop Independent School District*, a federal court ruled that segregation of Mexican-American children was illegal. This decision, like the one in California, was based on constitutional guarantees; and together with other decisions filed in the 1950s, the Delgado and Mendez cases established that purposely maintaining segregated schools for Mexican-Americans was illegal.

Nevertheless, the desegregation cases filed in the Southwest in the late 1960s and early 1970s indicate that segregation still exists. In 1970, a federal judge ruled that the Corpus Christi Independent School District was operating a dual school system. He found that the practices of the school board created a *de jure* segregated school system. There were separate schools for Mexican-Americans, who comprise almost half the school district's enrollment, as well as for blacks. Throughout the Southwest, the federal courts found that school districts often had overestimated their attempts at desegregation progress by counting Mexican-Americans in the same category as the Anglos, rather than grouping them along with the blacks. While some school districts' desegregation progress might look good on paper, all they had done was to mix blacks and browns. Ultimately, the courts declared that Mexican-Americans indeed constituted a distinct minority group, and they imposed tougher desegregation standards on school districts in the Southwest.

Ironically, at the same time that Mexican-Americans have moved to the forefront of the struggle for better schooling, the very idea of "equal educational opportunity" has become a source of controversy. Certain social scientists argue that no amount of extra money spent on schools will make much difference in how the children perform. Nothing that schools do in the name of reform, they say, seems to alter the gross inequalities which separate poor children from rich children, white children from brown and black children, when they begin their schooling—and when they finish it. This is heretical stuff. It attacks the common notion that money buys solutions to social problems. More important, it challenges a basic article of American faith—that schools are the great "equalizers" of our national life, that education "frees" the poor from poverty, the blacks from the ghettos, and the Chicanos from the *barrios*.

Among the leading critics of educational reform has been Christopher Jencks of Harvard who does not attack as such reforms like integration and compensatory education, but questions whether educational policy can have any significant effect on the adult earning power of poor children. But mixed in with the doubts and the skepticism is the intriguing conclusion that nothing short of a massive, top-to-bottom restructuring of our economic order can equalize people's earning potential.

As Jencks himself stated it: "In America, as elsewhere, the long-term drift over the past 200 years has been toward equality. In America, however, the contribution of public policy to this drift has been slight. As long as egalitarians assume that public policy cannot contribute to equality directly but must proceed by ingenious manipulation of marginal institutions like schools, this pattern will continue. If we want to move beyond this tradition, we must establish political control over the institutions that shape our society. What we need, in short, is what other countries call socialism. Anything less will end in the same disappointment as the reforms of the 1960s."

This is an argument that is at once utopian and, in effect, defeatist. Yet it is a conclusion that touches the nerve of what the Mexican-American protest against the educational system in the Southwest has been all about. It may have begun only as a labor-organizing struggle in the California grapefields, but by the mid-1970s, the Chicano movement had blossomed into a broad legal and political effort to affect and to control institutions, including the educational system, that have shaped the plight of the Mexican-American.

EL MOVIMIENTO

5 CHICANO ECONOMICS: "VIVA LA HUELGA!"

Social movements and revolutions are built around causes and martyrs, and it might seem surprising that the Chicanos waited as long as they did before rallying behind an issue. The idea, *la causa*, that finally triggered the Chicano movement in the 1960s was the economic problem, which the Mexican-Americans experienced as the intolerable gap between what they sought and what they received. Call that gap poverty. It was only one of the problems besetting Mexican-Americans in the Southwest, but it was by far the most volatile.

No one showed up the economic plight of the Chicano more effectively than the hundreds of thousands of Mexican-American farm workers whose back-breaking labor demanded long hours, often under a flaming sun and in choking dust. Their work, seasonal and sporadic, rarely provided a total income above the poverty level. Even in the 1960s, job security for farm workers was unheard of, and fringe benefits were few. Housing often amounted to shacks without lighting or plumbing. Prospects for the future were only slightly less promising for adults than for their children, who usually lagged behind in school, particularly if they belonged to a migrant family, and who probably would drop out, join the ranks of farm workers, and be caught in the cycle of poverty with little chance of escaping.

It was among the farm workers that the Chicano movement began in 1965 as César Chávez, a small, determined son of migrant farm workers (described later as "one of the heroic figures of our time" by Senator Robert F. Kennedy), led farm laborers on a strike against table-grape growers in Delano, California. Buoyed by support from organized labor, liberals, Democrats like Kennedy, and a unique mysticism that surrounded Chávez, the grape strike—or *la huelga,* as even the Anglo press came to call it—developed into a phenomenon that touched the public consciousness and became both a national and a household issue.

The irony of *la huelga* is that it was not particularly successful in the fields. Chávez failed to get all the grape pickers out of the vineyards, and he was never able to get large numbers of workers to join the strike. Instead, the real troops in the battle were the American consumers who joined in a national grape boycott—the most effective boycott in American labor history—that eventually forced the California grape growers to their knees. In 1970, Chávez's United Farm Workers Organizing Committee (UFWOC) made a significant breakthrough, signing with growers and winning an historic victory for the young union and its struggling grape pickers.

The grape strike was just the first step in an effort to accomplish the impossible: to organize the nation's hordes of farm workers. Previous efforts, dating back to the turn of the century, always failed, except in Hawaii where in 1945 a rugged longshoreman's union helped win a contract for sugarcane workers. One of the major problems was that agriculture fell outside the realm of the National Labor Relations Board, which has provided safeguards to union workers since 1935. The transience of farm workers' lives added another hurdle, as did the vast reservoir of impoverished migrants willing to work for low wages. And until 1964, the wage levels were kept at low levels by Mexican aliens who were imported for temporary labor under the *bracero* program approved by Congress in 1942, during the wartime labor shortage. Despite the objections of organized labor and farm workers, the growers' lobbies managed to keep using *bracero* labor until 1964 when

Congress ended the program. Finally in 1970, when the union forced the table-grape growers into concessions, it was clear that the Chávez formula of organization, strikes, and boycotts would make unionization of other farm workers inevitable.

By 1973, the United Farm Workers Union (UFWU) was a fully accredited affiliate of the AFL-CIO, having graduated from its organizing committee status in early 1972. UFWU had signed collective-bargaining agreements with more than 200 growers, and its membership had grown from a few hundred to an estimated 40,000. From the tiny office in Delano, the small farm town 150 miles north of Los Angeles, where Chávez's movement began, the union spread to twenty-seven field offices in California, Arizona, and as far east as Florida, where Chávez organized 2,000 citrus workers who came under contract in early 1972. Like no rural leader before him, Chávez managed to project *la causa* of the farm workers on a largely sympathetic nation. He dramatized the issue in front of millions of television viewers during the 1972 Democratic National Convention, when newsmen gave national exposure to the lettuce boycott, the latest of Chávez's organizing efforts and probably his most important.

The lettuce conflict is a classic economic and political power struggle, and it has become the watershed of Chávez's project of creating a national farm workers union. The major issue was symbolic—if Chávez succeeded in California's Salinas Valley, where a third of the nation's lettuce supply is produced, there would be no stopping either him or his union. Initially, Chávez called a strike of up to 7,000 workers, but a court order banned picketing. Chávez was jailed briefly in late 1970, and then he spent most of 1971 in fruitless negotiations that finally broke off with Chávez resorting to another boycott. This time, though, Chávez met the strongest effort ever mounted to stop him. A coalition of the American Farm Committee and the Western Growers Association launched a national drive to strip Chávez of his chief weapons—the secondary boycott and harvest-time strikes. In August, Chávez himself admitted before the California Labor Federation AFL-CIO convention that a proposition on the November ballot in California would destroy his union. "If they succeed," he told the convention, "you're next."

While there were plenty of parallels between the lettuce and grape strikes, the differences were more striking. In 1971, Chávez was an established labor boss with a full-fledged union that no longer received economic assistance from the AFL-CIO or the United Auto Workers but relied on dues, investments, and contributions. The lettuce workers were not living in dire poverty, although UFWU literature made it clear that their income was often below the national poverty level. Because their work involved a grueling stooping posture and some specialized techniques, the lettuce workers were an economic elite among farm laborers. They could make up to $12,000 in a good year and rarely less than $5,000, working year-round with the same firm as it moved from Salinas to the Imperial Valley to Arizona. The union already had produced fringe benefits for the lettuce workers never before enjoyed by farm workers — paid vacations, holidays, and leaves of absence for family death and jury duty. The most sweeping benefit, though, was the Robert F. Kennedy medical plan, which cost employers ten cents an hour per worker beyond the regular rate, and which paid out $1.8 million in health benefits in its first two years. But the biggest difference between the grape and lettuce *huelgas* was that the lettuce boycott failed to achieve anything like the momentum of the grape boycott. At the same time, the anti-Chávez forces and growers were fighting their strongest battle against the union, a last-ditch effort.

Despite Chávez's troubles, the UFWU began to have an economic impact on the vegetable growers. And soon, just like the grape growers, the lettuce growers began to bow to the union. The growers saw that the threat was no longer unions per se but Chávez's union in particular, and not simply because of wages. The growers saw Chávez's movement as part of a national social force threatening to take from them their traditional right of control over their farms. Ultimately, who controls agriculture was at stake.

This century has been marked by violence, exploitation, and futile attempts at organization, and Chávez's UFWU was the first field workers' union to gain a toehold in California agriculture. Ever since the 1860s, the growers have been able to thwart all organizing efforts because they could always get cheap labor. First, they used the California Indians, then the Chinese, the Japanese, the Filipinos, the Okies, and finally the Mexican-Americans. Through the century, California agriculture thrived and grew into a $4-billion-a-year business, the largest in the nation in the 1970s. California growers kept the unions out by lobbying to keep farm laborers from getting legislative protection. The 1935 Wagner Act, giving workers the right of collective bargaining, excluded farm laborers.

There were sporadic bursts of labor-organizing activity, but the growers managed to retain complete freedom and power over their work force, a power sometimes exercised with a kind of benevolent paternalism. Often, though, this was a power backed by selfish and arbitrary authority; labor contractors hired and fired on impulse, took bribes, and herded migrant workers into hovel-like labor camps.

With the coming of César Chávez, this social order was reversed. The standard UFWU contract radically upset the power relationships in agriculture, eliminating the contractor, for instance, in favor of hiring halls controlled and administered by the union. The grower could no longer hire outside the union, except when the union work force was depleted. The contract stipulated that workers be sent out to growers through the hiring halls on the basis of growers' requests. The idea was to assign workers to a ranch on the basis of an elaborate system of seniority, designed and administered by the union. A detailed grievance procedure protected workers from arbitrary dismissal. Even more significant was a system of ranch committees elected by the field crews. Now the growers faced their once lowly field hands across conference tables to negotiate grievances and contract conditions. "The union," one disgruntled rancher told an interviewer, "wants to be the *patron*."

Yet, in the beginning, such a statement would have seemed absurd. In the mid-1960s, few observers gave Chávez a chance to succeed. Too many other farm labor-organizing efforts had failed. Of course most of the previous efforts had originated on the outside, and the money was quickly pulled out when defeat appeared imminent. But Chávez came from the ranks, and it soon became evident that he would not pull out.

In the years that followed, Chávez was able to meld self-sacrifice, non-violence, and nationalism into a force backed by the church, the *barrios*, labor, the radicals, the students, and the wealthy liberals. Marshall Ganz, the UFWU's director of boycotts, explained in an interview, "People everywhere can respond to a non-violent movement. It has great power. Also the aspect of sacrifice. It's a religious idea, in a way. The fasts, the pilgrimages. The religious content to the movement is part of the people who are the movement. Take salaries. The union couldn't survive with them. To build you have to have sacrifice. Work sixteen hours a day. It doesn't happen otherwise. That's why so few movements succeed."

And in Chávez, the farm labor movement had a leader who represented the bleak past of the Mexican-American. He was the son of migrant workers, attended dozens of schools but never got beyond the seventh grade, and as a teenager, became a *pachuco*, or Chicano street tough. During Chávez's boyhood, his parents tried to scratch a living from the arid desert earth of an eighty-acre farm in Arizona's Gila Valley near Yuma. But when the farm failed in the Depression, the Chávez family packed up and headed to California, where the father found little work. The family was forced to spend one winter in a tent, living on beans, tortillas, and an occasional potato. Finally the next spring, the family learned the harvest schedule and began the migrant workers' circuit, beginning in the Imperial and Coachella valleys of the south, going up through California to the area north of San Francisco and into the Napa Valley, working each crop in turn—asparagus, grapes, beets, potatoes, beans, plums, apricots. In 1941, the family settled in Delano, where Chávez met his wife, Helen Fabela, herself a worker in the Delano vineyards since she was fourteen. In 1948, César and Helen were married, and two years later, while working on an apricot farm in San Jose, Chávez met the man who changed his life and the future of agriculture in California.

The awakening of Chávez's social awareness came in a seamy San Jose *barrio* called *Sal Si Puedes* (Get out if you can). There he met Fred Ross, a tall, quiet organizer for Saul Alinsky's Community Service Organization (CSO), who got him working with Mexican-Americans in the cities. Chávez soon began to organize the poor for political and economic gain. At the same time he began to improve his reading and writing; he was determined to carve out a better life for himself, but he always had to push himself to assume a leadership role. Much of the organizing was done through house meetings, and Chávez always seemed concerned not to appear pretentious. "I would get to the meeting early and drive back and forth past the house, too nervous to go in and face the people," he later recalled in an interview. "Finally, I would force myself to go inside and sit in a corner. I was quite thin then, and young, and most of the people were middle-aged. Someone would say, 'Where's the organizer?' And I would pipe up, 'Here I am.' Then they would say in Spanish—these were very poor people and we hardly spoke anything but Spanish—'Ha! This kid?' Most of them said they were interested, but the hardest part was to get them to start pushing themselves, on their own initiative."

In 1962, after he had served as an organizer and director of the Mexican-American Community Service Organization for nine years, Chávez moved his family to Delano, in the San Joaquin Valley. There, with the $1,200 in savings, he began the National Farm Workers' Association (NFWA). During his first six months in Delano, Chávez drove his battered 1953 Mercury station wagon 300,000 miles across the valley and talked to more than 50,000 workers. Soon, the money ran out, but Chávez found that poverty could be a blessing. "I went to the people and started asking for food," he told an interviewer. "It turned out to be about the best thing I could have done, although at first it's hard on your pride. Some of our best members came in that way. If people give you their food, they'll give you their hearts." In September 1962, when the association had its first formal meeting, 287 people attended, and the Chávez farm labor movement was under way.

It took two years, though, for the NFWA to feel strong enough to wrestle the growers on a substantive issue. Finally, in 1964, the association took legal action against one grower who was paying less than the minimum wage of $1.25 an hour. After months of quarreling, Chávez's union won, proving that the growers could be beaten.

But it was not until May 1965 that the union had its first strike. A group of rose grafters who were discontented over low wages won a 120 percent wage increase after a strike of only four days. So intent was Chávez on making the strike succeed that on the first morning he and Dolores Huerta, his tiny, brash assistant, drove out to check the workers' homes.

They found lights in several homes where the workers were planning to go back to work, and they had to reconvince them to go through with the strike. In one instance, Mrs. Huerta, who later became vice-president of the UFWU, saw no other way to prevent four workers from going back to the fields than by blocking their driveway with her green panel truck, turning off the key, and putting it away in her purse.

The great grape strike did not begin until the end of that same summer in Delano. Ironically, Chávez did not start the strike; the largely Filipino grape pickers of the AFL-CIO's fledgling Agricultural Workers Organizing Committee (AWOC) walked off when some grape growers refused to pay the AWOC members wages equal to those given field hands imported from Mexico. On September 16, Mexican Independence Day, Chávez's union decided unanimously to join the strike. At the Roman Catholic church in Delano, a tumultuous meeting reverberated with cries of *"Viva la huelga!" "Viva la causa!" "Viva la union!"* Chávez's group soon merged with the AWOC, then headed by a Filipino named Larry Itliong, to form the United Farm Workers Organizing Committee. Itliong took a secondary role to Chávez in the movement, but in 1971, six years after the great grape strike began, Itliong left the union and bitterly complained about its direction under Chávez.

In 1965, however, Chávez and Itliong were locked arm in arm in the struggle against the grape growers. In 1966, the union signed its first collective bargaining contract. Soon, though, it became apparent that even with the sophisticated assistance of AFL-CIO organizers like William Kircher, Chávez would never pull large numbers of laborers out of the fields. It is estimated that only 3 percent of California's grape pickers joined the union during the strike. The growers, meanwhile, spent hundreds of thousands of dollars on an anti-union publicity campaign. What finally had an effect on the farmers was economics. In 1967, Chávez resorted to a boycott, and eventually this tactic threatened to squeeze the growers out of the grape business.

Also, it was the boycott that made *la causa* into a national issue as hundreds of farm workers, students, and volunteers carried the fight to the major cities in the country. On their holy crusade, bearing aloft a stylized banner, a black Aztec eagle on a red field, the representatives of *la causa* picketed supermarket chains that continued selling California grapes. The issue left virtually no middle ground, and at one point even the Pentagon took sides, substantially increasing its grape orders for mess-hall tables. And generally, the division broke along ideological lines. California Governor Ronald Reagan branded the strike and boycott "immoral," "attempted blackmail"; Senator Robert F. Kennedy and later his widow Ethel and brother Edward supported Chávez and the farm workers.

And while the boycott made its presence felt, the name of one César Estrada Chávez was becoming a household word. Chávez alone symbolized *la causa*, its determination, its sacrifice, and its attempt at non-violence. Though he was the leader of the union, he and his wife and eight children subsisted on a ten-dollar-a-week union salary and on food from the nearby UFWOC headquarters communal kitchen. They lived in a tiny two-bedroom house in Delano, where they steadfastly abstained from casual socializing, liquor, and cigarettes. As his models, Chávez looked up to Emiliano Zapata, Gandhi, Nehru, and Martin Luther King. Chávez more than anyone or anything else gave the movement its strong religious overtones. He opposed birth control for his people, and he received Communion daily. He and his union received the support of clergymen of all faiths, and later, when labor peace came to the Delano vineyards, the U.S. Bishops Committee on Farm Labor Disputes, a group of five Roman Catholic bishops, helped get the contract signed.

It is no accident, then, that six months after the great grape strike began, there was a 300-mile farm workers' march, like a religious pilgrimage, from Delano to the steps of the state capitol at Sacramento. Chávez wanted the march to be non-sectarian, and at the very front of it, alongside the union's own brilliant pennant and Mexican and American flags, there waved a banner depicting Our Lady of Guadalupe together with a large cross and the Star of David. On Easter Sunday, twenty-five days after the march began, the farm workers arrived in Sacramento, with Chávez's eighty-two-year-old father among them. The workers received no official welcome, but it was during this pilgrimage that the union got its first two contracts from Schenley Industries and the huge Di

Giorgio ranch. Both Schenley and Di Giorgio later sold their table-grape holdings.

Chávez himself was not reluctant in fueling the legend and mystique building up around him and his movement. In February 1968, he began a twenty-five-day fast "as an act of penance, recalling workers to the non-violent roots of their movement." When at last Chávez broke the fast, Senator Robert F. Kennedy came to kneel beside him to receive Communion, while some 8,000 other persons joined them in a Delano park for a bread-breaking ceremony.

Throughout the lettuce strike, Chávez's fear of possible violence never materialized, although on a number of occasions he and other union members were arrested in connection with picketing activities. Several times Chávez's union was blamed for packing sheds that were set ablaze, as well as tires slashed and windows broken. The union steadfastly · denied any responsibility for the incidents.

But these losses amounted to little compared to the millions of dollars that the grape growers lost as a result of the nationwide boycott, the most effective in American labor history. Through the impact they made on American consumers, the boycott workers got non-union grapes off the counters of most of the nation's chain stores. On July 29, 1970, Chávez accepted surrender from the Delano table-grape growers, among them John Giumarra, Sr., one of eleven members of a family that owns the largest table-grape vineyard in the world and was also the original prime target of the strike. The agreement between the union and twenty-six growers in the Delano area who produce half of the state's table-grape crop was witnessed by some 400 workers who packed the white-painted room at union headquarters (later a hiring hall). The workers, several carrying their black-eagle strike banners, sang, laughed, cheered, and applauded in a celebration that Chávez described as "the beginning of a new day." While Giumarra signed the contract on behalf of the growers, it was his son, John, Jr., who acted as spokesman and said: "It's dawned on everyone in agriculture that unionism has finally come to this industry and there's no sense pretending it will go away. The thing to do is come to the best possible terms." Only a few weeks earlier, however, the elder Giumarra had told one reporter: "If this outfit is successful, it will be one of the saddest days for America. It's not a question of wages, it's a question of harnessing all of agriculture and ultimately taking a bigger chunk of the consumer's check for food. I think Chávez is looking to get control of agriculture in the United States, and this is the jumping off place."

Even in his moment of triumph, though, Chávez had to face another major obstacle. The growers of crops other than grapes felt so strongly about Chávez's union that, even before the Delano table-grape war was over, the lettuce, strawberry, carrot, and celery growers in the Salinas Valley rushed to sign labor agreements with the Teamsters — they were trying to head off Chávez from organizing their own field hands. The Teamsters were already foes of the UFWOC, having opposed the union in the early grape-organizing days. But in its fight with the Teamsters, the Chávez union drew the support of the national AFL-CIO, also old enemies of the Teamsters. Basically, this was a struggle to represent the field hands in the Salinas Valley, known as the nation's "salad bowl." The battle went to the courts and then again to the consumer when Chávez called for a national boycott of non-UFWOC lettuce. He was jailed for pressing this boycott, and that experience did little harm to his martyr image. In the spring of 1971, with the lettuce boycott making its impact, Chávez reached a truce with the Teamsters, who chose to leave the field hands to the UFWOC while retaining representation rights over the processing workers.

Even six years after they signed their first collective bargaining contract, Chávez and the union were still struggling to consolidate their past gains while defending themselves against an increasing number of powerful attacks from a number of connected forces. The union had to engage itself in battles on so many fronts that its true effectiveness was questioned. Despair and fatigue drove off several union staffers, and one of the movement's major leaders resigned in anger.

Undoubtedly the strongest attacks on Chávez and his union were the growers' attempts to get measures through Congress, state legislatures, the courts, and the ballot to outlaw the chief weapons in Chávez's movement — harvest-time strikes and the secondary boycott. First time around, agribusiness failed to get congressional legislation that would have placed the UFWU under National Labor Relations Board jurisdiction. But in 1972, a coalition including the American Farm Committee, the Western Growers Association, and the American Farm Bureau Federation, continued their attack by introducing anti-UFWU legislation in seventeen states and again in Congress. In California, after several fruitless attempts to push a bill through the legislature, the agricultural interests raised almost $250,000 to have an initiative motion placed on the November 7 general election ballot. This referendum not only pitted Chávez against the growers but also pointed up a clash of philosophies and cultures. Known as Proposition 22, the initiative put Chávez and the UFWU on the run, as he found himself engaged in a political struggle against what he described as a threat on the life of his union. The UFWU got involved in a massive voter registration campaign, and on election day several thousand farm workers were carried from the fields to the cities to build up the vote. In what Chávez later hailed as a victory comparable to Delano, California voters overwhelmingly rejected Proposition 22.

In three states, though, the UFWU was unable to prevent anti-union legislation from being enacted. Arizona, Idaho, and Kansas enacted statutes that outlawed secondary boycotts, prohibited the union from contacting workers while on the growers' property, gave the growers right to a ten-day restraining order in the threat of a harvest-time strike, and outlawed all strikes unless approved by a secret ballot supervised and certified by a seven-man state board appointed by the governor. By far the heaviest burden on the union was the ban of secondary boycotts, which had proven to be the farm workers' decisive weapon in winning the great grape strike. Through this technique, union workers and sympathizers urged the boycott of a product at the place where it was being sold, or else urged that the store or chain of stores be boycotted. The state legislation would allow primary boycotts limited to naming the specific grower of the produce. But a supermarket picket with a sign reading, "Don't buy non-union lettuce" would be subject to a $5,000 fine and a year in jail.

Caught off guard by the legislation in Arizona, Chávez responded by selecting that state as a prime battleground for the running feud with the growers. The union began with a campaign to recall Governor Jack Williams, a Republican, who had signed the bill, and had described it as being comparable to right-to-work legislation. Shortly after the bill was passed in mid-1972, Chávez went on a dramatic twenty-four-day fast aimed at calling attention to *la causa* while galvanizing farm workers and other allies into the coalition that had won previous fights. During the fast, he wrote a letter to union members, telling them he was not particularly protesting the new law nor was he angry at the growers.

"My concern is the spirit of fear that lies behind such laws in the hearts of growers and legislators across the country," Chávez wrote. "Somehow these powerful men and women must be helped to realize that there is nothing to fear from treating their workers as fellow human beings. We only wish an opportunity to organize our union and to work non-violently to bring a new day of hope and justice to the farm workers of our country."

At Chávez's call, union supporters marched through Phoenix to a downtown hotel where more than 5,000 attended a memorial mass for the late Senator Robert F. Kennedy, and Chávez broke the fast with Communion bread, while a dozen clergymen, most of them in red vestments with the farm workers' black eagle on their chests, stood nearby, holding hands and singing together, "We shall overcome."

Both Chávez and the agricultural interests were prepared for a long, bitter fight in Arizona, where the growers felt they were making a last stand against the UFWU's dream of unionizing all agricultural workers. At the same time Chávez and his union felt they were cornered into taking a position in Arizona and California, where they had begun building an important new political force. An indication of the union's growing strength came earlier in 1972 when Chávez and UFWU supporters forced the National Labor Relations Board to withdraw an attempt to seek an injunction against the union's use of the secondary boycott. Union sympathizers saw the injunction as an effort by the administration to place farm workers under NLRB jurisdiction for the first time in history. Movement supporters, including U.S. Representative Edward R. Roybal, a Democrat from California, accused the administration of attacking the UFWU in order to attract healthy campaign contributions from the agribusiness interests that had suffered financially from the nationwide boycotts against non-union grapes and lettuce.

Not all the criticism of Chávez and the union, however, came from outside. The sacrifice and demands that the union required of its leadership burned out several staff members through the first years of organizing. The biggest ripple of dissension came in 1971 when Itliong, second in command of the union since merging his AFL-CIO-backed Filipino farm workers with Chávez's group, resigned as vice-president of UFWOC. This move came as a shock because Itliong had been with the farm labor movement from the very beginning. Itliong's AWOC started the great grape strike in Delano, and Itliong teamed up then with Chávez, Dolores Huerta, Gilbert Padilla, and Antonio Orendain to continue organizing and pushing *la causa.* (Later, Padilla and Orendain each took a crack at the long, hard—and for the first years disappointingly unsuccessful—struggle to organize field hands in South Texas.)

Itliong was publicly critical of Chávez and the direction the union was taking, but he also refused to cooperate with anti-UFWOC forces. He felt the union was creating future problems for itself by relying so heavily on volunteer social activists. He said the doctors at the Delano clinic and the programmers computerizing the union's records were transients who would soon move on. He accused Chávez of risking alienating the minority-group members by keeping Anglos in key union positions, and he maintained that the "Anglo brain trust" was more concerned with influencing long-range social change than with the immediate welfare of the farm workers. He complained bitterly in one interview that the union's leadership had been deliberately antagonistic to the growers and that Chávez had increasingly removed himself from personal contact with his constituency and had delegated authority to others. Moreover, Itliong felt that the union had gone beyond the purpose originally conceived for it and was now risking its past gains. "What I'm worried about really," he said in one interview, "is we are going to go back fighting again with the growers, and people are going to be asked to sacrifice and suffer. It doesn't look like a bright future."

But Chávez and the union's leadership felt there was no other choice in the matter and viewed their movement as one that was just, perhaps even divinely sanctioned. Much of the criticism failed to affect Chávez, but the charge of Anglo influence is one that really raised his ire. In an interview, Chávez explained his position and insisted he would never allow Chicano union members to dominate the union to the exclusion of the deprived groups.

"A poor black worker in Florida hurts me as much as a poor Chicano worker in Texas," he said. "Now the union has a Chicano thrust, but that will change as we spread to other areas. This is an economic movement by poor workers and [it] will stay that way as long as I'm around to influence it."

In the early 1970s, though still beset by problems in California, Chávez began laying the groundwork for future organizing efforts in the Pacific Northwest, Texas, the Midwest, and the South. An indication of this expansion came when Chávez and the growing UFWU headquarters staff moved away from the old union center at Delano, called Forty Acres, which was reduced to field office status. They set up a new headquarters in a former tuberculosis sanitarium near the Kern County hamlet of Keene. Rented from a union sympathizer, the old wood-frame hospital buildings were scattered in one corner of a rolling 280-acre plot. A forest surrounded the area and the pine-studded Tehachapi foothills in the background provided a sense of quiet isolation fitting *La Paz*, meaning the peaceful place, the nickname the union members gave the new headquarters. Officially known as *Nuestra Senora de la Paz* (Our Lady of Peace) Educational Center, the buildings are used to house farm workers who are being trained for union leadership roles.

In 1973, in addition to coordinating the new organizing efforts, the union also found itself continuing its old fights. It had internal problems both in staff and services; and the opposition from the agribusiness, despite the California voters' rejection of the anti-UFWU proposition, was renewed in the state legislature. On top of that, the union had to administer its 200 contracts, including the all-important grape contracts that were up for renegotiation.

When those contracts began expiring in the spring of 1973, Chávez and his union found themselves in trouble. Most of the growers gave up on negotiations with the UFW and quickly signed with the Teamsters in what the AFL-CIO called "sweetheart" contracts that were not as far-reaching as the Chávez union wanted. But the most striking difference in the contracts was that the Teamsters' pact did away with the controversial hiring hall system that Chávez insisted upon. By the latter part of the year, Chávez by his own count lost 150 out of 182 contracts, and his membership was down from 40,000 to 10,000. The reasons for this are disputed. To the Chávistas, the defection of the grape growers was a clear case of collusion and a conspiracy by the growers and the Teamsters aimed at destroying the UFW. The growers denied the charges and laid Chávez's problems to a too-rigid stance on renegotiating the contracts and the sincere revulsion among many farm workers against the UFW's heavy-handed treatment of its members.

Near the end of 1973, Chávez's union and the Teamsters reached a surprising settlement. The Teamsters gave up their claim of representing farm workers and agreed to allow the UFW to negotiate new contracts with the Coachella Valley grape growers. The agreement came only after a bitter battle in which Chávez resorted to the two weapons that had won the first grape war: the strike and the boycott. But the settlement merely closed one hostility and reopened another for Chávez and his union. Having been wounded severely by the fight with the Teamsters, the UFW faced an uphill struggle in renegotiating old contracts with the growers, while at the same time continuing its efforts to expand the unionizing drive to other agricultural products.

These troubles, though, were indications of how much more Chávez and his union were becoming involved in large-scale labor problems that went beyond specifically Chicano issues. In 1972, the UFW-Teamster struggle itself became a political issue, with support of the two sides clearly divided along party lines.

At the Republican National Convention at Miami Beach, Governor Reagan and Agriculture Secretary Earl Butz told a press conference that the Teamsters had begun to package their workers' lettuce in red, white, and blue boxes stamped with a "Reelect the President" label. During the 1968 presidential campaign, at the height of the great grape strike, Richard M. Nixon had made it a point to be photographed eating grapes as he wooed not only the California voters but the financial backing of the state's corporate agricultural interest.

The political climate affecting Chávez and his union's lettuce fight was much different a month earlier in Miami Beach, at what Senator Edward M. Kennedy later described as "the most widely publicized lettuce boycott rally ever held—the Democratic National Convention." This was the first time an entire Democratic National Convention, from delegates to party platform to party nominees, committed itself openly and publicly to the cause of the nation's farm workers. During the convention, boycott signs were periodically unfurled by the California delegation, including in its midst Dolores Huerta; and about a dozen states prefaced their votes during each of the roll calls with remarks supporting the lettuce boycott.

Above all, the attention given Chávez and the UFWU by both conventions showed the strength of the union's threat— and that it was now political as well as economic. Chávez's farm labor movement had developed as a reaction to the farm workers' economic deprivation, which itself was representative of the plight and disenfranchisement of Mexican-Americans in the country. And in one decade, Chávez and his union managed to imbed themselves in the mainstream of American politics. In 1972, Chávez himself was given a mandate of sorts by the California voters who defeated the proposition on the state ballot that would have brought the union's assault to a virtual halt. At the same time, though, Chávez and the UFWU were drifting away from the heart of the Chicano movement, and the Mexican-American activists had begun looking elsewhere for new leadership and direction.

6 CÉSAR CHÁVEZ: FATHER, SON, AND HOLY GHOST

In the early 1970s, César Chávez was the only Mexican-American leader with a major national reputation. After gaining almost legendary status in the farm workers' struggle, he was caught in the wave of the civil rights movement. Chávez took his place next to the Reverend Martin Luther King, Jr., and Delano was coming to be a Chicano version of Selma. Now, Chávez was moving in circles beyond the grapefields. As a celebrity he acquired both a following of believers and some powerful antagonists: the Kennedys embraced him, but Richard Nixon snubbed him, just as one segment of society assailed him as a troublemaker while another hailed him as the Chicano Moses—the man who would lead his people out of the socio-economic wilderness. Chávez seemed content to perpetuate the sanctimonious air surrounding himself and his movement. He had fasted not just once but twice, and the media made due note. His travel around the country increased. And he became less easily accessible to his constituency of farm workers. But Chávez had reason for his eccentricities. He was an American hero of sorts, and he had public opinion behind him.

Ironically, while Chávez was building his base nationally, his stature within the Chicano movement diminished. By the end of 1972, Chicano activists no longer regarded him and the United Farm Workers Union as the leaders of the movement. This was a major break within the movement that Chávez had initiated, but it was a split that went largely unreported, possibly because most of the reporters who occasionally covered the movement did not understand it.

By 1972, the Chicano movement and La Raza Unida were synonymous. The movement had grown into an independent national party intent on breaking past ties to the Democratic party and asserting its own role in the political system. The party's national organization was skeletal, at best, with the major stirring centered in a handful of states in the Southwest. With 3.1 million Mexican-Americans living in California, that state and Texas had long been the two most obvious targets of La Raza Unida organizers, who quickly learned that many Chicanos have an almost religious devotion to the Democratic party. Even so, in Texas, getting the party off the ground was relatively easy. La Raza Unida had been born in South Texas, and its parent organization, the Mexican-American Youth Organization, had been developing chapters throughout the state since 1967. In California, however, La Raza Unida organizers had to begin from scratch. There was no major group behind the California party, which became a shifting coalition of students and other activists without the know-how or resources to organize.

Chávez and his union stayed at arm's length from La Raza Unida, and the party leaders who expected organizing assistance from the farm labor movement soon realized that Chávez wanted no part of the party.

From a purely political standpoint, Chávez could hardly be blamed for avoiding La Raza Unida. To aid the party would have meant siphoning away voters from the Democratic party, with its historical ties to his own movement. Since the mid-1960s, Chávez and his farm labor struggle had been befriended by liberal Democrats who saw both the Chicano and labor aspects of the movement as ingredients of the old Rooseveltian Democratic coalition. The AFL-CIO, with its own strong ties to the Democratic party, provided financial support to the young union. And when Chávez focused the thrust of the great grape strike on the nationwide boycott, both the AFL-CIO and the Democrats helped the union succeed.

Consequently, Chávez realized that to desert the Democratic party would be to jeopardize the future of his movement. In fact, Chávez needed the Democrats' support more than ever in the early 1970s. The agricultural interests were trying to pass legislation, both nationally and at the state level, that would drastically curb the UFWU's use of harvest-time strikes and the secondary boycott. Through its own lobbying efforts and with the help of sympathetic Democratic legislators, the union had succeeded in defeating such legislation in all but three instances. Now there were indications that the growers were stepping up their assault. And La Raza Unida, without a legislator or a congressman to its name, would be of no help to the union in its struggles in Congress and the state houses.

When La Raza Unida found its voice, in 1970, there soon came a steady stream of criticism against Chávez. Much was said privately, and the party leaders hesitated to make their gripes public for fear of giving an impression of discord and disunity among the Chicanos. Something like discord affects all movements, Chicano, black, or any other. La Raza Unida, at first, was afraid to show a weakness or uncertainty that would only bolster the confidence of the establishment. The leaders worried about the reaction among other Mexican-Americans to an attack on the nation's Number One Mexican-American. Criticizing Chávez would be like criticizing the father, who in the Mexican-American patriarchal family structure represented ultimate authority and a living sanctuary.

In fact, Chávez had come to represent a father figure both to the Chicano movement and to Mexican-Americans in general. The pattern reflected the traditional rural society of Mexico, and many of these values could be traced back to Spanish practice and the social caste system that grew up in her New World colonies. Spanish Catholicism played an important part in developing fatalism and resignation, and closely tied to religion was the authority of the father. In the process of acculturation into a second language and culture, many Mexican-American families experienced upsets or disruptions in the orderly pattern of the patriarchal structure. In such instances, the father's *machismo*, or maleness, suffered, and his role as the dominant figure in the family would suffer as well. Gradually parental control and authority tended to slip away, threatening the entire traditional structure.

In late summer of 1972, after months of private bickering, the collapse of the united Chicano movement finally occurred. The split came in El Paso, where about 4,000 delegates and visitors from eighteen states and the District of Columbia met during the Labor Day weekend to organize La Raza Unida into a national political party.

Though never active in La Raza Unida nor particularly sympathetic to it, Chávez was invited to the convention along with President Nixon, Senator George S. McGovern, and a long list of others. The leaders never really expected either presidential nominee to attend, but at the same time they announced they would not accept any representatives of the two candidates as substitutes. The party leaders thought there was a strong possibility that Chávez would come, and they were concerned what influence the farm labor leader might have on the delegates.

By their own admission, none of La Raza Unida leaders could approach Chávez in stature. The farm labor movement had gone beyond militancy and protest, and in California, at least, it had begun to modify the social order. Chávez's leadership was acknowledged by organized labor leaders and Democratic politicians. But the Raza Unida organizers were disappointed that Chávez, for all his connections with the Anglo establishment, had failed either to push Chicano issues or to demand political concessions for other Chicanos. Chávez appeared to be willing to work toward achieving parity for his people through a slow but steady process that eventually would meld Mexican-Americans without a trace into American life. Such a pattern was a long-standing, traditional formula for ethnics to achieve equality in America, whenever the dominant white Anglo-American culture would tolerate portions of the ethnic culture to give American society a unique and exotic blend. Such was the idea of the American "melting pot," undoubtedly the most popular but least substantiated of all theories on American society.

The differences between Chávez and La Raza Unida made for philosophical as well as political conflict. Chávez subscribed to something like the melting-pot concept, and he was faithfully leading his movement of poor, downtrodden, and alien followers toward prosperity, equality, and assimilation. On the other hand La Raza Unida rejected the old paradigm and believed strongly in Chicano nationalism. The Raza Unida leaders advocated community control of local schools and institutions as a first step toward creating a Chicano system and a new Chicano self-identity. The young Chicanos were saying that their advancement in the face of what they considered a hostile Anglo society depended on their ability to develop a countervailing power that would require its own organizational structure and leadership—Chicano power. They felt that assimilation was self-defeating in its present token form because it dissipated Chicano militancy, absorbed Chicano talent, and dimmed Chicano consciousness, while giving little substantive return to the Chicano masses. La Raza Unida looked upon the Mexican-American official or leader who replaced an Anglo but continued with the same values and traditions as merely an extension of the white power structure in a dark face.

La Raza Unida's separatist philosophy rejected the view that with more time and more education, Chicanos would assimilate into an Anglo-American culture and social structure, as had the immigrant groups. Indeed, there were strong indications that such an assimilationist ideology, based on a misapprehension of what actually did happen to the other minority groups, was outdated and incorrect. The white minority groups, the "white ethnics," had not moved up but had moved in at certain modest levels of the social structure. Upward mobility of the ethnic groups just did not take place. The Irish, Poles, Italians, Jews, and others who took over semi-skilled and moderately skilled jobs did not move on to greater heights but instead remained in control of their positions. And, instead of following up the experience of the white ethnics, the Chicanos—like the blacks—were victims of it. La Raza Unida activists maintained that anyone who insisted on total social assimilation into American life was either ignorant or indifferent to the fact that no prominent ethnic group had achieved such assimilation. And in the early 1970s, no one was more committed to the ideology of limitless assimilation for Chicanos, and understandably was more resistant to the ideas of Chicano power and Chicano separatism, than white liberals and Chicano moderates like Chávez.

So when Raza Unida leaders met in El Paso the week before their convention to plan strategies and policies, only a loose, uneasy truce held together the national coalition of strident, nationalistic activists and Chávez. To the dismay of the Raza Unida leaders, Chávez had not replied to the invitation, and they chose to use this moment to put him on the spot.

Working secretly, a pre-convention planning committee composed of a handful of party leaders, including La Raza Unida founder José Angel Gutiérrez and Texas State Chairman Mario Compean, decided to withdraw the invitation to Chávez. In its place, they extended an invitation that would make Chávez the guest of the Texas delegation. Chávez would be allowed to address the convention, but only on the condition that he limit himself to the Chicano and farm labor movements. The idea was to prevent Chávez from seeking an endorsement for Senator McGovern or from talking about the Democratic presidential nominee, whom Chávez already had endorsed.

Chávez's endorsement of McGovern had turned off the Raza Unida leaders. During the California primary, when both McGovern and Senator Hubert H. Humphrey were courting the Mexican-American vote, Chávez endorsed McGovern as the man who "has consistently stood with us on issues most vital to our people."

On at least one occasion, Compean, a temperamental party organizer who had been with Gutiérrez since the beginning of the movement, confided that the only presidential aspirant La Raza Unida could support was McGovern, but not as a Democrat. As La Raza Unida saw it, to support any Democratic presidential nominee would be a severe blow to the party's own chances as well as a contradiction of the movement's philosophy of political independence. Traditionally, Mexican-Americans voted Democratic, and the only political education many had received was to "pull *la palanca*" (the big lever) at the polls. In Texas, where La Raza had earned a place on the general election ballot, party leaders realized the difficulty involved in simply getting Mexican-

Americans to switch from pulling the Democratic *palanca* to the Raza Unida *palanca*. Teaching much of the Mexican-American electorate to split a ballot, though seemingly simple, would complicate matters and perhaps only frustrate the voter who might decide just to continue pulling the Democratic *palanca*. So, in addition to the ideological differences involved, endorsing McGovern might only result in the Chicanos' continuing to vote the straight Democratic ticket.

As the convention neared, party leaders contacted Chávez and notified him of the conditions under which he could attend and address the convention. Seething, Chávez turned down the invitation, leaving La Raza Unida with what many of its leaders wanted—a break with the movement's past leadership that would allow the new leaders the freedom to give the movement a new tone and new direction.

The split with Chávez was the result of power struggles long developing within the Chicano movement. Less than two months after La Raza Unida's convention, New Mexico land-reform leader Reies López Tijerina broke with the party. And at the party's first national meeting after the November general election, Gutiérrez and Denver activist Corky Gonzales exchanged heated words that resulted in Gutiérrez and Ramsey Muñiz's walking out of the meeting.

All the different divisions within La Raza Unida, along with the break with Chávez, made it seem likely that the Chicano movement, like the black movement, would become a collection of local and regional movements, each with its own leader but with no individual as a national spokesman. By the early 1970s, most black leaders realized that no one leader was going to follow in the footsteps of the late Martin Luther King. Several black leaders—the Reverend Jesse Jackson of Chicago and the Reverend Ralph David Abernathy of Atlanta in particular—described the black movement as operating on several fronts with local leaders who were more familiar with local problems. In their own way Reverend Jackson and Dr. Abernathy paralleled the split between Chávez and La Raza Unida. Jackson, the flamboyant young face of the black movement, parted with Dr. Abernathy and the Southern Christian Leadership Conference in the early 1970s and started his own civil rights group, Operation PUSH (People United to Save Humanity).

La Raza Unida's split with Chávez was only one mani-
festation of the anti-Chávez sentiment within the Chicano
movement and also among middle-class Mexican-Americans.
Chávez had become a public figure and thus a political target.

In the home stretch of the presidential race, President
Nixon's top Spanish-speaking campaigner was vehement in
criticism of Chávez, to counter the farm labor leader's en-
dorsement of Senator McGovern. At a press conference in
Dallas, Henry M. Ramirez, a California educator and chairman
of the President's Cabinet Committee on Opportunities for
Spanish-Speaking People, described Chávez as merely a labor
leader who was concerned only with the small percentage of
Mexican-Americans who were farm workers. Under tense
questioning, Ramirez called Chávez "only a minor [Mexican-
American] leader" who had no relevance to the average
Mexican-American. "He speaks for only 5 percent of the
Spanish-speaking people in the country," Ramirez said. "I'm
concerned about the other 95 percent. He's not. I'm concerned
about the Mexican-Americans in East Los Angeles and other
urban areas. When has he ever done anything for the urban
Mexican-American?"

In California, McGovern easily captured the Mexican-
American vote, even by the GOP's own sampling, and this
preference came as no surprise—in 1968, Nixon received only
10 percent of the Mexican-American vote. So Chávez's endorsement of McGovern could be seen as reinforcing the
Democratic cause. Yet whatever political influence Chávez
might wield did not carry into other parts of the country,
particularly Texas, where, to everyone's surprise, President
Nixon carried the Chicano vote.

Ramirez's criticism of Chávez went beyond politics, since
it lent credibility to La Raza Unida's charge that he had lost
relevance to the movement and to non-rural Mexican-Americans. The Raza Unida leaders themselves had been concerned about what effect their break with Chávez would have
on the rank and file party members who attended the El Paso
convention. Party leaders never told the convention of the
rift; even when he was confronted by a member of his delegation, Compean blamed Chávez for imposing his own conditions and creating the incident. The party leaders' concern
was well placed: the convention unanimously passed a resolu-

tion supporting the farm laborers, although Chávez was never mentioned by name.

Of course, Chávez had been criticized previously by individual leaders who were maneuvering to unseat him as the movement's most influential spokesman. Chávez himself had never sought to be the voice of all Chicanos, and lumping Chávez together with Tijerina, Gonzales, and Gutiérrez was to some degree a misrepresentation of both the farm labor and the Chicano movements. To be sure, the Chicano movement was a collection of several different movements, some of them with obvious differences but all asserting Chicano rights. In the beginning, Chávez's farm labor movement was seen as reflecting the plight and aspirations of all Mexican-Americans. The farm workers not only helped create other activism, but they also prepared the country for the militancy that followed. The philosophical differences between Chávez and other leaders did not become pronounced until after the Chicano movement turned to politics, an area where Chávez's detached attitude could not be tolerated for long.

Gonzales, the ambitious leader of the Crusade for Justice in Denver and organizer of the 1969 Chicano Youth Liberation Conference, longed to be recognized as the voice of the Chicano movement. On several occasions he spoke harshly of Chávez, once implying that the farm leader was an idiot. As colorful as Gonzales's rhetoric was, it only echoed more dramatic stirrings in California and New Mexico. Much more significant was the criticism that came from Tijerina shortly before La Raza Unida's national convention. Tijerina had long supported Chávez, and he sought to include him in La Raza Unida and in a series of "brotherhood awareness" conferences in New Mexico. But in a lengthy, introspective interview, Tijerina defended Chávez's decision to concentrate on the farm labor movement. "It has become a labor movement," he said. "César has never said he wanted to lead the movement of Indo-Hispanos or Chicanos, however you want to describe our people. He has been part of the [Chicano] movement, but he has his own problems and he has to solve them the way he sees best. He has his people to worry about first. You have to understand César as he is now. He is a union man—a union leader. He might not want to admit it, but I think it's fair to say César at this moment has more in common with your other union leaders, Meany and them, than he does with many other Mexicanos."

Tijerina's criticism was typical of the new wave of disenchantment with Chávez, when even old friends began to view him with discontent. The hierarchy of organized labor, including AFL-CIO President George Meany, expressed disapproval of Chávez and other maverick labor leaders who announced their support of Senator McGovern's presidential candidacy. Meany and the AFL-CIO, which for years had provided Chávez's union with financial and moral assistance, took a neutral stance in the 1972 presidential election and expected labor bosses like Chávez to follow in their path.

Chávez's willingness to cross his allies displayed not only his stubborn independence but also his confidence in the union. People sometimes forgot the enormous amount of power and influence that Chávez himself had amassed. Indeed, so steep a rise from so humble a beginning was notable in itself. But even more notable was the way in which Chávez had prospered. He had put up relatively little money, and his *huelga* had never succeeded in clearing the fields of farm workers. What had won the great grape strike and what had been the farm labor movement's most effective weapon was the boycott. By Chávez's own admission, his union organizing effort would probably have floundered and failed without the nationwide economic boycott.

It was the American public that turned the tide for the farm workers and contributed most heavily to Chávez's climb. Chávez, like the Black Panthers, was "radical chic," for the Beautiful People in New York; to liberal politicians, he was the voice and ears of the growing Chicano electorate; to the students, he became either a sociological phenomenon come to life or a modern-day Robin Hood ripping off the establishment; and the blue-collar working man saw him as a reminder of labor's own days of struggle earlier in the century. The sympathy and support of this section of the American public— the backbone of the old Democratic coalition—had come together behind Chávez and, in doing so, his supporters fashioned him as their own kind of establishment leader.

By the early 1970s, the young activist Chicanos who formed La Raza Unida saw Chávez as the establishment's tool. For them, he had begun to take on the characteristics of other Mexican-Americans appointed or elected to leadership roles by the established political system. Such an image encouraged La Raza Unida to reject Chávez; leaders ought to be selected by the Chicanos, not by the establishment. Actually, La Raza Unida saw almost every Mexican-American official as an Anglo establishment leader. In Texas, La Raza Unida hurled such labels at its two Mexican-American congressmen, Representatives Henry B. Gonzalez of San Antonio and Eligio (Kika) de la Garza of Mission. The criticism against de la Garza was supported by Ralph Nader's *Citizens Look at Congress,* a compilation of profiles on all congressmen released less than a month before the 1972 general election. De la Garza's 15th Congressional District comprised the southernmost part of the state, and it was extremely poor, populated largely by Mexican-American farmers and migrant workers. The report claimed there were 25,000 persons in the district who did not have potable water but that de la Garza appeared uninterested in alleviating the condition. According to the report, 90 to 95 percent of the federal funds that had gone into the district were channeled to support the interests of the 25 percent Anglo population of the district. De la Garza came off as an official who looked out for the district's moneyed Anglo establishment and was indifferent to the needs of his Mexican-American constituents.

Though Chávez never openly claimed the mantle of spokesman for the Chicanos, he likewise never hesitated to foster and encourage his public image. In what appeared to be a conscious effort, Chávez managed to maneuver both the movement and himself in such a way that to criticize him would be like criticizing the Church and everything else that was sacred.

Pitted against the Holy Virgin, the Church, and the clergy, the California growers could not help but come off as villains. Their criticism of Chávez and the farm labor movement, in fact their entire defense, took on the appearance of attacks against an entire nationality. Indeed, this was a conflict between cultures and philosophies, but the issues were blurred when the clash raised a religious issue with a connotation of the righteous against the damned.

Chávez and the farm workers were unique in seeking to instill in their movement the aura of the Church, religion, and self-proclaimed righteousness. Other Chicano-movement groups had shied away from linking themselves with the Church, which they blamed for cultivating passiveness among the Mexican-Americans. "The emphasis the Church places on misery and penance and suffering does nothing but buttress the condition we're in—and it's one hell of a condition," said José Angel Gutiérrez.

In fact, on the Sunday after Christmas in 1969, the Chicano movement showed real contempt for the Church. In Mission, Texas, about 100 young Mexican-Americans painted a statue of the Virgin brown, or actually metallic bronze, with paint from spray cans. Dressed in berets, brightly colored ponchos, and serapes, one by one they climbed a five-foot high pedestal to take a turn spraying the life-size gray stone statue while two guitarists and three singers provided an accompaniment of revolutionary songs. *"Yo soy Chicano, tengo color,"* they sang, *"Americano pero con honor."* ("I am Chicano, I have color/American, but with honor.") When the Virgin was brown from head to toe, the crowd cried, *"Viva La Raza! Viva la causa!"* The statue was cast against a great brown hulk of an Oblate Mission, founded and run for almost two centuries by white missionaries. Later, an Oblate priest complained that the mission had been desecrated, and he hinted that "Communists" had been at work.

But the young Chicanos saw the painting of Our Lady as an affirmation and a challenge. In the crowd were members of activist groups in Texas, California, and other parts of the West; they were celebrating their brownness and symbolically throwing down the gauntlet before the Catholic Church. No institution stands higher in Mexican-American esteem than the Church, but the affront to the Virgin shows how the Chicanos were challenging institutions and policies that had always been untouched or tolerated.

An overwhelming majority of Mexican-Americans are devout Roman Catholics, whose deep traditional respect for civil authority is surpassed only by their adulation of sacred authority. Chicano activists such as Gutiérrez were not critical of the divine authority of the Church or its theology but rather of its human dimension. Activists were saying it was the human expression of the Christian message, not the message itself, that had failed the Mexican-American; they contended that the Catholic Church had failed the Chicano on sociological grounds. With the election of John F. Kennedy as the first Catholic president of the United States, the Church could no longer be questioned as an accepted American institution. It was no longer considered an outsider, associated with immigrants; nor could it still be considered, in some corners, un-American. The Church was fully assimilated into American society, and it reflected all the same biases and prejudices of the majority Anglo society. Like other American institutions, the Church was geared to serve the majority, and, consequently, it discriminated within its system because the minorities were not taken into consideration in its planning. Only in May of 1970 was the first Spanish-surnamed bishop named to serve in the American Catholic hierarchy. Until that time, although one out of every four Catholics in the United States was a Spanish-surnamed person, they had no representation on the policy-making level of the American Catholic Church.

Culturally, there was a great gap of relevance between the clergy and the Spanish-speaking community. In the United States, the Church is administered mostly by clergymen raised in the German or Irish Church traditions. Sociologically, these traditions are in strong contrast to the Latin-American cultural pattern. Similarly, the Anglo-Saxon tradition in law and ethics differs from its Latin counterpart, if not in content, at least in cultural expression, on which religious expression is based. Mexican-Americans follow the Latin emphasis on personalism and the customs of a people, while the Anglo-Saxon tradition places its emphasis and respect on the written law. Logically, for instance, when a Catholic raised in the Irish-German tradition no longer complies with the laws of the Church, Mass attendance and marriage laws, he usually considers himself an ex-Catholic because he is outside the realm of the Church's written regulations. A Mexican-American Catholic may not have been at Mass for twenty years, but he still considers himself a Catholic because he recognizes other values than mere compliance to laws.

The language barrier has compounded the relevance gap between Mexican-Americans and the Catholic Church in America. Together, the cultural and language differences have led the Church, out of ignorance, not to see the crushing social needs of the Mexican-American. As the Chicano movement gained momentum, activists inevitably criticized the Church for its failure to respond to the problems and inequities in the educational, legal, economic, political, and social systems.

In March 1968, an estimated 15,000 Mexican-American students walked out of five East Los Angeles high schools to protest the mistreatment of students and the irrelevance of the educational system. They demanded a revised bilingual, bi-cultural curriculum that would point out the contributions of Mexican-Americans to the development of the Southwest and the United States. In the next two years, there were dozens more student walkouts in other parts of the Southwest. The protests came with the support of many of the students' parents, and they gained the backing of some teachers, educators, and individual priests. But the official Church remained silent.

The Church made no official comment even in August 1971, when an East Los Angeles parade and rally to demonstrate Mexican-American opposition to the war in Southeast Asia erupted into a riot that resulted in three deaths. Among the dead was newsman Ruben Salazar, a columnist for the *Los Angeles Times,* who was killed by a ten-inch long tear-gas projectile which, according to law enforcement officials, was designed to penetrate a door or wall. The Right Reverend Patricio Flores, auxiliary bishop of the San Antonio diocese (the first American bishop with a Spanish surname), was the only Church official to question the official reports of Los Angeles County deputies, whose statements contrasted sharply to statements made by members of the Mexican-American community.

Even in the case of César Chávez and the farm workers' movement, the Church remained uninvolved at the official level, although many priests and Church-related groups had supported *la causa* from the start. It took the Church more than five years and a lot of pressure from priests and other individuals and groups to exercise its moral leadership. When the great grape strike ended in 1970, it was the U.S. Bishops' Committee on Farm Labor Disputes, a group of five Roman Catholic bishops, that acted as the negotiator between the union and the growers.

By the early 1970s, though, Chávez and the Church appeared to be closely tied to each other. At the height of the iceberg-lettuce boycott, Bishop Raymond Gallagher of La-fayette, Indiana, chairman of the U.S. Bishops' Committee on Social Development, called on all the nation's Catholic bishops for public support of the boycott. This was a new step for the Catholic bishops who had carefully avoided endors-ing the table-grape boycott.

The bishops' support only reaffirmed Chávez's accept-ance by Anglo institutions; it served to justify the Chicano movement's criticism and their break with the labor leader. Chávez himself refused to discuss his relationship or his union's to La Raza Unida or any other segment of the Chi-cano movement. Despite the differences and animosities with other Chicano leaders, Chávez felt that the thrust of his con-cern should be concentrated where his union faced its most serious troubles.

Among those problems, one came from the time he began battling California grape growers: Chávez worked under the shadow of an alleged plot on his life, and the tension ham-pered his aides' efforts. Much as he had encouraged the re-ligious image that had become associated with him, Chávez carefully cast himself in the role of the suffering servant. He preached non-violence and self-sacrifice. During Lent in 1968 he offered his body in a "Lenten fast for peace and non-violence." By the end of the twenty-fifth day, subsisting on water, a few ounces of bouillon, and unsweetened grapefruit juice, Chávez could hardly speak or move.

Chávez spent the twenty-five days praying and shivering in the unheated garage of the union's cooperative gasoline station at Forty Acres, where an altar was built on the rear of a truck. Hundreds of farm workers came every day in a pilgrimage to the garage where Mass was celebrated daily for Chávez's act of sacrifice. Nearby, the farm workers built a thirty-foot high cross that became symbolic of the Passion of César Chávez. In his own way, Chávez expected to be mar-tyred; and in the months after he ended his fast, the possi-bility became much more real. First, the Reverend Martin Luther King, whom Chávez had held up as a model, was killed in Memphis. Then, Senator Robert F. Kennedy, who had joined Chávez in Communion when he broke his fast, was assassinated as he accepted his victory in the California presidential primary.

A few of Chávez's followers worried that perhaps some warped, sick mind would see Chávez's death, along with Kennedy's and King's, as completing a crazy trinity, and they feared the worst. Antonio Orendain, the UFWU secretary who is close to Chávez, best described the feeling when he wrote in the union's newspaper, *El Malcriado:* "Perhaps some of us will follow the path that Kennedy was made to follow, but we are ready for that journey, if it is necessary."

By 1973, however, the only journey Chávez was taking was a path away from the mainstream of the Chicano movement. In its rebellion against traditional institutions and authority, the movement found that its father had become an establishment legend.

7 TIJERINA: RISE AND FALL OF A MILITANT

César Chávez always urged peaceful protests, but the Chicano movement also knew violence and militance. One incident in particular infused the movement with an angry, impatient tempo. On June 5, 1967, Reies López Tijerina and six carloads of his armed followers descended on the courthouse at Tierra Amarilla, New Mexico, to make a citizens' arrest of the Rio Arriba County district attorney. Instead, there erupted a two-hour shootout in which two deputies were wounded and a third deputy abducted, and the violence, in turn, prompted the callout of the National Guard and a wholesale roundup of Mexican-Americans in the area. The courthouse raid terrorized New Mexico and served to galvanize federal, state, and local agencies for a three-year campaign of criminal charges and trials. Tijerina's militancy was neutralized and he himself was imprisoned.

But the raid brought more national attention to the Chicano movement, and it made Tijerina the leader of the militants. Meanwhile, outside the Southwest, his cause went largely unnoticed in the glare of his reputation as a romantic revolutionary.

Tijerina headed the *Alianza Federal de los Pueblos Libres* (Federal Alliance of Free City States), a group he founded in order to reclaim millions of acres of old Spanish land grants dating from before the Mexican War of 1848. The grants were honored by the territorial government, and most of the land was owned communally by Mexican-Americans until the end of the nineteenth century when the Anglos began legal manipulations that took advantage of the owners' unfamiliarity with the U.S. system of land titles and taxation—which contrasted sharply with Mexican and Spanish land laws and traditions—to take over the land.

Complicated as it was, Tijerina's cause struck at the root of the Chicanos' civil and legal rights as Americans. Actually, Tijerina and the *Alianza* were raising the issue of the Treaty of Guadalupe Hidalgo, which ended the Mexican War, and also guaranteed to the Mexicans in the new territories their citizenship and the right to their land, language, and culture.

Tijerina spent his early years as a Pentecostal preacher and evangelist. He came to New Mexico from Texas, via Mexico, in the early 1960s, armed with documentation and a vision of 100 million acres of property reclaimed by Mexican-Americans. His timing was apt, for thousands of Chicanos in the poverty-stricken northern part of the state looked back on the old arrangements with more than just nostalgia. They were in strong contrast to the present, when the Anglos were forcing the Mexican-Americans into smaller and smaller pockets of subsistence land, and the federal government, using most of the ancestral land grants for national forests, was increasingly restricting the Chicanos' grazing rights and access. Tijerina's style—fiery and romantic—served to mobilize what was already a growing bitterness and resentment among rural Chicanos. The *Alianza* was a populist movement, and unlike the urban militancy in the cities, its followers were mostly middle-aged, conservative, and driven by a deep obsession with land and rather naive faith in justice. Finally, after more than a century, they were looking for the law to be fulfilled.

After Mexican independence in 1821, the Southwest belonged to the new republic, even though the Anglo-Americans were already moving into the area. Before 1821 Moses Austin obtained permission from Spain to bring 300 families into Texas, then part of the Mexican State of Coahuila. Through later negotiations with the new Mexican government, Austin's son Stephen raised the number of families to 2,000; and by 1830, about 20,000 Anglos had settled in Texas. Soon, though, troubles arose between the Anglo immigrants and the Mexican government, principally on the slavery question—a new constitution had abolished slavery in the State of Coahuila. Stephen Austin tried unsuccessfully to get permission from the Mexican government to split Texas from Coahuila and to form another state; and in 1836, the Anglo-Americans in Texas revolted against Mexico. In a series of battles, including the famous massacre at the Alamo, the Mexican forces under General Santa Anna were well on their way to crushing the rebellion until the Texan army led by Sam Houston defeated the Mexicans at the battle of San Jacinto in April 1836. Santa Anna was captured and signed away Texas to the Anglo-Americans, although he later repudiated his concession.

No peace treaty was ever negotiated, though, and consequently the boundary between Mexico and the new republic of Texas was never established. The Texans laid claim on all the land on their side of the Rio Grande, while Mexican authorities held firmly that the boundary was on the Nueces River. This dispute led to further animosities and fighting throughout the brief history of the Republic of Texas, which was annexed to the United States in 1845.

Shortly after, the U.S. government began to press the state's boundary claims, and President James K. Polk sent Major General Zachary Taylor and an army of more than 3,000 men into the disputed zone and up the Rio Grande in order to provoke the Mexican government into a conflict. In April of 1846, General Taylor's forces blockaded the mouth of the Rio Grande and got the Mexican army to retaliate. This gave President Polk the opportunity to ask for a declaration of war. In his message to Congress, he said: "The cup of forbearance has been exhausted. Now after reiterated menaces, Mexico has passed the boundary of the United States, has invaded our territory and shed American blood upon the American soil. As war exists, and notwithstanding all our efforts to avoid it, exists by act of Mexico herself . . . I invoke the prompt action of Congress."

The U.S. launched an all-out offensive throughout Mexico, but as the war widened, President Polk faced growing

opposition to the war in Congress and increasing resistance
from the Mexicans that threatened to draw out the struggle.
In January 1848, the House of Representatives went on record
declaring that Polk had started the war "unnecessarily and
unconstitutionally." In his memoirs, Ulysses S. Grant, who
was a young officer under General Taylor during the war,
wrote: "We were sent to provoke a fight, but it was essential
that Mexico should commence it. . . . The occupation, separation, and annexation were, from the inception of the movement to its final consummation, a conspiracy to acquire territory out of which slave states might be formed for the American Union. Even if the annexation itself could be justified, the
manner in which the subsequent war was forced on Mexico
cannot." The war came as a fulfillment for the Americans'
feelings of superiority and their commitment to territorial
expansionism summed up in the slogan "manifest destiny."
Americans tended to see the entire western hemisphere as
their backyard—land that was theirs to dominate. In the
1830s, the Americans were engaged in incorporating all
the adjacent lands they could acquire, in order to impose on
them the benefits of American institutions and ideas. To justify their expansion the Americans came to rely on a mixture
of doctrines, including idealistic views of their providential
mission, questionable notions of national development, con-
cepts of social duty and legal rationalizations. Ultimately, the
Americans believed that the United States was destined to
spread to the Pacific and to lead the sister republics of Latin
America along the path of Anglo-Saxon virtue and justice.

Midway through the war, President Polk sent Nicholas
P. Trist, the chief clerk of the State Department, to Mexico
to negotiate a treaty ending the war. On February 2, 1848, at
the town of Guadalupe Hidalgo, Trist and Mexican officials
signed the treaty, guaranteeing to Mexicans in the new U.S.
territories all the civil rights that went with American citizenship. The new boundaries gave the United States the area that
now makes up California, New Mexico, Arizona, Utah, and
Nevada and parts of Colorado, Oklahoma, Kansas, and Wyo-
ming, increasing the area of the United States by more than 50
percent. Then, four months before the treaty was signed,
President Polk revoked Trist's credentials as a representative
of the U.S., triggering a storm of controversy over the legality

of the treaty negotiations. But Polk sent the treaty on to Congress, where it was ratified only after cutting out Article X. This section would have guaranteed Mexican land-grant owners in Texas that their titles to land would be honored. Deleting the article was intended to wrest the land grants away from Mexicans who either had not sided with the Texas revolution or who had failed to carry out requirements for land possession before Texas declared its independence.

The U.S. government, however, gave its assurance in a protocol that land grants in territories other than Texas would be protected. This document was signed on May 26, 1848, by Mexican officials and U.S. Attorney General Nathan Clifford and Senator Ambrose H. Sevier, chairman of the Senate Foreign Relations Committee. It explained that deleting Article X "did not in any way intend to annul the grants of lands made by Mexico in the ceded territories. These grants, notwithstanding the suppression of the article of the treaty, preserve the legal value which they may possess, and the grantees may cause their legitimate [titles] to be acknowledged before the American tribunals."

But when the war ended, the new Anglo immigrants began jockeying to get the land grants in the new territory. In the typical village, or *pueblo,* each farmer owned his house and the land he worked, but the surrounding grazing and forest land was owned collectively by the community. In one of the first violations of the Treaty of Guadalupe Hidalgo, the U.S. government chose not to recognize the communal system of land tenure, which immediately opened the question of ownership to the village grazing and forest lands. The villagers' own trusting spirit and unfamiliarity with the new tax system facilitated the Anglos' effort. The Mexicans saw no threat to their ownership of the land. As a result, before the end of the century, many of them had their lands taken away for unpaid, accumulated taxes and sold to newly settled Anglos for ridiculously low prices. Thousands more acres were victims of less legal schemes that capitalized on the Mexicans' difficulties with the Anglo language, laws, and traditions.

Among the new Anglo landowners was Thomas B. Catron, New Mexico's first U.S. senator, whose name became anathema to the Mexican-Americans. A speculator and for years a U.S. attorney general, Catron obtained more than a million acres of land, becoming the largest landowner in the country by merely "patenting" the uninhabited land grants in his own name. He was aided by the disappearance of titles and other documentation in old Spanish archives that were burned or sold as wrapping paper during the administration of Governor William A. Pike in 1870. In 1960, some of the old Spanish records were recovered from a Missouri book dealer, who said he had bought them from the family of Catron, the attorney general in New Mexico territory at the time they disappeared.

The federal government was accused of complicity in taking land grants from the Mexican farmers; in any event, the U.S. wound up as the major recipient of the lost and stolen land. By the turn of the century, the government had control of more than 52 million acres of land in New Mexico, much of it taken from former land grants that had been considered by a court of private land claims in 1891 and turned over to the federal government.

The extent to which Mexican landowners and their heirs were stripped of their land surfaced in 1969, during the trial of the Tierra Amarilla courthouse raid case. In 1832, it turned out, the heirs to the Tierra Amarilla Land Grant owned more than 580,000 acres compared to 10,000 acres that belonged to the heirs in 1969; and the heirs to the San Joaquin del Rio de Chama Land Grant, who in 1806 owned up to 600,000 acres, possessed only 1,411 acres in 1969. These two land grants were the largest, and they became the heart of Tijerina's land-grant movement.

The movement began with legal claims on the land grants, but Tijerina moved increasingly to confrontation-style tactics in the face of government indifference. Finally he led the courthouse raid. Four years after the raid, Don Devreux, a community organizer in Santa Fe who mediated during the raid controversy, saw Tijerina's militancy as a tragedy. "The state and federal government, in a sense, entered into a conspiracy," he said. "It was a lot easier to deal with the [land-grant] problem as a police problem rather than a political problem. Thus the courthouse raid played right into their hands. It was the end of *Alianza* as a political threat. Unfortunately, Reies was not wise enough to understand what they were doing."

Tijerina's understanding of the Chicanos' problems was shaped by his own life and his memories of his family's troubles with the Anglo-Americans. Born September 21, 1923, near Falls City, Texas, to a poor migrant family, Tijerina grew up amid bitter border fighting between Anglo ranchers and Texas Rangers and the Mexican-Americans who owned land in the lower Rio Grande Valley near the border. Tijerina's mother's family once owned part of what is now the King Ranch in Texas. She died when he was young, and his father raised the family of ten children by sharecropping. According to Tijerina, three times his family was driven away from Anglo farms at gunpoint when his father attempted to collect his share of the crop at harvest time. And his great-grandfather, who owned a small ranch on a land grant near Laredo, was hanged by six Texas Rangers on fraudulent cattle-rustling charges. Later, Tijerina's grandfather became a border raider attacking Anglo ranches and settlements along the Texas-Mexican border.

When he was seven, Tijerina began working as a migrant field hand with his family, and he hardly went to school until a Baptist missionary presented him with a copy of the New Testament. Already in his teens, Tijerina became fascinated by the book, struggling through it and learning to read at the same time. The night he finished reading it, he had a vision that God had chosen him to lead his people out of their misery and poverty. Although he had been baptized in the Catholic Church, at age eighteen Tijerina enrolled in the Assembly of God Institute at Ysleta de Sur, Texas, now part of El Paso. He dedicated himself to becoming an evangelist, and he quickly became known as a spirited, unconventional preacher. Within a few years, however, he lost his license to preach. Tijerina drifted around northern New Mexico until, in his early twenties, he settled for a period in Tierra Amarilla, where Mexican-American land-grant heirs kept on raiding and burning the Anglo ranchers' land and property. After leaving Tierra Amarilla, he drifted around the country for several years as an itinerant Pentecostal preacher. Finally, in 1950, Tijerina and seventeen families who had become his dedicated followers pooled their savings and bought 160 acres of barren land in Casa Grande and Eloy, Arizona. The settlers built their own community, naming it Valle de Paz (Valley of Peace), but as the value of the land increased, the valley quickly developed into a troubled area, and the community was burned out. In 1957, Tijerina left Arizona a fugitive and fled to Mexico, where he remained for six years, poring over documents and archives in the Mexico City public library and studying the Treaty of Guadalupe Hidalgo and the land grants in the Southwest.

In the early 1960s, Tijerina returned to Tierra Amarilla, and the Anglo ranchers were quick to accuse him of raiding their property. He had to move his family to Albuquerque, where his first wife left him, and the only work he could find was as a church janitor. Even at this low ebb, Tijerina began the slow job of organizing the land-grant heirs into a movement to reclaim the ancestral lands. Through speeches, meetings, and radio and newspaper announcements, Tijerina began his appeal to the people. He later talked about the strength of his movement: "The people were totally dependent on this land, physically, morally, spiritually. I saw the land question as the hope of the Southwest."

Organized orginally as the *Alianza Federal de Mercedes* (Federal Alliance of Land Grantees), Tijerina's movement attracted primarily the elderly, poor, landless Mexican-Americans who had been forced out of their rural homes and into the slums of Albuquerque and Santa Fe when the Anglos took their land and wrecked the village economic system. These people lived on welfare and on their dreams of one day recovering their land. It was not until around 1965, though, that hundreds of embittered Mexican-American small ranchers and farmers joined the *Alianza* and drastically changed the organization's membership. They were angered by a series of National Forest Service decisions, and they gave the *Alianza* its distinct shade of militancy. Dependent on their small herds of cattle and sheep, these Mexican-Americans suddenly found their grazing permits to use the National Forest lands drastically cut. The Forest Service reduced the grazing season from nine to six months and cancelled the permits for milk cows and work horses. The Service also forced these Mexican-Americans to fence their land allotments. Supposedly, these measures were taken because of erosion in the grazing lands, but the farmers were convinced that the Forest Service was trying to run them out of the area.

When they were denied a hearing on their appeals to state and federal officials, the farmers turned to the *Alianza*. Soon, *Alianza* members were accused of shooting at Forest Service rangers and of setting a rash of fires in the national forests. But the *Alianza* warned in a widely distributed pamphlet in both Spanish and English: "There are many trespassers on these land grants who have through various and devious means seized these lands both contrary to law and the true owner's interest. The true owners of these lands have the legal right to use all the force necessary to oust these trespassers."

Tijerina and the *Alianza* chose the Tierra Amarilla and San Joaquin del Rio de Chama land grants out of more than fifty land grants in the state as the focus for the movement. Rio Arriba County was certainly one of the poorest areas in poverty-ridden northern New Mexico. In 1970, 34 percent of the county's population had incomes below the federally established poverty level, compared to 19 percent in the state as a whole. Of the county's 25,170 population—20,691 of them Spanish-surnamed—less than a third of the adults had finished high school. The county was dotted with squalid adobe shacks, and 58 percent of the houses lacked plumbing facilities. In October 1966, the *Alianza* dramatized its claim to the San Joaquin del Rio de Chama grant when 350 members took over a portion of the land, then part of the Kit Carson National Forest, and proclaimed the area the Republic of San Joaquin del Rio de Chama with officials selected from the *Alianza* membership. On October 22, there was a confrontation between the *Alianza* and about two dozen Forest Service officers. The resulting incident, along with the courthouse raid, served to curb Tijerina and the *Alianza* movement.

The angry Mexican-Americans harassed three of the Forest Service Rangers and then held them prisoners and took their trucks away. In a "trial" at the campsite, the rangers were convicted of trespassing on the land grant, and then they were given suspended sentences and released along with their trucks. Four days later, Tijerina, his brother Cristobal, and three other *Alianza* members were arrested by FBI agents on federal warrants charging them with assault on two Forest Service Rangers and converting government property to personal use. More than a year later, in November 1967, a twelve-man jury with only two Mexican-Americans on it found all the defendants guilty. Tijerina was sentenced to two years in prison, although he did not begin serving until 1969 when his bail was revoked and the U.S. Supreme Court denied the defendants a review.

While Tijerina was awaiting trial in early 1967, there were more fires in the national forests and raids against the Anglo ranchers. Public pressure against the *Alianza* mounted, and the organization disbanded and regrouped as the *Alianza Federal de Pueblos Libres.* They called a mass meeting for June 3, at Coyote, a village within the San Joaquin Land Grant, to make plans for recapturing the land. Then, the day before the meeting, Governor David F. Cargo, a liberal Republican who was married to a former *Alianza* member and who was sympathetic to the Mexican-Americans' problems, flew off to Michigan for a fund-raising ceremony. His departure opened the way for a major confrontation and one of the most massive violations in U.S. history of civil rights.

Alfonso Sanchez, the district attorney for Rio Arriba County, tried to stop the Coyote meeting by declaring it illegal. Sanchez threatened anyone attempting to attend with prosecution, and he issued arrest warrants for Tijerina and other *Alianza* leaders. Describing the *Alianza* movement as Communist-inspired, he joined the state police force in setting up roadblocks along the highways leading to Coyote. When people tried to get through, Sanchez arrested eleven men and charged them with unlawful assembly. But Tijerina and other *Alianza* leaders slipped through the roadblocks and met near Canjilon, where they decided to take Sanchez in a citizen's arrest at Tierra Amarilla, where the arrested *Alianza* members were to be arraigned.

At mid-afternoon on June 5, twenty *Alianza* members armed with hunting rifles and a warrant burst into the Tierra Amarilla courthouse and caught its occupants by surprise. Despite a warning from the men to drop his pistol, State Patrolman Nick Saiz drew his weapon and was shot in the chest. Panicking, some of the court employes fled through the windows, and District Judge James Scarborough, before whom the arrested *Alianza* members had been arraigned only a few minutes earlier, locked himself in the toilet of his court chambers. Among those who tried to escape through a window was Deputy Sheriff Elogio Salazar, who was shot twice as he jumped. The raiding party checked the courthouse but found no trace either of the men who had been arraigned or of Sanchez, who had not appeared for the arraignment.

Tijerina's own role in the raid later became clouded by conflicting testimony. Tijerina swore that he had waited in a nearby home while the arresting party went to the courthouse. Then, he said, he went to the courthouse in an attempt to stop the shooting. Saiz testified that he saw Tijerina with "a rifle strapped to his arm," along with the rest of the raiding party. A clerk testified she had heard Tijerina tell the group *"Acaben con todos* (Finish them all off)."

Two hours after they had entered the courthouse, Tijerina led the raiding party away to the mountains near Canjilon with two hostages, a deputy sheriff and a newspaper reporter, whom they released before fleeing into the hills.

For the next few hours, panic and confusion swept through the state as rumors began circulating that Cuban guerillas were leading *Alianza* raiders on an indiscriminate rampage against Anglos. National Guard troops with tanks and artillery under General Jacob Jolly, adjutant general of New Mexico, joined up with state and local law enforcement officers and the Apache tribe police at Tierra Amarilla to set up a force of more than 2,000 men to blockade the roads and make a massive search for Tijerina and his men. The posse stormed into villages in the area, breaking into homes and confiscating property without warrants. At Canjilon, the lawmen imprisoned about fifty Mexican-Americans, old men, women, and children, for twenty-six hours in a muddy sheep pen without food or water. They hoped this bait would lure Tijerina into the open. A *New York Times* reporter quoted General Jolly as saying, "Let's don't get involved in civil liberties."

Governor Cargo returned to New Mexico the day after the courthouse raid and within two days he called off the massive manhunt, giving assurance to Tijerina and his men meanwhile that their lives would be spared once they surrendered or were arrested. When he was caught, Tijerina was charged on fifty-four criminal counts including kidnapping, and District Attorney Sanchez announced that he would seek the death penalty. In the next year and a half, the judicial handling of Tijerina's case itself became a source of controversy. The state supreme court shifted jurisdiction of the case from District Judge José Angel, who had reduced the capital charge and dismissed others, to District Judge Paul Larrazolo, in whose court Tijerina was tried for the original charges. The issues grew cloudy when Deputy Sheriff Elogio Salazar, a star witness for the prosecution, was found beaten to death on a road near Tierra Amarilla in January 1968. The murder went unsolved while law enforcement officers accused Tijerina and the *Alianza,* and they in turn blamed the death on militant Anglos who were trying to make the *Alianza's* reputation seem even worse. With the assistance of two court-appointed lawyers, Tijerina conducted his own defense. And on December 14, 1968, Tijerina was acquitted on all the charges stemming from the courthouse raid. The verdict stunned the state's establishment, but it was wildly cheered by the *Alianza* and its sympathizers and supporters. It also offered the hope that Tijerina and the *Alianza* would again become a political and economic threat in northern New Mexico.

That threat was short-lived. In 1968, Tijerina founded the *Pardido Constitucional del Pueblo* (Peoples' Constitutional Party), which received only a few thousand votes but openly placed the land-grant issue in the political arena. In early 1969, Tijerina stepped up his activity, adding such causes as increased social services to the poor and higher wages for Albuquerque garbagemen to his own movement to reclaim the land grants. He began making more speeches and appearances in front of college audiences and civil rights groups around the country, and he joined the movement opposing Warren E. Burger's nomination as chief justice of the United States. At one point, he filed a citizen's warrant with the Supreme Court for the arrest of President Nixon's chief justice appointee. In New Mexico, meanwhile, Tijerina and the *Alianza* faced their own opposition. Tijerina's office in Albuquerque continued to be the target for an occasional round of bullets, and several buildings housing *Alianza* clinics and cultural centers were burned. In one previous attempt to bomb Tijerina's office, a Bernalillo County deputy sheriff had lost part of one arm when he fell on the dynamite.

Then, in June 1969, the threat of Tijerina, and, in effect, of the *Alianza,* came to an end. Tijerina, his wife Patsy, and several others were arrested by Forest Service Rangers and charged with burning a government sign at the Santa Fe National Forest. Tijerina's bail on his November, 1967, conviction was revoked, and on June 11, 1969, he was sentenced to the La Tuna Federal Prison in El Paso. In the days that followed, Tijerina was convicted of assault on another ranger and aiding and abetting the destruction of government property in the Santa Fe National Forest incident, and he received a three-year sentence. Finally, in late 1969, Tijerina was tried again on other charges stemming from the Tierra Amarilla courthouse raid and was convicted of assaulting Deputy Sheriff Salazar.

Chicano activists throughout the Southwest were certain Tijerina's imprisonment was "politically motivated," to neutralize his influence and to take the land-grant leader out of the mainstream of the Chicano movement. Whatever its motivation, Tijerina's imprisonment had its effect. When he was released on parole in July 1971, and placed on five years' probation, Tijerina was a changed man. He could not take an active role in the *Alianza,* and to the disappointment of the Chicano movement's new leadership, he turned his back on violence and returned to preaching brotherhood and love among all men.

"I have outgrown militancy," Tijerina said at a press conference in Albuquerque the day he was freed from a federal prison hospital in Springfield, Missouri. "I can see beyond it. There is more than one way to change the rich and the powerful. . . . In my 775 days in prison, I found justice in my heart. I want to dedicate these 775 days to bringing peace and understanding among the people of New Mexico and the whole Southwest. The future of the Southwest has greater racial perspective and consequences than the blacks and whites in the South. . . . As the Indo-Hispano gains his frozen spirit, he will become a greater and greater threat unless his spirit is channeled in the right direction."

Tijerina returned to Albuquerque suffering a chronic throat ailment that had required two operations in prison, and badly handicapped by the provisions of the parole. When he arrived home, he found that new organizations such as the Black Berets in Albuquerque and La Gente in Santa Fe had taken center stage with their focus on community organizing, parallel institutions, and confronting the Anglo establishment with an array of sophisticated techniques. In Tierra Amarilla, the Chicano movement activists had formed a clinic and an agricultural cooperative and were in the process of framing a master plan for the entire town. Antonio Cordova, a young writer for *El Grito del Norte,* a movement newspaper, summed up the change that had taken place: "The young people are getting away from the Messiah thing. They're more politically aware. They can get more done through group action. You can't rely on one man. What happens if, like Tijerina, he goes down? The thing stands still or collapses completely."

In many ways, Tijerina had remained his old self. He was still a strong, dynamic speaker, capable of ranting at the top of his lungs for long periods before audiences at colleges and meetings. He screamed, he banged the podium, his arms still waved and shook, and he might jump up and down, almost comically, in the midst of delivering a serious message. But the message was far different from what he had said in the 1960s. Now he spoke of "brotherhood awareness" and of a calling for the "bilingual people to bring harmony and brotherhood between North America and South America and between the blacks and the whites."

Chicano leaders shook their heads and said Tijerina had been more useful to the movement as a jailed martyr and political prisoner. Tijerina, however, was intent on resuming a leadership role and he began a struggle that culminated in the new leaders' humiliating him and causing him to break with the young Raza Unida national party.

Tijerina organized the Institute to Research and Study Justice, Inc., that was to help promote his idea of brotherhood awareness which he described as the "God-sanctioned destiny of the Indo-Hispano in the world." Along with "Indo-Hispano," Tijerina liked another descriptive term, "Mexicano," and in this he typified the diversity on names and group identity within the movement.

In 1966, Tijerina returned from Spain, where he had gone to secure additional documentation on the New Mexican land grants, with three volumes of old Spanish decrees. He described one of the decrees, issued in the late sixteenth century by King Philip II, as "the first civil rights law in the Americas," establishing equality for the offspring of Spaniards and Indians in the New World. According to Tijerina, the decree created a new race, the Indo-Hispano, or Mexican-American. Tijerina made an effort to regain his leadership through the brotherhood cause; and in an interview in early 1972, he said: "I have paid the price to lead. History will be the truth, for the role of leadership is not premeditated or calculated. There will be no doubt as to who is to lead the Indo-Hispanos in the Southwest. José Angel [Gutiérrez] will tell you who. It doesn't have to come out of my mouth. It's a role that is developed around you. It's not one that you're elected to or get appointed to. If history and the forces of nature put me there, how can I back out?"

And despite his lack of a formal education, Tijerina had an acute sense of history, and he was convinced enough of his own importance to assume he would play a major role in twentieth-century American civilization. He saw himself as the target of a government-inspired assassination plot because he alone stood in the way of the rich robbing the poor. Tijerina felt that his only crime was to uphold his people's rights as protected by the Treaty of Guadalupe Hidalgo and to demand respect and protection for Mexican-American property. He thought that the comparison of the Chicano struggle to the black movement was too obvious, preferring as more accurate a comparison to the plight of the Hebrews in Egypt or to the Jews in Germany. Unlike the black civil rights struggle, he thought, the Chicano movement had failed to arouse widespread guilt and sympathy around the country. He remembered how the Pope of the Roman Catholic Church had been criticized for his silence while Hitler and the Nazis persecuted the Jews; and he found that same silence in New Mexico, where he believed too many had kept their mouths closed and contributed to the exploitation of the Indo-Hispanos. Tijerina saw an advantage in the United States' troubles in Vietnam and elsewhere abroad. Any criticism of America's involvement in Southeast Asia served only to support Tijerina's long-standing contention about the United States' entry into the Southwest and the government's role in taking the land grants from their original Mexican owners.

Tijerina saw history's shadow in his role in the 1968 Poor People's March on Washington where he, Corky Gonzales, and black leaders such as the Reverend Ralph Abernathy led thousands of marchers to Resurrection City. Tijerina carried his plea for a hearing on the land-grant question to the State Department and to Galo Plaza, secretary general of the Organization of American States (OAS), who met with the *Alianza* leader. Tijerina saw himself not as a revolutionary or peasant anarchist but as a visionary of the millennium who would bring parity to the Chicano and salvation to the Anglo.

Strange as it may seem, Tijerina, despite his rhetoric on the land claims and the militance he encouraged within the *Alianza*, appeared less of a revolutionary than the Jefferson Davises and Robert E. Lees of a century earlier. In October 1969, while in jail awaiting his second trial on the courthouse raid charges, he angrily resigned as president of the *Alianza* and broke with the organization over the hypothetical issue of seceding the Southwest from the United States. At its annual convention, the *Alianza* passed a resolution petitioning President Nixon and demanding the Southwest be turned over to the Chicanos, who would create the nation of *Aztlan* as declared by the Chicano Youth Liberation Conference earlier that year in Denver. Tijerina was irate, saying, "I am not for separatism from the United States. My motto is justice, but not independence from or revolution against the United States."

Perhaps that statement should have been a warning to Chicano leaders of Tijerina's new low profile and soft rhetoric. Out of prison, he was no longer "King Tiger," as some reporters had described him in erroneously translating his name. Actually, Tijerina should literally be translated "little scissors," although Tijerina claimed the name was derived from the Tejas Indian tribe and given a Spanish ending. To the movement people, however, he had been simply "Tijerina." And into the 1970s, Tijerina was still a legend among Chicano militants even though he was no longer their hero. In September, 1972, Tijerina went to the Raza Unida national convention in El Paso as a special guest, and his speech to the 4,000 delegates and visitors had more the tone of fatherly advice than activist exhortation. "This is a magnificent display of the new political awareness of our people," he said. "There is a powerful expression of our yearnings. But now that we have the revolutionary spirit, we must not lose sight of the brotherhood awareness. Temper the revolutionary spirit. Cultural identification is needed, but we must not let it lead us to hatred. We can become intoxicated and lose sight of our real goal to fully participate in the political system of the United States."

Much as in New Mexico, however, the national Chicano movement had blossomed without Tijerina's presence or direction, spawning new, young leaders and a pragmatic organizational style that minimized individual personalities. And those leaders who had survived or emerged were not willing to give Tijerina even an honorary role of leadership. It was no surprise, then, that two months after the convention, the new, young leaders exerted their power and embarrassed Tijerina at the National Chicano Congress on Land and Cultural Reform, which he had called in his hometown.

About 1,000 persons attended the congress, whose theme Tijerina outlined as "unity before ideas, leaders, or organizations." He wanted to use the congress as a springboard both for his own role in the movement and for unifying Chicano support on the land-grant issue and the Treaty of Guadalupe Hidalgo. Tijerina wanted to eliminate politics from the congress; but to his surprise, La Raza Unida party activists grabbed control of the meeting and passed resolutions with Raza Unida positions, including a resolution naming the party the official spokesman of the congress. Tijerina stormed out of his own congress and blamed La Raza Unida and Corky Gonzales, who did not attend, for usurping his own role and the purpose of the congress. "The *congreso* was a failure," Tijerina said later in an interview. "It accomplished nothing that it was supposed to. I am disappointed in Corky, very disappointed. I wouldn't be surprised to learn that he wanted the *congreso* to fail. . . . At least we found out which individuals and organizations will not sacrifice their names for the sake of unity, and they will never be invited again to another unity attempt by honest people."

The congress fiasco came as an ironical setback for Tijerina, who suddenly found himself on the receiving end of the movement's militance. Being on parole circumscribed his freedom and, in effect, placed him in his own prison from which there seemed no escape. And as he approached the mid-1970s, Tijerina, still on parole and confronting other legal hurdles, found himself seeking justice both within the law and within the movement.

8 CORKY GONZALES:
A RETURN TO
AZTLAN

In 1969, almost four years after César Chávez awakened
Mexican-American awareness and nearly two years after
Reies Tijerina led the assault on the Tierra Amarilla courthouse, the Chicano movement was a restless force of activist
groups and organizations marching, picketing, and boy-
cotting with a militance that was not customary for Mexican-
Americans. As the decade was ending, the movement showed
its need for a national spokesman and national direction.
Chávez was caught up in his union's organizing struggle in the
California grapefields, and as it turned out, he had no desire
to be the spokesman for the Chicano movement. Tijerina was
barely avoiding imprisonment in New Mexico, and he faced
a long legal battle that would surely take him out of action.
There was an impasse and a vacuum that left the way open for
Corky Gonzales, who otherwise probably would have been
overshadowed by Chávez or Tijerina.

Gonzales already had a strong track record in the movement. A product of the Denver *barrios,* he had vaulted from a
promising prize-fighting career into business, Democratic
party politics, and civic and social welfare programs. But in

the mid-1960s, he turned his back on the establishment and returned to the *barrio* to organize *La Crusada Para la Justicia* (the Crusade for Justice), a community service center that became synonymous with Chicano activism in Denver.

Unlike Chávez and Tijerina, Gonzales had not yet attracted national attention. He had neither Chávez's *huelga* nor Tijerina's land grants as an identifying issue, neither support for a boycott nor a revolutionary reputation. Yet the issue of justice that was an integral part of Gonzales' movement was important too in both the farm workers' struggle and the land-grant reclamation effort.

Finally, the week after Palm Sunday in 1969, Gonzales made his mark in the movement. The Crusade for Justice sponsored a Youth Liberation Conference at which Gonzales gave the whole Mexican-American movement a name, a language, and a country. In just a few days, Gonzales established himself as a major leader within the movement, and even without recognition by the national media, he was acclaimed by the 1,500 delegates who assembled in Denver.

Gonzales' major coup was christening the young Mexican-Americans in the movement "Chicanos," a name he resurrected from the past. Before the 1969 conference, the Chicanos had been described clumsily as "Mexican-Americans," "Indo-Hispanos," "Spanish-speaking," or "Spanish-surnamed." And before "Mexican-American" became popular, they were called "Mexicans," a term that in many instances carried a strong negative connotation, if not overtly then psychologically. Too often, "Mexican" became "Meskin" in much the same way "Negro" was slurred by Southerners as "nigra"; and along with "Meskin" went other derogatory terms like "greaser," "Mex," and "Spic." But "Chicano," like "black" for "Negro," cut through all the problems of tags and labels. "Chicano" was to become a badge of brown pride embraced by the activists while it was uncomfortably digested by the moderate and conservative Mexican-Americans.

The older Mexican-Americans could claim that "Chicano" was a throwback to the days of the *pachucos* in the 1940s. These were youth gangs from the *barrios*, who had styles of behavior at once outlandish and unsophisticated. Their name was probably taken from a Mexican town, and the *pachucos'* own identifying marks were the "zoot suit" and the duck-tail haircut, extreme styles that exaggerated, as a form of protest and contempt, the American norm. *Pachuquismo* was a rebellion against Anglo-America's social ostracism, unintelligent educational measures, and prejudicial economic practices. At the same time, the style was also an assertion of individuality. "The purpose of his grotesque dandyism and anarchic behavior," wrote Mexican poet-essayist-diplomat Octavio Paz, "is not so much to point out the injustice and incapacity of a society that has failed to assimilate him as it is to demonstrate his personal will to remain different." Perhaps the *pachucos* might have remained only another social anomaly in the country but for the infamous "zoot suit riots" of June 1943, a series of incidents that grew out of a fight between *pachucos* and U.S. sailors in Los Angeles. For several nights, hundreds of sailors drove through the *barrios* looking for Mexican-Americans and beating up the ones they found, while law enforcement authorities looked the other way and never arrested a sailor.

After 1943 the *pachucos* faded, to be replaced by the *vatos locos* (crazy guys), *barrio* toughs who were influenced by the social stirrings within the *barrios*. But in the 1970s, it was the *pachucos* who were revered as folk heroes. Some Mexican-Americans saw them as predecessors not only of the Chicano militants but also of the hippies, the New Left, and the wave of social protest in America. And it was the *pachucos* who first used the term "Chicano," giving it a negative connotation for moderate and conservative Mexican-Americans, who, like most of middle America, could neither accept nor understand the extrovert young.

Actually, the word "Chicano" dates back to the early sixteenth century when the Spaniards invaded Mexico and conquered the Aztecs, who under their other name, "Mexicas," gave their name to the country. The Castilian of sixteenth-century Spanish sounded the letter "x" as "sh," a sound that no longer exists in the language. Mexico was pronounced *Meh-shee-ko*, and the Indians, "Mexicanos," *Meh-shee-kah-nos*. In the eighteenth century, Castilian changed the letter "x" and the "sh" sound to the "j." Mexico and the Latin American highlands maintained most of the original Castilian speech but accepted the "j" sound in place of "sh" while at the same time keeping the letter "x." However, the uneducated rural Méxicans who lived in the mountain villages, isolated from urban areas, held on to the "sh" sound; and when they left their villages, they still called themselves "Meh-shee-kah-nos." Many of them carried that pronunciation to the urban areas and into the United States, along the way dropping the "Me" and shortening the word to "Shicano," which later became "Chicano."

At the Youth Liberation Conference, Gonzales simply revived officially the name "Chicano," already coming into the new militant language or *barrio* slang called *pocho*, Corky's second major addition to the movement. In *pocho*, the jargon of other movements was given Chicano flavor; brothers became *carnales*, Uncle Toms were now *Tío Tacos*, and sellouts were known as *vendidos*.

Last, Gonzales gave the movement a homeland, *Aztlan*, the mythical fatherland of the Aztecs. According to legend, the Indians Cortes conquered were the descendants of the Chichimeca nomadic tribes that had migrated in the eleventh century from what is now the southwestern United States southward to the present-day Mexico City where, as Aztecs, they founded the ancient city of Tenochtitlan in 1325. By the end of the fifteenth century, Tenochtitlan was the principal city in central Mexico and it was noted for militarism and human sacrifice to a host of deities, among them Huitzilopochtli, whose anger held the wrath of *El Quinto Sol* (the Fifth Sun) that threatened to destroy the earth. But in 1519, the Spanish conquistadores landed in Mexico and within two years Cortes had seized Emperor Montezuma II and had conquered Tenochtitlan. The Spaniards introduced radical changes in religion, technology, and government, and since few Spanish women came to the New World, they eventually created as great a change in the physical and cultural worlds of their subjects. The mixture of the Spanish and Indian bloods, a process later described as *mestizaje*, resulted in creating the *mestizo*, the present-day Chicano, who had returned home to *Aztlan*.

So, with a homeland, a language, and a name, the Youth Liberation Conference proclaimed themselves a "bronze continent" and adopted a moving declaration entitled the "*Plan Espiritual de Aztlan* (Spiritual Plan of *Aztlan*)" stating:

In the spirit of a new people that is conscious not only of its proud historical heritage but also of the brutal "gringo" invasion of our territories, we, the Chicano inhabitants and civilizers of the northern land of *Aztlan,* whence came our forefathers, reclaiming the land of their birth and consecrating the determination of our people of the sun, declare that the call of our blood is our power, our responsibility, and our inevitable destiny.

We are free and sovereign to determine those tasks which are justly called for by our house, our land, the sweat of our brows, and by our hearts. *Aztlan* belongs to those who plant the seeds, water the fields, and gather the crops and not to the foreign Europeans. We do not recognize capricious frontiers on the Bronze Continent.

Brotherhood unites us, love for our brothers makes us a people whose time has come and who struggle against the foreign "*gabacho* [Anglo]" who exploits our riches and destroys our culture. With our heart in our hands and our hands in the soil, we declare the independence of our *mestizo* nation. We are a bronze people with a bronze culture. Before the world, before all of North America, before all our brothers in the Bronze Continent, we are a nation. We are a union of free *pueblos.* We are *Aztlan. Por la raza todo, fuera de la raza nada* [Everything for the race, nothing outside the race].

The plan was a call to nationalism, in Gonzales' view, the common denominator that could unite the Mexican-American people. Gonzales saw nationalism flowing naturally from the family, developing into tribalism, and finally transforming itself into alliances that brought about changes within the political, economic, educational, and social systems of the United States. Eventually, Gonzales felt, the movement would have to be politicized, but there had to be a common ground in nationalism. And the idea of *Aztlan,* with its own people and language, was carefully calculated to stir the Chicanos to embrace nationalism.

In late 1969, as the newly named Chicanos were spreading the concept of *Aztlan* to the *barrios* of the Southwest, Gonzales explained the idea behind Chicano nationalism and the ingredients of culture and history he had injected into the movement. "We have to be able to identify with our past, and understand our past, in order that we can dedicate ourselves to the future, dedicate ourselves to change," he said. "And we have to understand what humanism really is. We can tie the cultural thing into it, but we also have to tie in the political and the economic. We tie these things together and we start to use the common denominator of nationalism. . . . We have to understand that liberation comes from self-determination, and to start to use the tools of nationalism to win over our *barrio* brothers, to win over the brothers who are still believing that *machismo* means getting a gun and going to kill a communist in Vietnam because they've been jived about the fact that they will be accepted as long as they go get themselves killed for the 'gringo' captain; who still think that welfare is giving them something and don't understand that the one who is administering the welfare is the one that's on welfare, because about 90 percent of the welfare goes into administration; and who still do not understand that the war on poverty is against the poor, to keep them from reacting. We have to win these brothers over, and we have to do it by action. Whether it be around police brutality, the educational system, whether it be against oppression of any kind—you create an action, you create a blowout, and you see how fast those kids get politicized. Watch how fast they learn the need to start to take over our own communities. And watch how fast they learn to identify with ourselves and to understand that we need to create a nation."

Gonzales' rhetoric of self-determination, nationalism, *machismo*, and the need to "use more forceful methods" reflected the changed mood the Chicano movement took in the 1970s. The militancy of Tijerina and the *Alianza* in New Mexico generated additional activism in East Los Angeles, in Denver, and in Texas, where Chicano students staged massive "blowouts" or walkouts from schools. New organizations sprang up, such as the Brown Berets in California, the Black Berets in New Mexico, and the Mexican-American Youth Organization (MAYO) in Texas. On the college campuses, Chicano students organized their own groups, among them the *Movimiento Estudiantil Chicano de Aztlan* (MECHA), the United Mexican-American Students (UMAS), the Mexican-American Student Association (MASA), and the Mexican-American Student Confederation (MASC). These organizations spoke through Chicano activist newspapers and publications such as *El Grito del Norte, El Gallo, El Papel, El Grito, Con Safos, El Chicano,* and *El Deguello*. Both organizations and newspapers protested discrimination and injustice, criticizing and attacking the Anglo-dominated system and calling for a redirection of the system to include the Mexican-American. Part of their message was the threat of violence that accompanied the civil rights movement in the 1960s, and some activists made no attempt to veil their warnings of extremism.

In Texas, every Texan remembers the Alamo, and Beto Martinez was no exception. But the man Martinez admired in 1970 was Santa Anna, the Mexican general whose army of thousands slaughtered the 187 defenders of the old Spanish mission in San Antonio. "He had the right idea of what to do with white men," Martinez said in one interview when he predicted: "The day will come again when any 'gringo' in this part of the country will be shot on sight." Martinez, an ex-convict in his early thirties who served time in Texas prisons for possession of marijuana and for sodomy, was minister of war for the Mexican-American Nationalist Organization (MANO), a clandestine group in San Antonio that believed all Anglos were racists who should be driven out of the Southwest. Most members of MANO were either ex-convicts or Vietnam veterans with experience in guerilla warfare and demolition techniques, and he likened his organization to a Chicano Minuteman group of the left. Martinez and MANO were discounted by other Chicano activists as publicity-hungry *vatos locos;* but MANO got a story on the front page of the *Wall Street Journal* that brought a wave of angry protest from San Antonio leaders — including Mexican-Americans. A prominent story in such a prestigious paper reflected a new awareness of the Chicano movement and the deepening frustration it represented.

In 1967 the Brown Berets organized in East Los Angeles as a paramilitary group, patterned after the Black Panthers, and they were highly vocal in complaining about police mistreatment of Mexican-Americans. At the height of their activism, the Berets were accused of criminal conspiracies, bombings, arsons, and disturbances of the peace. No member better exemplified the group's aggressiveness than David Sanchez, who was in his early twenties when he helped found the group and served as prime minister of the organization. Sanchez served two jail terms in connection with the disturbances in 1968—the East Los Angeles school walkouts and a street demonstration—and he was acquitted on a firebombing count in 1970 and on draft evasion charges in 1971. Carlos Montez, another cofounder of the Berets, was convicted on arson and other charges after a series of fires and disturbances at the Biltmore Hotel in Los Angeles in 1969. The police maintained that the Berets created the incidents to disrupt a speech by Governor Ronald Reagan, while Sanchez blamed the disturbances on a police infiltrator into the group. The Berets' last activism came in September 1972, with a month-long "occupation" of a hillside on Catalina Island, twenty miles off the Southern California coast, where the group protested the island's acquisition from Mexico after the Mexican War ended in 1848. A month later, Sanchez, no longer sporting a beret and khaki uniform, announced at a press conference that the organization of ninety national chapters and 5,000 members was dissolving in order to avoid strife within the Chicano movement. He said he feared violence between factions that conceivably could spill out into the community.

This was a fear already widely expressed, even by moderate Mexican-Americans. In June 1969, at a Senate subcommittee hearing, Senator Abraham Ribicoff, D-Conn., asked a witness; "How is it they [the Mexican-Americans] have taken this lying down all these years?"

"It is probably because of the Church, who has taught us to obey," answered Vicente T. Ximenes, a native of Texas and a commissioner of the U.S. Equal Employment Opportunities Commission. "It is probably because we have felt that somehow the law, the government, or someone will come forth with the proper solution. I do not think that that is going to go on any longer. I can tell you that, because at this point there are students in the elementary grades and in the high schools who are now walking out of the schools with parents' consent. Now, this is something I have never heard as long as I can remember. . . . So I think you must have a rising awareness in the nation, and especially in the Southwest, of the obligation of government officials, education officials, and certainly the people, the obligation to a very important segment of the population. It would seem to me that we are taking five million people in this area . . . for granted at our own peril. I think it would be a tragedy if we had to wait for something explosive to happen before we acted."

Two years before this subcommittee hearing, the Johnson administration made a token effort to act on the problems of the Mexican-Americans. On June 9, 1967, just four days after Tijerina's raid on the Tierra Amarilla courthouse, President Johnson announced the creation of the Inter-Agency Committee on Mexican-American Affairs to be composed of four cabinet officers and the director of the Office of Economic Opportunity. The President had met the previous year with a handful of Mexican-American leaders from the Southwest, and this committee came out of what he learned then. These Mexican-American spokesmen, hand-picked by the White House, were: U.S. District Judge Alfred Hernandez, a past president of the League of United Latin American Citizens (LULAC); Dr. Hector P. Garcia, founder of the American G.I. Forum; Bert Corona, president of the Mexican-American Political Association (MAPA) of California; Roy Elizondo, president of the Political Association of Spanish-Speaking Organizations (PASSO) of Texas; and Augustín Flores, a past president of the G.I. Forum. At first, the White House had promised to convene a White House conference on Mexican-American affairs, but the conference was postponed indefinitely and never held. Instead the White House asked Ximenes, the chairman of the new Inter-Agency Committee, to call for hearings on Mexican-American affairs to be held in October 1967, in El Paso. But the hearings did nothing to establish rapport with the Mexican-Americans. Actually, the Chicanos' growing disenchantment with traditional institutions and systems showed clearly in a "rump" Mexican-American conference held in the heart of El Paso's *El Segundo barrio* at the same time as the official committee's hearings. Chicano leaders such as César Chávez, Corky Gonzales, and Bert Corona ignored their invitations to the government hearings. Others boycotted the hearings, and some, like Tijerina who was not invited, simply became too concerned with the business of the rival conference to worry about the government meeting. Still, the conference marked a time of rising Chicano awareness, as was signified in the rallying cry of unity adopted by the conference — "La Raza Unida."

The government's hearings resulted in no noticeable change in attitude, and Ximenes' warning that "something explosive [is going] to happen" came true in August 1970, when East Los Angeles' *barrio* exploded in violence. On August 29, the National Chicano Moratorium Day Committee organized the Mexican-Americans' largest demonstration, assembling more than 25,000 people in the unincorporated county territory of East L.A. to protest the disproportionately large number of Spanish-surnamed soldiers who were being killed in Southeast Asia. Studies of casualty reports for the first eight years of the Vietnam War showed that Mexican-American military personnel had a higher death rate than all other servicemen. Mexican-Americans felt that Spanish-surnamed servicemen were over-represented in the Vietnam casualty reports because they were over-represented among those who were drafted for military service and those who volunteered. Only a small fraction of Mexican-Americans had been able to dodge obligatory military service by college deferments. And, cast against a low-income background, military life offered an attractive way out of the economic plight of the *barrios*.

So, in summer of 1970 a parade was called to urge young Chicanos to resist military service in favor of fighting for social justice at home. The protesters marched without incident along a two-and-a-half-mile route through the heart of the nation's largest *barrio* to Laguna Park, where they were to hear a series of speakers, including César Chávez and Corky Gonzales. But the speeches never took place. Instead, Los Angeles County Sheriff's Department officers, concerned about a disturbance and possible looting at a nearby liquor store, moved into the park area in what they said was an attempt to control the crowd from going to the area of the liquor store. Moratorium leaders later charged that the armed deputies moved into the crowd without warning and created a panic. Bombarded with rocks and bottles, the deputies fired tear gas into the crowd, and the crowd went on a rampage down Whittier Boulevard, breaking windows, burning, and looting. When it was over several hours later, one person was dead, 2 others were dying, 74 had been wounded, more than 250 people had been arrested, and property damage in the area was estimated at more than $1 million. The Chicano community was hard hit by the violence, and its biggest loss was the man who died during the riot—award-winning *Los Angeles Times* columnist Ruben Salazar, forty-two, a leading spokesman for Mexican-American rights, who was killed by a twelve-inch bulletlike tear-gas shell fired by a sheriff's deputy into a bar.

In late 1969, the editors of the *Times*, which had been making a slow, deliberate march to the leftward borders of moderate Republicanism, belatedly recognized that California's Mexican-American community outnumbered the blacks and made up almost 16 percent of the state's population. East of the Los Angeles River, in the smog-enclosed eastern portion of Los Angeles County, lived more than a million Mexican-Americans, more persons of Mexican descent than in any metropolitan area except Mexico City. The *Times* decided it was time to print a column about Chicano life in Los Angeles; and to write the column, the paper chose Salazar, a Mexican-American political moderate, who had put in ten years as a reporter with the *Times* and was about to accept a $25,000-a-year position as news director of KMEX, a local Spanish-language television station. For all its cautious new liberalism, however, the *Times*, with Salazar's hard-hitting columns attacking Anglo racism and voicing Chicano grievances, found itself taking a far more radical position than it ever intended. In one column, Salazar charged that the word "Mexican" has been "dragged through the mud of racism since the Anglos arrived in the Southwest." In another, he noted that Mexican-American "culture predates that of the Pilgrims and that Spanish was spoken in America before English and so the 'problem' is not theirs [Chicanos'] but the Anglos' who don't speak Spanish." He explained that Chicanos feel "Fourth of July oratory . . . tends to paint God as a super-American who has blessed this country with its great wealth and power because right-thinking people—like those who attend Honor America Day celebrations and wave the flag vigorously—run the place." And another time, he asked: "If Daniel Moynihan speaks of 'benign neglect' for the black, what is in store for the Chicano?" Los Angeles law enforcement officials, who often received the brunt of his criticism, seethed at Salazar's columns. But the reporter went right on: "I think what we ought to do is shake up the establishment so that it will include us," he said in one interview.

When trouble broke out at Laguna Park at the end of the moratorium march, Salazar left the area and stopped by the Silver Dollar Cafe on Whittier Boulevard. While he was having a beer in the cafe, sheriff's deputies received a report of a gunman inside the bar and gathered outside where they said they warned the people in the cafe to evacuate the building. Apparently nobody inside heard the warning, and Deputy Thomas Wilson leaped across the cafe doorway and fired a tear-gas projectile into the building. The long shell, unlike a tear-gas canister, was a projectile built to penetrate a door or wall. Fired at close range, the shell struck Salazar on the head and killed him instantly. Testimony at a coroner's inquest later revealed that there was nobody armed in the bar, and consequently no shots had been fired at deputies during the course of the disturbances. The inquest took testimony from sixty-one witnesses and covered 2,025 pages, but District Attorney Evell J. Younger decided that no criminal charges would be filed against the deputy who killed Salazar.

Salazar's death intensified the Chicano community's frustrations, and for several weeks he was a martyr and rallying cry of the movement. This was a role, though, that Salazar would have had a difficult time in fitting. His life-style was anything but radical. He lived in conservative Orange County, was married to a blonde Anglo wife, and called himself "pretty middle-class establishment." Later, William J. Drummond, a black who worked with Salazar on the *Times* staff, described Salazar as "a man in the middle." "We were both close enough to our people to feel affronted by the day-to-day indignities that they suffer," he wrote, "but we were trained to swallow emotion, because they would trim that from your stories. You had to be low-key and factual. Ultimately, nowhere were you secure. The Chicanos (or in the case of blacks, the 'soul brothers') distrusted you because you were part of the establishment, because you weren't angry enough. And at the same time, you felt that those you worked for sometimes thought you were an informant first and a reporter second."

Despite the tragedy of Salazar's death and the explosion in East Los Angeles, that was the end of the violence for the time being. A year after the riot, Chicano activists in East Los Angeles looked back on the tragedy with an attitude of subdued bitterness, claiming there had been no substantial improvements in the *barrio*. A series of bombings in the East Los Angeles area in 1971, for which a clandestine group calling itself the Chicano Liberation Front took credit, appeared to be an extreme reflection of the frustration felt by many in the Chicano community. "I sometimes feel," said Richard Martinez, president of the Congress of Mexican-American Unity, "that out of the ashes just came more ashes."

Meanwhile, the National Chicano Moratorium in Los Angeles provided another chapter in the saga of Corky Gonzales, who along with twenty-five of his staff members and followers were among the Chicanos arrested there. But by 1970 Gonzales was a veteran of run-ins with police over civil disobedience. In his own eyes he was being jailed for political reasons, while trying to live up to the standard of Joaquin Murieta, the first prominent revolutionary in California after the Americans took over the territory more than a century ago. Murieta was eventually captured and beheaded and his head put on public display as a lesson to future would-be revolutionaries. Gonzales immortalized Murieta in one of the best-known pieces of recent Chicano literature on both sides of the border, an epic poem, "I Am Joaquin":

I am Joaquin.
I am lost in a world of confusion,
Caught up in the whirl of
    an Anglo society,
Confused by the rules,
Scorned by the attitudes,
Suppressed by manipulation,
And destroyed by modern society.
My fathers have lost
    the economic battle
And won the struggle of
    cultural survival.
And now!

I must choose
Between the paradox of
victory of the spirit
Despite physical hunger
Or to exist in the grasp
Of the American social neurosis,
Sterilization of the soul
And a full stomach . . .
And in all the fertile farm lands,
The barren plains,
The mountain villages,
Smoke-smeared cities
We start to move.
Mexicano, Espanol, Latin, Hispano, Chicano.
I look the same.
I feel the same.
I cry and
Sing the same.
I am the masses
Of my People
And I refuse to be absorbed.
I am Joaquin
The odds are great,
But my spirit is strong.
My faith unbreakable.
My blood is pure.
I am an Aztec Prince
And Christian Christ.
I shall endure!
I will endure!

"I Am Joaquin" reflected many of the conflicting ideas of urban Chicanos, *barrio* youth, and the poem's wide circulation made Gonzales one of the most influential voices within the movement. The poem may almost have been autobiographical, for it was only in the 1960s that Gonzales made his own self-discovery. By the mid-1960s, Gonzales had long since departed from the Denver *barrio*, where he was born in 1929, the son of a Mexican emigrant. He was working with his family in the fields by the age of ten, and after graduating from high school at sixteen, he went to work at a slaughterhouse.

But his route out of the *barrio* led through the boxing ring, where he won both the National Amateur Championship and the International Amateur title before turning professional. He won sixty-five out of seventy-five pro fights and at one point was rated the third-ranking contender for the world featherweight title by the National Boxing Association. After ending his fighting career, Gonzales returned to Denver and went into the insurance and surety-bond business, while being befriended by the Anglo establishment. At twenty-nine, he became the first Mexican-American district captain in the Denver Democratic party, and in 1960 he was the Colorado coordinator of the "Viva Kennedy" campaign. Gonzales, whose Chicano background was an asset among the Mexican-American electorate, was a rising star in Denver Democratic political circles. He became the chairman of Denver's antipoverty program and served on countless boards of other community and social programs.

"I was held up as the beautiful example of what a Chicano kid could do if he worked hard and lived right," Gonzales later said. "It didn't work. I was just being used by the politicians. . . . The poor were just as poor."

In 1966, Gonzales, as director of an antipoverty program, found himself at the center of a controversy, being accused of discriminating against non-Chicanos in his antipoverty agency. Although federal officials in Washington supported him, Gonzales acted in his own defense; with a political activist group known as *Los Voluntarios,* he picketed the *Rocky Mountain News,* the paper that printed the stories about him. Then, under severe pressure from local officials, Gonzales resigned as head of the program in a strongly worded letter to Democratic Party Chairman Dale R. Tooley in which he said: "The individual who makes his way through the political muck of today's world and more so the minority representatives, suffers from such an immense loss of soul and dignity that the end results are as rewarding as a heart attack, castration or cancer. . . . You and your cohorts have been accomplices to the destruction of moral man in this society. I can only visualize your goal as complete emasculation of manhood, sterilization of human dignity, and that you not only consciously but purposely are creating a world of lackeys, political boot-lickers, and prostitutes."

Thus Gonzales made a complete break with his establishment past. He organized the Crusade for Justice, operating out of an old church in downtown Denver that contained a bail bond and legal aid office, a nursery, art gallery, library, theater, newspaper, gymnasium, and dining room. Almost overnight, Gonzales had returned to the *barrio;* and while building the Crusade center, he rejected the temptation of asking for grants or federal funds. "The Crusade is living proof of self-determination," he said in one interview. "It is the embodiment of nationalism that now exists here in the Southwest. It has been a dream in the past, but now we're creating a reality out of it—a home for La Raza."

Gonzales' call for nationalism and devotion to La Raza came to a climax in the week-long Chicano Youth Liberation Conference. Like Delano and Tierra Amarilla, this meeting left a lasting impression on the movement. The conference drew activists, students, professionals, and other Mexican-Americans from all classes and walks of life. Here was the rejuvenation of Chicano pride, a "brown is beautiful" gathering, even though the meeting came only days after a major student-police confrontation. In what was called the worst street disturbance in Denver's history, protesters pelted the police with rocks and bottles and were countered with clubs and tear gas. Thirty-six Chicanos were arrested, but as many police officers were sidelined, too. The conference praised the courage of the demonstrators, whom Gonzales described as "the real revolutionaries."

The Youth Liberation Conference developed into an annual meeting, following the course that Gonzales had set out. In addition to adopting a name, a homeland, and a language, the delegates agreed to work for the creation of an independent Chicano political party, which Gonzales felt could help achieve the independent power base he sought for the movement. He went on to suggest that the party be called the *Congreso de Aztlan* (Congress of *Aztlan*).

With a mandate from the conference, Gonzales made himself the driving force behind the movement to organize La Raza Unida into a national party in 1972. At first, he experienced opposition from José Angel Gutiérrez, who had founded La Raza Unida as a local party in 1970 and who wanted to concentrate on turning it into a strong regional party. But at Gonzales' insistence, Guitérrez and Texas party leaders called the national convention in El Paso to group the various state organizations into an independent political party.

But the convention proved to be a major disappointment for Gonzales, who went to El Paso expecting to be selected either the party's 1972 presidential candidate or the national chairman of the steering committee. Gonzales felt that he, more than anyone else, had been responsible for giving La Raza Unida its political philosophy and ideology, for guiding its evolution from the Chicano Youth Liberation Conference to the Spiritual Plan of *Aztlan*. But in El Paso, Gonzales found a formidable challenge in Gutiérrez, the youthful Texas leader whose organization already had gone beyond simple political rhetoric. Through La Raza Unida, Gutiérrez had captured control of his hometown and several other South Texas communities since 1970; and Gutiérrez also went to El Paso with the intent of being named the party's key national spokesman.

In El Paso, Gonzales suffered two major setbacks. First, the party hierarchy, influenced by Gutiérrez and other Texas leaders, refused to accept Gonzales' nomination as the party's presidential candidate; the party, instead, decided not to endorse any presidential candidate and to sidestep the presidential race entirely. Secondly, the convention chose Gutiérrez over Gonzales as the party's national chairman after a bitter pre-dawn floor fight during which some Gonzales backers shouted insults and obscenities at Gutiérrez. At the close of the marathon session, both Gutiérrez and Gonzales made appeals for unity and stood on the auditorium stage with raised, clasped hands before the convention. The moment of unity, though, did not last long. Three weeks after the November 7 general election, Gutiérrez and Gonzales confronted each other again in Albuquerque at the first meeting of the *Congreso de Aztlan*.

The differences between Gutiérrez and Gonzales are partly ideological and partly a matter of style. Gonzales is outwardly aggressive, even tactless at times; he doesn't care about the impression he leaves. His harshly worded letter of resignation to the Denver Democratic party typifies his free use of rhetoric and language. And in a highly inflammatory speech to La Raza Unida's national convention, Gonzales called "hard drugs . . . the invention of the 'gringo' because he has no culture." He labeled the majority of Americans "stupid—that's why we have a silent majority." And he accused the federal government of using Chicanos for "experimental biological subjects." Gonzales made his appearances before the convention surrounded by about a dozen muscular Chicanos wearing berets as protection from physical harm.

By stark contrast, Gutiérrez and other Texas party leaders, once highly vocal members of the Mexican-American Youth Organization (MAYO), have curbed their rhetoric. They figured it would be politically astute not to offend the Anglos openly and not to turn off the masses of Mexican-Americans. The Texas leaders want to attract some of the growing number of middle-class Mexican-Americans, no longer calling Chicanos outside the movement *"Tío Tacos"* or *"vendidos."* There is a feeling among La Raza Unida leaders in Texas that the militancy and verbal attacks on the gringo badly crippled MAYO in the long run, and they now shy away from the tactics being used by Gonzales and his followers. Even the idea of self-styled bodyguards seems a bit outdated in an era when not even the Secret Service can guarantee security.

By late 1972, there was no doubt of Gonzales' intent to establish himself as the movement's principal leader, regardless of the humiliation it would cost other Chicano leaders or the divisions it would create and intensify. In October, the Raza Unida activists, influenced by Gonzales' hard-line party stance, grabbed control of the National Congress of Land and Cultural Reform held in Albuquerque away from Tijerina, who had organized the congress, and they succeeded in making it an instrument of the party. Dejected and badly shaken by the personal affront, Tijerina walked out of the meeting, blaming Gonzales for what happened and vowing to exclude the party from his own activities. Gonzales himself did not attend the meeting, protesting the presence of Mexican-American Democrats such as New Mexico Lieutenant Governor Roberto Mondragon and Colorado legislator Betty Benavides who had been invited to participate in the meeting. "In the past years, I have disassociated myself from these people who confuse and mislead the gullible members of our Raza," Gonzales said in a statement. "I can no longer bargain with despotic government representatives. . . . I want no part of alignment with political prostitutes. . . . I have no intention of creating reaction for the profitable benefits of the professional program managers."

A month later, when the *Congreso de Aztlan* met behind closed doors over the Thanksgiving Day weekend, Gonzales and his forces confronted Gutiérrez in the same manner. Through a bit of politicking among members of the *congreso*, Gonzales secured enough votes to pass a series of strong, highly isolationist positions that fit in nicely with his push for nationalism and self-determination. Unfortunately these measures were likely to limit drastically the party's appeal to blacks, students, poor whites, and liberals, whom La Raza Unida had been able to attract in Texas. Infuriated, Gutiérrez told Gonzales and other members of the *congreso* he would have no part of the business and, along with Ramsey Muñiz, the party's Texas gubernatorial candidate, he stormed out of the meeting.

Gonzales could not have cared less. Gutiérrez's departure left him in control, although there was no assurance he could keep power, either for himself or for the party as a national organization. From the outset, it appeared that La Raza Unida's chance of making an impact on national politics would be as part of a "new majority" coalition including other minority groups and white liberals disenchanted with the two major parties. As the movement approached the mid-1970s, however, the Chicanos had to face a dilemma over the two men who had emerged as leaders. Gutiérrez, the titular head of the party, is the founder of La Raza Unida and probably the most ingenious thinker in the movement. Gonzales, on the other hand, is the old-style militant who appears to fit the mood of the movement's nationalists, whose militancy and *machismo* perhaps is outweighed only by their political naïveté. Under Gonzales' influence the Raza Unida national party is destined possibly toward achieving some semblance of Chicano nationalism and self-determination but most certainly also toward a fatal stance of isolationism.

9 JOSÉ ANGEL GUTIÉRREZ: A CHICANO PRODIGY

José Angel Gutiérrez is not like the other leaders of the Chicano movement. A generation gap separates him and the older threesome, Chávez, Tijerina, and Gonzales. Young, college-educated, the son of a doctor, Gutiérrez may have the most brilliant mind of any of the civil rights leaders of his lifetime. He represents the new breed of Chicano professionals produced by the colleges and universities, but he is still a Chicano with the old dream of revolution. Yet, even in revolt, there are contrasts between him and the older leadership: Chávez is cautious, Gutiérrez self-confident; Tijerina is aggressive, Gutiérrez cunning; Gonzales is uncompromising, Gutiérrez fluid. Gutiérrez is a Chicano prodigy, a well-read intellectual by Anglo standards who can just as comfortably organize *barrio* youth to counter the very system that taught him.

But Gutiérrez has two major enemies—the dreaded gringo, of course, but also himself. And it is often unclear which is worse. Sometimes Gutiérrez is too sharp-tongued, too self-confident, and too daring, particularly when accusing the gringo of racism and cultural genocide against the

Mexican-American by stripping him of his language and culture. The word "gringo" itself carries racist overtones, and some people think it is equivalent of "nigger" and "spic." For Gutiérrez, "gringo" describes a certain breed of Anglo: " 'Gringo' is an attitude. Blacks have called it racism, or honky. In South America or the Far East, it's called yankee imperialism. It's the whole paternalistic, ethnocentric, xenophobic attitude. It's typical among the people who come from sections of Europe, of Anglo-Saxon origin. You call them bigots, racists, animals. We Chicanos use the word 'gringo.' It doesn't go back too far. I think it [dates back] to Argentina. It has been widely used within the last forty years. It just means a foreigner. People who come from the north, who are blue-eyed blondes. It's rather significant [that] Hollywood always shows the barbarians coming from the north. If you ask a Chicano what a gringo is, he knows, especially if he lives in South Texas. If you live across the tracks from the 'gringo,' he's the guy who puts the shaft to you when you go into the employment office; the one who makes you feel as if you're getting a hand-out when you're on welfare, the sheriff who kicks your ass, then sticks you in jail without any regard for family or friends. It's the whole damn society that exists in South Texas. It's also an institution—like the Democratic party in Texas. That thing just typically fits the definition of 'gringo.' They have no regard for anyone. They are built to propagate themselves. They have no program for the people. They simply want to stay in power and keep building the same kind of political leaders."

But at a press conference in the spring of 1969, Gutiérrez's rhetoric continued to heat up: "We have got to eliminate the gringo, and what I mean by that is if the worst comes to the worst, we have got to kill him."

Gutiérrez meant what he said, but his strongest statements were open to interpretation. A champion debater in high school, he has a sense of the dramatic and of the simplified over-statement. He did not hestitate to say "eliminate the gringo," but he added that eliminating an individual could be done in various ways. Killing was one way, but, as he explained later, literal death for the gringo was not the immediate goal. Instead, Gutiérrez wanted to remove the gringo's economic, political, and social base of support; and in South Texas, where Mexican-Americans made up as much as 90 percent of a community, the base of support was largely Chicano. Killing the gringo, Gutiérrez later said, would come only as a last resort, in self-defense. But his initial interpretation is the one most people remembered.

Gutiérrez became the major spokesman for MAYO, the Mexican-American Youth Organization, which he and four other Chicano youths organized in 1967 while they were students at St. Mary's University in San Antonio. The group, which also included Mario Compean, Willie Velasquez, Juan Patlán, and Ignacio Perez, reacted against existing Mexican-American organizations considered not to be "geared for the *barrios*." Gutiérrez and his friends chose the name MAYO partly because the word means "May" in Spanish, and several successful Mexican revolutions culminated in that month. MAYO got off to a slow start, but after a year it began to take hold.

In 1968 the Ford Foundation report concluded that the Mexican-Americans were the most disorganized and fragmented minority in American life and that they needed national organization to serve their social, economic, and political needs. Ford's help to the Chicanos was channeled through two organizations—the Southwest Council for La Raza, located in Phoenix, and the Mexican-American Legal Defense and Education Fund (MALDEF), originally located in San Antonio and later moved to San Francisco. Ford gave $630,000 to the Southwest Council and $2.2 million to MALDEF to function along the lines of the National Association for the Advancement of Colored People (NAACP) and the NAACP Legal Defense Fund.

Among the leading spirits in both the Southwest Council and MALDEF was Albert Peña, Jr., a tough, middle-aged liberal who had been prominent in San Antonio Democratic politics for years and in 1968 was a member of the Bexar County Commissioners Court. His philosophy: "Take to the streets, demonstrate more, raise more hell." His objectives: to end the racial stereotypes of Mexican-Americans; to end wage, job, and educational discrimination of all kinds; to obtain better welfare and housing programs; and to stimulate political activity aimed at "electing people sympathetic to your problems." Peña attracted like-minded politicians and a tough-talking group of young Chicanos dedicated to social action and political change. These included the founders of MAYO, who were all in their early and mid-twenties. With assistance from Peña, the Southwest Council set up the Mexican-American Unity Council in San Antonio with a $110,000 grant. Velasquez was installed as its director and he proceeded, with his MAYO colleagues, to create a number of subsidiary organizations in the city's *barrios* to function as pressure groups and to be the Chicanos' voice in public affairs. Under the leadership of the Velasquez cadre, there were many and productive rallies and marches in the *barrios* of San Antonio in 1968 and early 1969. Among the targets were public schools that failed to function bilingually. Operating out of the dingy Unity Council offices over the Aztec Liquor Store on Guadalupe Street, Velasquez and his associates also gave MAYO a grant of about $10,000 and chose Gutiérrez to run the organization. With the Ford money, indirectly bestowed, MAYO began to attract notice.

MAYO recruited the young. Its tactic was confrontation in the streets. Its rhetoric, at times, was raw: "It is the gringo who we need to fight. He is the real enemy and cause of our miserable plight. We have to be revolutionary in our demands and make every sacrifice necessary, even if it means death, to achieve our goals. The name of the game is militancy in our actions." Such talk did not go down well with many people in San Antonio, despite the fact that MAYO's militancy never went beyond words. "We haven't burned down anything," Velasquez said once, "and we don't intend to." In 1969, MAYO made an overt plunge into San Antonio politics that also did not go over well. Compean ran for the city council with MAYO's backing and received almost enough votes to get into a runoff against the city's eighty-year-old mayor, W. W. McAllister. The mayor got so upset at MAYO that he called the local Ford dealers and asked them to protest to the Ford Foundation.

MAYO's most implacable and most effective adversary, however, turned out to be a fellow Mexican-American — U.S. Representative Henry B. Gonzalez, a bitter political enemy of Peña's but also a liberal Democrat from San Antonio, whose voting record for years received perfect marks from the Americans for Democratic Action. Shortly after Gutiérrez's "eliminate the gringo" statement in 1969, Gonzalez took after the Ford Foundation and the MAYO activists with a vengeance. In a series of interviews and speeches on the floor of the House of Representatives, he accused MAYO of promoting "racial hatred" and blamed Ford for supporting a group of "Brown Bilbos," equivalent in their own way to the late Senator Theodore Bilbo of Mississippi, whose name became synonymous with white racism during the States Rights controversy of the late 1940s. Gonzalez took the offensive, declaring: "I cannot stand silently by if an organization like the Mexican-American Youth Organization . . . publishes hate sheets containing statements like: 'The gringo took your grandfather's land. He took your father's job, and now he's sucking out your soul. There is no such thing as *mala suerte* [bad luck]; there is only *malos* [bad] gringos.' MAYO styles itself as the embodiment of good and the Anglo-American as the incarnation of evil. That is not merely ridiculous; it is drawing fire from the deepest wellsprings of hate."

In time, Gonzalez's own inflammatory rhetoric brought a reply from Patlán: ". . . [He is] finding himself for the first time in eight years without an 'in' to the administration, to the Kennedys, and beginning to lose ground with the Mexican-American people, particularly because he has sought to build an alliance with the racists and Birchers who don't give a damn about the poor. He is mad and crazily jealous of another Mexican-American from his own community who does have an 'in.'"

The conflict between MAYO and Gonzalez became a full-scale feud that is significant for several reasons. It marked the first outright confrontation between the new Chicano activists and the older, established Mexican-American leadership. It also set the stage for the split between the old-style "liberal" and the new-style "militant" camps that developed in the early 1970s, with lines sharply drawn over the leadership and the direction of the movement. At the same time, Gonzalez set himself up as a prime target for angry epithets: *Tío Taco, vendito, malinche* (whore) and the like. His headstrong opposition to MAYO unfortunately earned him the disrespect and contempt of the young Chicanos, whose civil rights cause he had championed for years.

In 1961, when he was thirty-five, Gonzalez was the first Mexican-American ever elected to Congress from Texas. Five years earlier he had won a state senate seat and thus had become the first Mexican-American to serve in the Texas Legislature in 110 years. In the late 1950s and early 1960s, Gonzalez had a reputation as a radical of sorts within the state's conservative-dominated political circles. He was a pariah, but his political strength lay in being a liberal Democrat in the state's most liberal urban area where fellow Mexican-Americans accounted for about half his district's constituency. Next to El Paso, on the Texas-Mexican border, San Antonio has the largest concentration of Mexican-Americans in any U.S. urban area, and the city was home for Gonzalez, whose father had fled from Mexico in 1911 to avoid that country's political and social upheaval. For forty years, Gonzalez's father edited a Spanish-speaking newspaper, remaining so Mexican in his ways that he refused to become a naturalized U.S. citizen.

Gonzalez's election to the House of Representatives was one of the first major achievements by a Mexican-American in American politics, but he sidestepped ever assuming a role of spokesman for the millions of Mexican-Americans in the Southwest, a role to which he easily could have laid a claim. Instead, Gonzalez saw himself as a congressman for all his constituents; by the early 1970s, he had virtually ruled himself out as a widely accepted spokesman for his people.

"I don't claim to represent so many millions of my people like so many others are doing," he said in one interview. "I don't think that's possible to do. Our people are a pluralistic group—diverse, not homogeneous. The so-called movement is imitative, a takeoff on Negroes in other sections of the country. I don't want to be the Moses of the Mexican-American people. I don't pretend to be. I don't have that ambition, and I don't think any one person can say he represents all the Mexican-Americans in this country. . . . The progress of the Mexican-American has been overlooked. In San Antonio, for example, in thirty years the character and classification of employment patterns has changed radically. Thirty years ago, the majority of Mexican-Americans were in semi-agricultural or rural categories. This has changed radically. In education, thirty years ago you didn't even have 15 percent [of Mexican-American youth] in high school population. Today, you have over 80 percent maybe more."

This basically was the difference in approach between Gonzalez and the old-style "liberals" on the one hand and MAYO and the new-style "militants" on the other. Gonzalez pointed to the problems of the past, saying that the Mexican-American had made significant strides. MAYO pointed to problems of the day, saying that the Chicano's progress had been neither far enough nor fast enough. And even by the most conservative of standards, the MAYO activists had a strong case.

In San Antonio, the *barrio*, even into the mid-1970s, was a sprawling collection of dilapidated wooden houses on the wrong side of town. Many of the *barrio's* streets remained unpaved, and many of the houses were jammed with big families, or sometimes several families. The yards were tiny, often surrounded by fences and decorated with bird baths and plaster religious statues. Many of those who lived in the *barrio* were migrant farm workers, who usually spent months in the Midwest during the growing and harvest seasons and returned to San Antonio for the winter. Unemployment remained high— nearly 30 percent on the Mexican-American west side of the city—despite a Labor Department "concentrated employment program" under way since the late 1960s. The city's Urban Renewal Authority was prevented by state law from using its land for badly needed public housing, and the only two projects the authority had completed since the late 1950s were devoted to commercial interests and headquarters for local government offices. The problems of the *barrio* were reflected in the statewide census statistics that showed that the median annual family income for Mexican-Americans in 1970 was $5,897, compared with $8,930 for Anglos; 31.4 percent of the Mexican-American families lived on incomes below the government-established poverty level, while only 12.4 percent of the Anglo families were in the same plight. The median educational level for Mexican-Americans was 7.2 years but 11.9 years for Anglos; and 33.8 percent of the Mexican-Americans had less than five years of schooling as compared to 8.6 percent of the Anglos. And the *barrio* was part of the only area in Texas where as recently as 1968 there had been cases of five unusual communicable diseases: diphtheria, leprosy, polio, whooping cough, and measles.

Still, Gonzalez felt that MAYO had gone beyond the limits of protest, and he broadened his attack to include the Ford Foundation. He accused it of supporting, through MAYO, "the spewing of hate, and rather than creating new political unity, it has destroyed what little there was. Rather than creating new leadership, it is simply financing the ambitions of some men who are greedy and some who are ruthless and a few who are plainly irresponsible." Officials at the Ford Foundation monitored this debate with care, as at the same time they were monitoring the progress of a tax bill in Congress that would impose a maximum forty-year life span on all foundations.

To an outsider, this threat to the Ford Foundation hardly seemed plausible. With its $3.1 billion treasury, its granite walls, and heroic glass portals on Manhattan's East Side, Ford appeared built for a millennium of good works secure from the connivances of mere men and public laws. The foundation was as firmly emplaced in the mythology of American wealth as Henry Ford the First and his Model T, and although it was the constant target of radicals, reactionaries, populists, and foreign powers, it had endured these occasional slings and arrows with patrician stoicism. In 1969, however, the people at Ford were uptight. The proposed legislation not only would impose liquidation within forty years but also would greatly restrict the way the foundations could use their money. They would be barred from such projects as voter registration drives and from investing in anything that smacked of "lobbying" or "influencing" public policy, meaning that up to 70 percent of Ford's activities in the fields of "national affairs" and "social development" would be banned. Ironically, Ford had taken few chances; it tended to let other foundations take the initial risks in underwriting social and political innovations. Even so, there were a few areas where Ford had played the pioneer and had got in trouble, and one of these was its decision to create the Southwest Council of La Raza and MALDEF as national organizations to represent Mexican-Americans.

Ford sent investigators into San Antonio to check out MAYO, and they filed a report that was not wholly flattering. In mid-June of 1969, Velasquez, Peña, Gutiérrez, and others

involved in the Southwest Council's operations were sum-
moned to New York for what turned out to be a stormy meeting in the tenth-floor office of Mitchell Sviridoff, a former
Connecticut auto worker who headed up Ford's division of
national affairs. Sviridoff bluntly announced that there would
be no more Ford money for MAYO, and Peña told Sviridoff
what he could do with all $3 billion of the foundation's assets.
Even before Peña and the young Chicanos returned to San
Antonio the next day, Ford took the unusual step of issuing a
press release to announce that it had declined MAYO's request for additional funds. This was a highly unusual step,
because the foundation ordinarily did not issue a public statement to announce turning down a grant application. "MAYO,"
one Ford official said, to justify their action, "got overtly
involved in the city election. They were campaigning openly.
. . . Their main concern was political. We just can't finance
that kind of thing." The MAYO leaders were outraged, and
some of them accused Ford of capitulating to Gonzalez out of
political expediency.

By mid-1969, though, there was no stopping Gutiérrez
and what had become the MAYO movement. MAYO chapters
were organizing around Texas and in several other states, and
Gutiérrez and MAYO members were now talking in terms of
state and national chairmen. MAYO showed its impact on
Palm Sunday, 1969, the same day the Chicano Youth Liberation Conference began in Denver and about a week before
Gutiérrez's "eliminate the gringo" press conference, when
about 2,000 Chicanos from throughout the Southwest marched
in Del Rio, 160 miles west of San Antonio, to protest the
closing of a VISTA program in Val Verde County. Indeed,
Governor Preston Smith had stopped funding VISTA workers,
mostly Chicanos, when the local county commissioners
complained that the workers took part in a MAYO-backed
protest of police brutality. The march on Del Rio pushed
MAYO to the forefront of the movement, and Gutiérrez, playing out the role of a modern-day Martin Luther, taped a copy
of what became known as the Del Rio Manifesto to the plate-
glass front door of the county courthouse. In a statement that
pledged both national loyalty and cultural identity, the protesters warned local and state officials of future "serious
social unrest," with Gutiérrez himself declaring: "La Raza

is the affirmation of the most basic ingredient of our personality, the brownhood of our Indian ancestors wedded to all the other skin colors of mankind. Brown is the common denominator of the largest number among us—a glorious reminder of our Aztec and Mayan heritage. But in a color-mad society, the sin of our coloration can be expiated only by exceptional achievement and successful imitation of the white man who controls every institution of society. La Raza condemns such a system as racist, pagan, and ultimately self-destructive. We can neither tolerate it nor be a part of it. As children of La Raza, we are heirs of a spiritual and biological miracle where in one family blood ties unite the darkest and the fairest. It is no accident that the objects of our veneration include the black Peruvian Saint Martin de Porres, the brown Indian Virgin of Guadalupe, the blonde European madonnas, and a Jewish Christ of Indian and Spanish features.

"We cannot explain our survival and our strength apart from this heritage—a heritage inseparably linked to Spanish, the soul language of La Raza. On this day, we serve notice on Del Rio and the nation that for their sake and ours we are willing to lay down our lives to preserve the culture and language of our ancestors, to blend them with that which is best in these United States of America, our beloved country. Let no one forget that thousands of our Mexican-American brothers have gallantly fought and died in defense of American freedoms enjoyed by us more in hope than reality. We shall escalate the defense of such freedoms here at home to honor those who fell for them yesterday, and to sustain those who live for their fulfillment tomorrow. We are committed to non-violence, even while living in the midst of officially tolerated violence. We are prepared, however, to be as aggressive as it may be necessary, until every one of our Mexican-American brothers enjoys the liberty of shaping his own future."

Gonzalez's opposition and the Ford decision to cut funding only further convinced Gutiérrez and other MAYO leaders that what the gringo opposed must be the movement's right direction. Shortly after Christmas in 1969, at a MAYO conference in the Rio Grande Valley town of Mission, MAYO leaders disclosed their Winter Garden Project: to redirect the political, social, and economic resources in a ten-county South Texas area and ultimately to install Chicano control there. It was during this same conference that about one hundred young Chicanos painted brown a statue of Our Lady of the Immaculate Conception.

The centerpiece of MAYO's Winter Garden Project was Crystal City, a small dusty town of about 8,000 situated in the chaparral- and mesquite-studded Rio Grande plain 125 miles southwest of San Antonio. The town is overwhelmingly Mexican-American; in 1969 the mayor and the majority of the city council were Mexican-American, but the Anglos still held the political and economic power. A railroad line ran through the heart of downtown dividing the Anglos from the Mexican-Americans, whose neighborhood was an array of wooden shacks on unpaved, muddy streets; on the other side of the tracks, concrete sidewalks and roadways weaved past modest middle-class homes and high-priced ranch-style structures.

Crystal City is also the home of José Angel Gutiérrez, born there in 1944. Gutiérrez's doctor father was himself a revolutionary who fought with Francisco (Pancho) Villa in support of Carranza's insurrection against the government of General Victoriano Huerta. The elder Gutiérrez fled to Texas during the continual upheaval in Mexico of the 1910s, and he settled in Crystal City, where he became one of the community's leading Mexican-American citizens. Being the son of a doctor, young Gutiérrez was admired by other Mexican-American youngsters and, unlike most of them, respected by his Anglo counterparts, who found that Gutiérrez could easily compete with them in school and that he quite often outsmarted them. But when Gutiérrez was twelve, his father died suddenly of a heart ailment, and respectability among the Anglos was soon gone. Though a doctor, the elder Gutiérrez had not accumulated much money. His son later recalled that his father often refused to collect money from poor Mexican-American patients. After the death, the family's small savings were quickly exhausted. The local merchants who once had been friends of the family now denied credit, and Gutiérrez's mother went to work along with other Mexican-Americans in the fields. Gutiérrez was jarred to realize that in the eyes of the Anglo community he was now just another Mexican. As time passed, he became more keenly aware of the racial issue. In high school, he was elected president of the student body and saw first-hand how the faculty manipulated school elections to give Anglo students a winning edge in school honors and positions.

Gutiérrez developed into a champion debater, and he was usually the only Mexican-American to make out-of-town trips with his team. While most of the other boys were housed two or three to a hotel room, Gutiérrez was always assigned to a room by himself. And when the students ate together on the out-of-town trips, Gutiérrez was usually given a place at a separate table with the teacher-sponsor. "I started having an interest in girls, and at that time, my concept of pretty was white—you know, a blonde chick with blue eyes, something I couldn't have. And when I started messing around with them I got burned." Later, Gutiérrez came to see this preference as part of the Mexicans' cultural genocide in trying to assimilate into the Anglo world. It is no wonder that a large number of successful Mexican-Americans are married to Anglo women.

While he was in high school Gutiérrez received his first taste of politics. In 1963, the Political Association of Spanish-Speaking Organizations (PASSO), sponsor of the Viva Kennedy Clubs in 1960, chose Crystal City as the target for a Mexican-American political takeover. With the assistance of the Teamsters Union, PASSO elected five poorly educated Mexican-Americans to the city council. They were dealt a humiliating blow when the newly elected city officials, lacking in know-how and subject to economic pressures from the power structure, threw the city government into chaos. Gutiérrez worked in the PASSO campaign, and the political education he received there may have been the most significant development of the effort.

This event was also Gutiérrez's introduction to the Texas Rangers, who were called into the area to monitor the election and who, understandably, had little love for anyone trying to disturb the status quo of South Texas. According to Gutiérrez, a group of Rangers "beat the crap out of me" several days before the election, setting off the defenses that six years later in a similar situation led him to threaten that he would "kill the gringo." "I guarantee you that the Rangers are not getting more than six feet from me," Gutiérrez said in an interview. "And if he makes any funny moves, it's either me or him. That's the kind of life it is down here, and I'm just tired of getting pushed around. I'm not going out looking for fights, but I am not going to run away from one. Psychologically, if you give in to one of those bastards, you've had it. That's been the life of our parents. That's why they go around with their hats in their hands. This has to be stopped. We've just got to be as arrogant."

In mid-1969, after having moved MAYO to the front line of the Chicano movement, Gutiérrez returned to Crystal City with the Winter Garden Project. Dissatisfied with nine-month's attendance at law school, he had transferred from the University of Houston to St. Mary's University in San Antonio, where, while earning a master's degree in political science, he, Compean, Velasquez, Perez, and Patlán had organized MAYO. The Ford controversy forced Gutiérrez out of a job, and so he decided to turn the leadership of MAYO over to Compean and return home to carry out his blueprint for giving control of the political, economic, and social systems of South Texas to Chicanos.

Crystal City was to be a test case in over-all MAYO strategy, and the planning was for Chicanos to take over the school board, the city council, the county government, and several businesses in the space of two years. The strategy began unfolding in December 1969, when a three-week student boycott crippled Crystal City's school system and ended with the Anglo-dominated school board capitulating and granting most of the students' demands. In the previous two years, Texas and other southwestern states had been hit by school boycotts, with the issues of discrimination and lack of bilingual programs dramatic and clear-cut enough for protest to form easily around them. The Crystal City boycott, however, showed several landmark differences: it was among the largest and most widespread actions, involving students from the first grade through high school; it had not only the approval of most of the Chicano parents but also their active participation; it attracted national attention, with representatives of the Department of Health, Education and Welfare and the Justice Department's Community Relations Service on the scene; it established the principle of student negotiation with school board trustees; and it resulted in victory for the protesters. The basic situation in Crystal City schools was summed up in statistics. Although Mexican-Americans made up about 85 percent of the city and school population, only a small percentage of the Mexican-American population actually got through school. As late as 1970, the city's Mexican-Americans twenty-five years old and over had attained a median educational level of only three years — less than a one-grade increase in ten years.

As elsewhere in the Southwest, much of the problem in Crystal City was the language. There was no provision for bilingual education in most schools, and until the late 1960s, use of Spanish in the classrooms and schoolyards was forbidden and punished by beatings. Children from Spanish-speaking homes grew up trying to learn in a foreign language. Frustrated and discouraged, many of them dropped out of school at the earliest opportunity.

In addition, the new young Chicano activists began pointing out other glaring inequities, even in the schools' methods of choosing cheerleaders and baton twirlers and the alumni association's selection of a homecoming queen. In every case the Mexican-Americans were excluded or given only token representation. And, underlying these problems, there was the long history of discrimination and tokenism in the schools. Finally, on December 9, 1969, about 700 high school students walked out of their classes and held a rally outside the school. Their signs said, "We want our rights now," "Chicanos want to be heard," and "We are not afraid to fight for our rights." Within a week, the boycott spread to the junior high and elementary schools, with most of the parents firmly behind the protest. Mrs. Olivia Serna, mother of one of the three boycott leaders, explained: "I went to high school here. We were in the minority then, so we didn't complain. We felt they had the right to run things. We have had the feeling of inferiority. We're made to feel that way. When my kids came and complained, I said maybe we should take it, even though we know it's wrong. I didn't want to push them until they were ready for it. What we're doing now, we're expressing to our children something we know has been important for a long time. Something good is bound to come. At least they have spoken. You can't keep people down."

The town's Anglos and a segment of establishment-minded Mexican-Americans were nervous and upset. They blamed the trouble on "outside influences," claimed the Chicanos' problems were exaggerated, and angrily pointed the finger at one person: José Angel Gutiérrez.

Of medium height, stocky, with a pencil-thin mustache and glasses, Gutiérrez does not give the expected impression of a modern-day Latin political leader. By contrast it is Ramsey Muñiz, La Raza Unida's Texas gubernatorial candidate in 1972 and 1974 who strikes that image: extreme good looks, an athletic build, and an air that quickly draws attention. Muñiz's charisma is instantly noticeable. With Gutiérrez, the charisma has to grow on you. Gutiérrez is an enigma. Behind his deceptively casual appearance there is an unusually quick mind directed toward political organization, infiltration, and agitation. Persuasive and self-confident, Gutiérrez is at his best when he is underestimated or is not taken seriously. In his research for a multi-volume series of books updating John Gunther's *Inside U.S.A.*, Neal R. Peirce, a highly respected national political writer, ran into such an experience when he was caught ill-prepared for an interview with Gutiérrez that he later described as "one of the most remarkable . . . I have ever had."

Gutiérrez, however, denied "masterminding" the boycott, claiming the students had followed their own lead, although his and MAYO's organizing hands were clearly in evidence. But there was no question who was behind the political revolt that began unfolding in the spring of 1970 when Gutiérrez introduced into local politics his new Chicano party—La Raza Unida. Relying on Gutiérrez's organizing skills, La Raza Unida won control of the school boards not only in Crystal City but also in nearby Carizzo Springs and Cotulla, the town where Lyndon Johnson first taught in a small Mexican-American school. Gutiérrez himself became the school board president, and by 1974, the new school leaders filled twenty-three of twenty-four administrative positions with Mexican-Americans; they had increased the school district's budget from $1 million to $3 million, had brought in a half-dozen experimental educational programs, and, most notably, had changed the composition of the faculty from 65 percent Anglo to 70 percent Chicano. At the same time, though, the district's Anglo enrollment dropped sharply from 175 students to less than two dozen.

By the end of 1973, Gutiérrez had fulfilled his immediate

goals for La Raza Unida with the party controlling not only the school board but the city council and the government of surrounding Zavala County. The new city officials took up a massive renewal program, pushing through a multi-million dollar school-bond program, arranging for federal home-improvement and rehabilitation loans, and assisting local contractors in launching their own business ventures with the aid of loans and grants offered by the Nixon administration. One new business, a Mexican-American-operated restaurant on U.S. Highway 83, was named after the two federal programs that spawned it—the SBANEDA Steak House, after the Small Business Administration and the National Economic Development Association.

At the same time, local activists went about establishing an economic base to withstand the pressures that foiled the 1963 political takeover. One by one, Anglo-run businesses in Crystal City became victims of a Chicano boycott aimed either at wresting economic control from the businessman or securing significant concessions in the form of employment and wages. "We boycott the businesses, bury them down into a hole, then we don't buy them out," Gutiérrez told one visitor as he showed him the businesses in the town mall that had closed down or were displaying closing signs. "We set up our own businesses, and then they lose their asses. It's interesting to see they [Anglos] can't take the pressure. Seven of those sons-of-bitches, seven, mind you, have died of heart attacks, maybe because we drove them out of business. Our people have died because of what they've done to them in the past. Maybe they didn't die physically, but they died in their spirit, in their brain, in different ways and the gringos never gave a shit. It's called capitalism and we're just practicing it. The gringos tell us, 'You guys are revengeful, racists in reverse, you're unfair.' Well, a racist in reverse is a humanitarian. And what we're practicing is just good, old American business sense. We don't buy from the competitor, and what happens is his business."

La Raza's success in Crystal City surprised even Gutiérrez, who, even while organizing the new party, commuted weekly to Austin where he was working on his doctorate in political science. He felt that if La Raza Unida worked in Crystal City, it could make an impact any place else, both urban and rural; but even he believed winning his hometown would be much more difficult than it turned out to be. "If you had told me then how far along we'd be in two years," he said in one interview, "I never would have believed it. I wanted to go slowly, to go conservatively. I was afraid if we moved too fast, we'd lose Crystal City and our other original bases. But the others [leaders in the party] saw it differently and outvoted me. It looks now that they may have been right to do it."

But by 1974, Gutiérrez had reason to be surprised by more than Crystal City. La Raza Unida was no longer his brainchild alone but the pride of the Chicano movement. Against his wishes, other Chicano activists thrust the party into statewide politics in 1972, and the Raza Unida idea slithered from his grasp and into the hands of the Chicano nationalists who forced upon Gutiérrez and the Texas leaders the El Paso convention where the movement organized La Raza Unida into a national party. While Gutiérrez wanted to keep the party at the regional level at least through 1972, Chicano activists throughout Texas were eager to become politically involved. To many of them, Crystal City presented a challenge; and if they lived in El Paso, Dallas, Fort Worth, or Houston, South Texas was too far out of the way to attract their enthusiasm. A statewide candidate, on the other hand, would give everyone in the state a chance to participate. At his own state party convention in October 1971, Gutiérrez was outvoted by the forces for a statewide party. Gutiérrez acceded, though he had his doubts about the party's decision. He wanted to be sure of each step, instead of seeing the party move ahead prematurely and suffer a morale-crushing defeat. At the same time, he hoped to monitor some of La Raza Unida's activity in other states. He had reservations about the party activism outside Texas, believing that the rhetoric and zealousness in states like California and Colorado might be blunted by defeats that he felt would be the result of poor organizing and political naïveté. But just as he had had no choice about the Texas party going statewide, Gutiérrez soon found himself in a similar situation in a nationwide setting.

In early 1972, the indomitable Corky Gonzales notified Texas party leaders that unless they acted quickly he would call a national convention to replace a meeting of the defunct

Spanish-Speaking Political Coalition. The coalition, formed in Washington, D.C., in October 1971, planned a series of regional conventions for early 1972 and a national convention later in Washington. The plans, however, ended at the regional level.

Gutiérrez was afraid of just such poor planning, which might seem to fit into the stereotype of lazy, half-way Latin methods. He was concerned that the movement might form a national political party prematurely and that it would fall apart within a short time. Or, worse yet, he was worried that poor organization would result in personal disputes underscoring another popular image of Latin leaders. Such a sequence of events would go well, Gutiérrez thought, with the white liberals who regarded the introduction of an independent Chicano party as a threat to the Democrats' traditional hold on Mexican-American votes. Gutiérrez was not opposed to having white liberals in La Raza Unida, but he had his doubts about the numbers who would be attracted and about their willingness to come into the party on La Raza's terms. Too often, Gutiérrez recalled, the liberals wanted to go into the *barrios* and help the Chicanos like Peace Corps workers in some underdeveloped country.

"When the Chicano sees a white," Gutiérrez said in an interview, "he doesn't see a liberal Anglo. . . . He sees a gringo, and they react this way because liberal Anglos have a facility for insulting people, especially our people. They can't conceive that we like steak, that we get tired of Mexican food because we eat it every day. They are the ones who buy a *molcajete* [mortar used to pound spices] and use it as an ashtray. They go to Mexico and say they saw the ruins of the Mayan tombs. Well, that makes me jealous and pisses me off because I can't even go see my own culture. Here they have it in arts and crafts, they have it laying around as ashtrays. They can't appreciate it. They only prostitute it. It's the same one that gets turned off when he listens to the *ranchera* [Mexican country] music or the polkas, but they like the Mexican music only when it's played by the Tijuana Brass. . . . If they hear the music played by the plain *conjunto* [Mexican combo], it's cheap stuff, but it's great when the Baja Marimba Band plays it in stereo. . . . The liberals haven't done a damn thing for the Chicanos. They have done things for themselves and used the Chicanos. I'm a bit critical, but that's the way I feel. I've gone to all those luncheons, this pisses me off. 'Ah, José Angel Gutiérrez, I want to shake your hand' . . . then they start flirting. I feel like a damn commodity. They don't even know what the hell to say. The 'gringas,' for example want you on their own timetable, not on agendas. They want to see if you're for real, if you really smell bad, or whatever. It's like the *molcajete* ashtray. I'm sure if I was for sale they would buy me, put me on their mantelpiece and say, 'Look, I have a live José Angel Gutiérrez.' "

This rhetoric, full of Chicano bravado, reflects the thinking of the movement. Within La Raza, there are a few Chicanos who differ strongly with Gutiérrez on the idea of openly alienating a potential ally. But above all things, Gutiérrez himself is a masterful politician, capable of soothing the whims and complaints of his divergent group of followers in much the same manner as his image can shift from an introspective student of political science to an angry revolutionary. Gutiérrez is predictably unpredictable, and his psyche can run the gamut of human emotion in such lightning fashion that occasionally it leaves the appearance of being part of carefully thought-out plans.

Gutiérrez is all these things — a planner, an organizer, a tactician, a realistic dreamer. In the mid-1970s, La Raza Unida continues to grow in Texas and painfully struggles to organize beyond the rhetoric stage in other states. If any one man in the Chicano movement symbolizes the hopes of the party and the forces that will either hold it together or split it asunder, it is José Angel Gutiérrez. He represents not so much the rise of a Chicano revolt as the decline of Chicano indifference to years of political frustration.

10 LA RAZA AND LA REVOLUCIÓN

More than any other leader in the Chicano movement, José Angel Gutiérrez is a student of revolution, and perhaps the greatest lesson he has learned is that revolution is always changing. In 1969 the Chicanos at the Youth Liberation Conference declared themselves in the tradition of other revolutions the heirs of *Aztlan,* "a nation . . . a union of free *pueblos.*" Reies López Tijerina, the Brown Berets, and others who looked to militance and physical force as the routes to freedom were following in the footsteps of the American colonists at the Boston Tea Party. As Gutiérrez was well aware, the great revolutions of the past, even those in his father's homeland half a century earlier, succeeded in countries that were largely rural; they came at times in history when communications and transportation systems were primitive.

But in twentieth-century America, or any other heavily urbanized country with a sophisticated technology, the revolutionary strategies that succeeded in toppling the old regimes in France, England, Russia, and the American colonies are outdated. In a country where it is possible to rush the National

167

Guard into such a non-urban area as Tierra Amarilla, New Mexico, there can be no successful storming of the Bastille. If revolutionaries are to be successful, they will have to revolutionize their own methods.

In the late 1960s, the Chicano activist leaders laid aside for the time being any notion of a violent swoop to recapture *Aztlan*. Instead, they were convinced that the path for revolution was the same political system that had failed them for more than 120 years. When the Youth Liberation Conference called for a national party in 1969, this was more a cry of protest than a realistic move that could have an immediate effect on the country's political structure. The national organization they were calling for would have to be a party with no financial backing, little political know-how, and an uncertain constituency. At best, the party was doomed to be a historical footnote like other third parties in American history; at worst, it could become another embarrassing example of ineptness by what the Ford Foundation described as the most disorganized minority group in the country.

The revolt needed as its leader a political pragmatist who would see *Aztlan* as an ultimate goal but in practice as a dream, someone who knew that political parties are built on tedious, dedicated planning and organization and not on rhetoric and weekend activism. The brute fact was that a Chicano party could not hope to begin successfully on a grand scale; instead the movement would have to start from scratch with the unglamorous work of politicizing the Mexican-American masses and organizing on a block-by-block basis. And then, maybe then, there would be a beginning. This revolutionizing of revolutionary strategies would have to be done within the movement, and there was only one man dedicated, patient, and capable enough to handle the task—José Angel Gutiérrez.

In his master's thesis at St. Mary's University, Gutiérrez concluded that "empirical conditions for revolution have been found to exist in South Texas. . . . If this is the case, then could not the Mexican-American revolt? Certainly, and as the rest of the evidence in this thesis indicates, the Mexican-American will revolt." A year later, in 1969, he was leading the revolution in Crystal City, masterminding the assault on the schools, the city, and the county establishment. The tools of the revolt were the school demonstrations, the economic boycott, and detailed organization, but these were overshadowed by activism and rhetoric. The very noisiness of the demonstration contributed to their being underestimated and misunderstood by other Chicano activists around the Southwest.

La Raza Unida's organization in Crystal City was a widely spread, carefully built, genuinely solid, old-fashioned structure in spite of its having been a do-it-yourself project. Gutiérrez's organizational technique was almost too simple: to establish personal contact—face to face or by phone—with as many Mexican-Americans in the community as was humanly possible; to identify the Raza Unida supporters and the waverers ripe for conversion; and to try to turn the waverers into supporters and the supporters into volunteer workers who would, in turn, spread the web of personal contacts. All this effort partook of the old politics of ward campaigning disguised as new Chicano politics, and it was a highly successful technique in what had previously been a disorganized community. The Crystal City success whetted the appetites of other Chicano activists who saw what could be done by turning the political system against the Anglo-dominated establishment, even though they failed to appreciate the long hours of diligent organizing work that supported the boycott. Chicano activists throughout the Southwest were eager to plunge into the political work, expecting to rely on a ready-made organization like the two major parties. But of course La Raza Unida had no such structure.

Gutiérrez figured it would take years to build up the same grass-roots organization in the ten South Texas counties of the Winter Garden Project, and even longer before the party could boast a structure of similar strength in most of the state's other twenty-six counties where Mexican-Americans constituted the majority of the population. In one interview, he said it could be as long as thirty years before there would be any future for Mexican-Americans in South Texas. Gutiérrez did not give much thought to immediately spreading the party to other parts of the Southwest, although the idea of a national Raza Unida party organizing some time in the distant future both intrigued and challenged him. But, unlike other visionaries of a national political organization, he saw the party evolving slowly from the work of statewide parties, themselves the products of assiduous organizing.

By 1972, though, the restlessness among the Chicanos outside South Texas was too strong, and the fervor and excitement building up in a presidential election year overflowed and touched the disenfranchised. In March 1972, more than 3,000 black activists gathered in Gary, Indiana, for the National Black Political Convention to settle on strategies for the fall. A month later, about 800 Mexican-Americans met in San Jose for what was mistakenly billed as the National Chicano Political Caucus. It was, in fact, only one of several regional meetings of Spanish-speaking groups that were to have led up to a national convention of the Spanish-speaking political coalition in Washington, D.C. But that convention never took place. Not to be outdone by the blacks, the San Jose convention organizers gave their meeting the most impressive name possible, though most of the major names within the movement, including Gutiérrez, Corky Gonzales, and Tijerina, did not attend.

In San Jose, the organizers planned a forum to hammer out a platform on social and political issues for Chicano activists of all political persuasions. Drawn to the convention were the militants carrying La Raza Unida's banner and also Mexican-Americans representing establishment organizations, including the Democratic and Republican parties. But the false atmosphere of unity was quickly broken as the Raza Unida forces, making up in sheer bravado what they lacked in organization, shouted their way into control of the caucus and in one of the first orders of business passed a measure endorsing the new separatist party. The caucus was thrown into further confusion when Raza Unida supporters adjourned the session being held in a downtown hotel and moved to the city's eastside *barrio* "to be closer to the people." The establishment delegates, however, refused to move and convened their own rump session in the hotel where state presidents of three major Mexican-American groups—the Mexican-American Political Association (MAPA), the League of United Latin American Citizens (LULAC), and the American G.I. Forum—told a press conference they could neither support nor endorse La Raza Unida. Reacting to Raza Unida charges that they were dupes of the two major parties, MAPA President Armando Rodriguez said La Raza Unida supporters had "imposed their will simply by shouting louder." Surprisingly, the chief Raza Unida spokesman at the caucus was veteran California activist Bert Corona, a past president of MAPA, who defended La Raza Unida's tactics as "clearly express-ing the will of the majority."

As an attempt at political unity, the San Jose caucus was a disaster, but it did dramatize the impatience, zeal, and reck-less abandon of young Raza Unida supporters. The caucus also indicated the support building up for a national meeting of Chicano activists.

So, when La Raza Unida's first national convention ac-tually got under way in El Paso over the Labor Day weekend, the leaders and factions within the movement confronted one another for the first time. Sadly, their meeting resulted not in a joyous beginning but a traumatic crisis for the Chicano party. Still, the convention was a landmark. El Paso marked the first occasion the whole Chicano movement had ever met to select its own leadership. By the traditional yardstick of political impact and influence, there was no question but that Gutiérrez and the Texas party towered over the other seven-teen states represented. They were the only Raza Unida party on a statewide ballot, and they were the only group with the semblance of a party structure.

Outside Texas, La Raza Unida activity, which rarely went beyond rhetoric, was limited to two states — Colorado and California — where, even by third-party standards, the results had been unimpressive. In Colorado in 1970, an entire slate of Chicanos, not under the name of La Raza Unida, ran for numerous offices, but had polled less than half of one percent of the statewide vote. In California, many party chapters sprang up in the early 1970s, but they were more tightly knit activist groups than political organizations. Outside Texas, La Raza Unida's only real political impact came in 1971 in California's 48th Assembly District where Raul Ruiz, a California college instructor, played the "spoiler" role in a special election to fill a vacancy. Although he was running as an independent, Ruiz carried La Raza Unida's banner, and he drew 2,786 votes in helping upset Democrat Richard Alatorre, a fellow Mexican-American. Alatorre, who was elected to the state assembly in 1972, lost the special election to Republican Bill Brophy by a mere 1,500 votes; and Los Angeles political observers readily conceded that with Ruiz out of the race, the overwhelming majority of the third-party candidate's votes would have swung to Alatorre to give him the election.

The difference between the Raza Unida parties in California and Colorado and the party in Texas was that the leaders outside Texas ignored the lesson of Crystal City, with its ward-style politics, and hoped that La Raza Unida's philosophy and platform would awaken the nationalism within Mexican-Americans. It was on nationalism, after all, that Corky Gonzales built his own movement, and the activists believed the nationalist sense of pride and belief in one's own people ought to override the pragmatism of traditional politics.

As the convention unfolded, then, Gutiérrez, as founder of the party, was challenged not only by Gonzales' own ambitions for leadership but also by a philosophy of political organization far different from the Crystal City idea. In a bitterly contested fight for the national chairmanship, Gutiérrez succeeded in thwarting Gonzales; but the zeal of the Chicano nationalists left an indelible mark on the convention. The nationalists spurned an overture from Senator George S. McGovern and adopted a highly nationalistic platform, even though they incorporated liberal Democratic planks like the redistribution of wealth, a guaranteed annual income, national health insurance, and immediate withdrawal from Indochina. Gutiérrez himself got mired down in convention disputes with results that hurt the Texas party later on.

So extreme was the nationalists' isolationism that they were able to prevent an address by the Right Reverend Patricio Flores, auxiliary bishop of the San Antonio diocese and a noted Chicano rights advocate. This was a direct affront to Bishop Flores, the only Mexican-American bishop in the country, and it humiliated the Texas party, whose leadership and activism had long received the bishop's support.

Two years earlier, when Bishop Flores was installed as the auxiliary in his diocese on *el Cinco de Mayo* — May 5, a Mexican political holiday — the ceremony included a *mariachi* mass and speeches by César Chávez and Gutiérrez. Flores was named chairman of the Texas Advisory Committee to the U.S. Civil Rights Commission and he became one of the state's most vocal spokesmen for Mexican-American rights. At Christmas time in 1971, he donated his episcopal ring to a raffle that raised about $2,400 for the defense of a young Mexican-American accused of murder in Houston. He testified at the trial, and when asked why he would give up such a valuable ring (which later was returned to him) he replied, "That's all I had to give." Two months later, he testified in behalf of Efrain Fernandez, a farm-worker organizer, MAYO member, and Raza Unida party activist, who was being tried on charges stemming from a 1971 riot in the Rio Grande Valley, charges of which he was later acquitted. Still in his early forties, Bishop Flores was established as the Church's Chicano advocate, intervening in a series of police brutality complaints and sponsoring a Mexican-American cultural center in San Antonio for training priests to deal with Mexican-American language and cultural needs and *barrio* leaders to plunge into politics.

And while he hesitated to give La Raza Unida his unequivocal endorsement, several months before the party's national convention Bishop Flores indicated in an interview that he was in sympathy with the movement: "La Raza is necessary in one way," he said. "We need our own thing. If we are given a machine that is already built, it defeats part of the purpose, which is development. If we invent our own thing, the development may be slower, but it is more profound. . . . In my native state of Texas, I have been witness to a lifetime of oppression and discrimination. The people are no longer willing to settle for a dream of equality and opportunity, but are determined to make that day happen here. . . . I may disagree with their [party activists'] techniques and rhetoric, but that has always happened in all areas with youth. They will always find a friend in me."

But Bishop Flores was an even closer friend of César Chávez, whose long association with the Democrats had brought him a barrage of criticism from La Raza Unida. In some secret dealings, the Raza Unida leaders managed to keep Chávez from attending the convention, thus severing the last ties between Chávez's farm labor drive and the Chicano movement that grew out of it. As a former migrant worker, Bishop Flores felt a natural affinity for Chávez and *la causa*. He still had hundreds of relatives in the migrant stream, and in past summers he had visited workers in migrant farm camps in the Midwest. Still, the major objection raised by the Chicano nationalists was Bishop Flores' past support of liberal Democratic candidates.

Colorado's delegation, still bitter about the defeat of Corky Gonzales, led the movement to bar outside speakers against the plea issued by Mario Compean, state chairman of the Texas party. Only a day earlier, before he defeated Gonzales, Gutiérrez announced that Bishop Flores would address the convention, along with a representative of the Southern Christian Leadership Conference and other speakers. Apparently the objection to Bishop Flores and outside speakers was directed as much at Gutiérrez as it was at the outsiders themselves.

The isolationists' intransigence came as a shock to supporters of Ramsey Muñiz and to Muñiz himself, who had been campaigning among students, white liberals, and blacks. Only a few weeks earlier, at the SCLC national convention in Dallas, Muñiz went to SCLC President Dr. Ralph Abernathy and other SCLC leaders and asked for their endorsement. Dr. Abernathy personally announced the endorsement, and Muñiz sought the help of other black leaders across the state. He received endorsements from more than a dozen college student-body presidents, and at the height of the campaign many liberal Democrats were working on his behalf. Muñiz's campaign, his issues, and his platform, in fact, were more in line with the McGovern Democratic party than with the Raza Unida national party that organized in El Paso and went on record pledging financial and manpower assistance to his campaign. Muñiz later reported that the national party's support was negligible. He wondered whether he might have been hurt more than helped by the confusion of the national convention.

El Paso, on the westernmost tip of Texas and just across the border from lively Ciudad Juarez, is a city of both wealth and extreme poverty, with perhaps the smallest middle class of any major American city. According to the 1970 census, Mexican-Americans make up 58 percent of the population, and many locals say that the figure is modestly low. The greatest single economic influence on El Paso is Fort Bliss, the army's air defense center and gateway to the massive

White Sands Missile Range, which served as a base for General John J. Pershing's punitive invasion of northern Mexico to curb Pancho Villa's border raids in 1917. Together, El Paso and Juarez make up an interdependent community of more than 800,000 people, giving El Paso the distinct look of a Latin American city. Thirteen thousand Mexicans in the international metropolis hold "green cards," remnants of the old *bracero* program, entitling the holder to work and live in the United States, though most prefer to commute to El Paso and live cheaply in Juarez. In addition, there are thousands of illegal aliens working as housemaids, sometimes three to a household in the affluent Coronado section in the western extreme of the city, who are paid no more than twenty dollars a week for six twenty-four-hour days plus room and board. The pay and the hiring of illegal help is usually justified by the rationale that the young girls, who usually can't speak English, would not find work elsewhere and probably would end up on the public assistance rolls. Whatever the reason, the employment of low-cost illegal aliens has a strong impact among the unskilled and semi-skilled workers who live in the *barrio.* In El Paso and throughout South Texas, where illegal Mexican aliens are hired in large numbers, wages are kept extremely low, and the large stock of cheap laborers has blocked any labor-organizing movement such as César Chávez's in California.

Since the mid-1960s, Chávez has had organizers in the area of Rio Grande City near the border. But almost a decade later the United Farm Workers Union had made little impact on the South Texas growers in what has been the Chávez drive's greatest failure. The most obvious evidence of a major organizing campaign came in 1966, during the first year of the great grape strike in California, when South Texas melon pickers rebelled and walked 490 miles from Rio Grande City to the state capitol in Austin, demanding a state minimum-wage law. This was a march modeled after the Delano-to-Sacramento march in California, with its heavy religious overtones and the assistance of liberal politicians and organized labor. The number of marchers reached 6,500 by Labor Day, sixty-four days after the march began, when the collection of leathery faced field hands, young Chicano activists, students, and a number of blacks and Anglos walked into Austin to be greeted by 4,000 supporters at the capitol. The *Texas Observer,* one of the few journals with insight into liberal thought in the Southwest, hailed the marchers as having "walked step by step from obscurity and exploitation into Texas history."

Two and a half years later a minimum-wage law was passed by the Texas Legislature, but the farm workers' strike in Rio Grande City failed in 1967, causing no heartbreak for the state leadership under Governor John B. Connally. Despite his great following among other Texans, Connally was considered the epitome of their past by the Mexican-Americans. A good reason for their animosity came up in the homestretch of the 1966 farm workers' march, when Connally and an entourage of politicians confronted the marchers just north of New Braunfels, midway between Austin and San Antonio.

Connally, distinguished-looking in his business suit, with suave manners and well-kept silvery mane, was not moved when a Catholic priest thrust a crucifix in his face; and he told the marchers that, despite their invitation, he would not be in Austin to meet them and even if he were in Austin, "I still would not have met with you . . . because I'm not un-aware of the difficulties that have arisen out of marches throughout this nation [that] for various reasons have resulted in riots and bloodshed." In his *Megastates of America,* Neal R. Peirce quoted a critic of Connally's as saying the governor "thought he was still on the ranch. He thought he was still the Anglo foreman talking to those little Mexicans back on the ranch in Wilson County, telling the people to go on back home."

The Chicanos' anti-Connally sentiment got a public airing a year later in El Paso where the governor was roundly booed by Mexican-Americans when he was introduced by President Johnson at ceremonies settling a century-old border dispute. A 437-acre area known as the Chamizal had been taken over by the United States in 1864 when a whim of the Rio Grande's meandering ways moved its course southward. After Mexico had pressed for its return for many years, President John F. Kennedy and Mexican President Adolfo López Mateos agreed the Chamizal should be returned to Mexico. At a ceremony on October 28, 1967, with President Johnson and López Mateos' successor, Gustavo Díaz Ordaz, the land was formally transferred in a peaceful settlement that contrasted with the violence of other disputes between the two countries. The ceremony coincided with the hearings being held in El Paso by the government's Inter-Agency Committee on Mexican-Americans, which had drawn Chicano activists who were turned off not only by Connally but also by the Johnson administration's failure to deal effectively with the problems of the Chicanos. But at the ceremonies, the ire of the activists aimed itself only at Connally, because his opposition to the farm workers' march had made him an easy political prey.

Alongside Connally at New Braunfels were Texas Attorney General Waggoner Carr and Ben Barnes, speaker of the Texas House of Representatives; they also incurred the wrath of the Chicanos. Carr was challenging incumbent John G. Tower for Sam Houston's old Senate seat—the post Lyndon Johnson had given up when he assumed the vice-presidency. Carr's stance on the farm workers' issue turned off large numbers of Mexican-Americans, who deserted the Democratic fold to vote for Tower, even though that conservative politician only two years earlier had been one of Barry Goldwater's staunchest supporters. By all accounts, the Mexican-American vote, of which Tower received about 30 percent, was pivotal in his victory.

In the late 1960s, Barnes became the rising star of Texas politics, following in the footsteps of Lyndon Johnson and Connally. The *Texas Observer* said he had become "perhaps in ways Lyndon Johnson never did, the consummate consensus politician." Barnes' political rise, paralleled by an unusual financial upswing, was touted by such admirers as former President Johnson. As much as Connally, however, Barnes came to be despised by the Chicanos; and in one interview, Mario Compean said that one of the party's aims in 1972 was to draw enough Mexican-American votes away from the Democrats in the general election to keep Barnes out of the governor's mansion. "He's who we want to beat," Compean said. "We want to get him bad." But the Chicanos never had a shot at Barnes when it came out that he was marginally connected with a stock-fraud scandal that shook the upper echelons of Texas politics. Barnes was defeated in the 1972 Democratic primary and went to the sidelines, his loss cheered by the Chicanos who viewed his fall as a deserved blow to the state's establishment. The Chicanos felt it was the state's leadership, symbolized by Barnes, that had turned its back on the plight of the Mexican-Americans in South Texas and in south El Paso, the *barrio* where poverty ranks with that of Mississippi and Appalachia.

South El Paso is known as *El Segundo,* after its designation as the city's Second Ward, and for generations it has been both a haven and a trap for the Mexicans moving across the border. It is a pocket of abject poverty, with 16,000 residents, virtually all of them Mexican-Americans, jammed against the Rio Grande in a population density of 145 per acre, mostly housed in two-story, two-room tenement units. In the city's newer subdivisions, the density averages fourteen persons per acre. An estimated 85 percent of the inhabitants in *El Segundo* are renters, living in 226 tenement structures with 3,500 dwelling units, most of them constructed before the turn of the century. Most buildings have no modern conveniences, with only a cold-water tap in a central courtyard, where on any hot, still day the stench of urine and human wastes becomes nauseating. Electrical wiring is primitive, and none of the buildings have central heating. Bathing facilities are non-existent, and the families are forced to use large tubs that they hang against the walls just outside their doors. Although local housing codes require a minimum of one toilet for every eight families, few toilets are in working order, and it is not uncommon to find one or two outside toilets serving two dozen people.

On the economic and educational fronts the conditions are not much better. In the early 1970s, the average family income was only one-third of the nationally established poverty level, unemployment was three times the national average, and almost a third of the heads of households were women. Less than a fifth of the family heads had a high school education, and more than a fourth of them were functionally illiterate.

This was the El Paso that somehow escaped the view of the tourists. More surprisingly, it had also escaped the efforts of the Chicano movement, which hardly existed in the city. The low-tuition, commuter-oriented state-supported school — the University of Texas at El Paso (UTEP) — had created opportunities for the bright Mexican-American students who might otherwise have put their minds to organizing the *barrio*.

It was this El Paso that drew about 4,000 delegates and spectators over the Labor Day weekend in 1972. They expected to see not only the creation of a national party but the kickoff of Ramsey Muñiz's campaign. Since the previous February, Muñiz had become La Raza Unida's best-known figure in the state, eclipsing even the reputation of Gutiérrez himself. But at the convention, he found himself pushed aside, as party leaders had made no plans for him to address the four-day gathering. They told him the best they could do was to try to find him a place on the agenda. Disappointed and angry, Muñiz left the convention for one day and flew to Lubbock to address several thousand delegates to the state convention of *Cursillos de Cristiandad*, a Catholic group. Back in El Paso, he waited to be recognized by the delegates, many of them drawn to the party and to the convention because of him. During one session, after the two keynote speeches by Gutiérrez and Corky Gonzales, a spontaneous chant erupted from the masses of delegates and visitors who filled the auditorium: "We want Ramsey! We want Ramsey!" This went on for several minutes until Muñiz, on instructions from party leaders, announced he would speak later.

In the end, Muñiz never addressed the convention. He was the victim of political jealousies within the party—he was in competition with other Texas Chicano leaders, many of whom had already spent years trying to establish themselves —and of a struggle among the delegations for control of the party machinery. Delegates from several other states objected to giving the Texans too large a role in the convention, and Muñiz's appearance before the convention apparently was traded away to help secure support for Gutiérrez's candidacy for the chairmanship.

But if party leaders would not let Muñiz speak, some 2,000 Mexican-American workers who were on strike against the Farah Manufacturing Company, one of the nation's largest pants makers, were willing to hear him. At a benefit dance, Muñiz gave an extemporaneous talk that was often interrupted by cheers and applause from the crowd of middle-aged, conservatively dressed Mexican-Americans. "What we're saying, brothers," Muñiz declared in a voice that reverberated in the huge El Paso Coliseum, "is that we're going to make a significant political impact, and we will become the balance of power in Texas and the Southwest. We don't care what the political pros say, because something needs to be done now. When you're hungry and when you're suffering, you need to get together real fast. And we don't care if you're brown, black, or white. . . . Today politicians are calling for law and order. They're saying they're worried about crime in the streets. Well, brothers, the real crime is being inflicted on browns, blacks, and poor and working whites. The real crime is in the White House and in the state capitol of Texas."

In spite of his effective speech, the convention failed Muñiz by denying him the exposure of state and national media. But the convention failed, too, to affect the Mexican-American masses even in the American city with the largest Spanish-speaking population. Muñiz arrived in El Paso telling reporters the party would "shake up this city like it's never been shaken." Muñiz's personal strategist, Roland Arriola, a young, intelligent Chicano whose journalism background gave him a realistic insight into politics, figured El Paso as fertile territory for the Muñiz campaign. Muñiz's own platform paralleled closely Sissy Farenthold's. Despite losing a runoff for the Democratic primary, Mrs. Farenthold had carried 60 percent of the vote in El Paso County, and her record made Arriola think that Muñiz could pick up a large percentage of the Chicano-liberal vote in El Paso, if only he could gain sufficient exposure and build an organization in the area. But El Paso was far removed from South Texas and the rest of the state, so as to make any personal campaigning in the area by Muñiz both inconvenient and costly. Arriola finally settled on launching a drive in El Paso by capitalizing on the convention for four days of heavy campaigning in the *barrio*, at UTEP, and among other Mexican-American groups such as the Farah strikers. But these plans, like Muñiz's request to appear before the convention, were nixed by party leaders who were involved in their own politics.

Despite a good deal of coverage by the local media, the convention failed to draw much attention for the Mexican-Americans in El Paso. Nor did La Raza Unida actively seek to involve the local Chicanos from *El Segundo barrio*—the party members went there only to attend the opening session, attended almost exclusively by delegates and out-of-town visitors. Two months later, when La Raza Unida's first major statewide campaign came to a close, Muñiz drew only 16 percent of the vote in El Paso, much of it attributed to a handful of campaign swings into the area he and Arriola made in the final two weeks. The vote in El Paso was a major disappointment, especially when Muñiz polled more votes in politically conservative Dallas, where Mexican-Americans make up only 10 percent of the population.

Gutiérrez later explained that Muñiz's low profile at the convention stemmed from the overriding need to establish a national party, though there soon arose doubts as to how well organized and how well united the party that formed in El Paso actually was. Gutiérrez's victory made him chairman of the *Congreso de Aztlan,* the equivalent of the national executive committees of the Democratic and Republican parties, composed of three members from each state with voting strength apportioned by the number of Mexican-Americans in each state. But the *congreso* did not meet until after the November general election, leaving the clear impression that La Raza Unida itself had doubts as to what role such an unwieldy confederation of state parties could play, other than simply refusing to endorse either presidential candidate, in the national general election.

It was not until Thanksgiving weekend, in the aftermath of the Nixon landslide and the party's failure to make any inroads except in Texas, that the *congreso* met in Albuquerque, where once again the Chicano nationalists were prepared to exert their power. Only a month earlier, La Raza Unida activists had embarrassed Tijerina at his own Congress on Land and Cultural Reform in Albuquerque, where they ran the land-grant movement leader out of the party. This was essentially the setting for the *congreso,* and Gutiérrez, sensing that the nationalists would outvote him and direct the party away from his program, chose simply to walk out of the meeting, after caustic verbal exchanges with Gonzales and his supporters.'

The future of the Raza Unida party was left at an impasse, with only one thing certain: the party as organized in El

Paso was no more unified behind any one leader nor any one course of direction than the movement it represented had been in the past.

Gutiérrez's and Muñiz's walkouts made party leaders see the deep divisions and factionalization within the movement. Muñiz in particular said that he would no longer pretend the differences did not exist. "Any movement, when it seeks to involve this many people representing different parts of the country, is going to have its conflicts," he said. "In that respect, we're no different from the struggling going on within the other political parties. It's no longer imperative on us to play consensus politics, though unity is certainly what we should strive for. The lesson that we learned at Albuquerque is that there's more involvement within the politics of the party, when there should be more involvement in the political system itself."

The Texas party leaders were content to withdraw from the whirlwind surrounding the national party and concentrate their efforts on building their party in the state. They saw themselves not so much parting from the rest of the party as having gone to the sidelines to wait while the Chicano nationalists burned out their zeal. Later, after defeat upon defeat, the others would finally acknowledge the leadership and political astuteness of the Texas party.

The rise of the nationalists within La Raza Unida was an example of revolution getting away from the revolutionaries — a swift, sudden swing of the political pendulum to the extreme left where there was more rhetoric than blood. The upheaval left Gutiérrez looking more the mild, studious intellectual he actually is. As revolutionary as his thinking may have been, it was Gutiérrez, the student of revolt, who, perhaps more than anyone else in the movement, realized that revolutionary strategies in twentieth-century urbanized America would bring change indeed, but at a slow, almost agonizing pace.

Buried in his master's thesis were words of patience for La Raza: "The young militants of today will not see the fruits of their efforts. Rather, it is the even younger Mexican-Americans, those in their early teens and pre-teen years, who will reap the benefits of the movement."

THE MELTING POT REDEFINED

11 THE EMERGENCE OF BROWN MIDDLE AMERICA

In early 1973, nine years after he joined the navy, Everett Alvarez, Jr., returned home to a world turned topsy-turvy. For eight years and five months Alvarez had lived suspended in the time capsule of a North Vietnam prison camp—longer than any other U.S. prisoner of war—through one of the most troubled periods in American history.

Alvarez was a twenty-six-year-old navy lieutenant (j.g.) when he left for Vietnam. When he returned, weakened and ill, he found that his wife, Tangee, had divorced him, remarried, and borne a child. His sister Delia, a shy young college girl when he went to war, had become a militant, vocal activist in the Chicano and antiwar movements and had picketed the 1972 Republican National Convention along with Jane Fonda. His mother, Soledad, whom he remembered as a conventional housewife in the Mexican tradition, had made public statements against the war, had studied the history of Southeast Asia, and had finally gone back to school to get a high school degree. His youngest sister, Madeleine, only twelve years old when Everett left, was engaged and married shortly after his return.

During the nine years of his absence, the other landmarks of Everett Alvarez's pre-Vietnam existence had become almost unrecognizable. His alma mater, the University of Santa Clara, a small, elitist, all-male Jesuit school when he had been there, had tripled in size, had gone co-ed—even in the dormitories—and had suffered its share of disruption, including a sitdown strike by Chicano students in the administration building. Even more dramatically, his hometown of Salinas, California, surrounded with the very same lettuce fields where he and his friends used to get smashed on beer, had become the battleground of an ethnic and social struggle whose dimensions he could not—and would not—have imagined when he was growing up.

As late as 1964, when Alvarez boarded the U.S.S. *Constellation* bound for Vietnam, there was no Chicano movement, no women's movement, no student rebellion. But in the mid-1970s, the Alvarezes suddenly found themselves caught up in the swirl of change. And, more significantly, Everett Alvarez, college-educated and with a bright future now that Vietnam was behind, found himself part of a new breed of Mexican-Americans who had placed the bad life—be it the *barrios* or a Vietnamese prison camp—behind them and were now "making it" in American society.

Call them Emerging Brown Middle America.

While Chávez was organizing the farm workers, and Tijerina and Corky Gonzales were fighting injustice in the law, and Gutiérrez was starting the Raza Unida party, a far more subtle Chicano movement was also under way in the country. Despite the drawbacks in their education, more Mexican-Americans than ever entered college in the 1960s, and they came out with degrees that set them apart from the Chicanos in the *barrios*. The college degrees opened doors rarely accessible in the past into the professional worlds of law, medicine, business, and education.

College meant better pay, a better life, and a more comfortable place in American society. Call it assimilation or whatever, the end result was the same: the economic advancements made by Mexican-Americans simply added to the numbers of Middle America. It's not surprising that the average Mexican-American professional has more in common with his Anglo counterpart than with his own people in the *barrio*. He may be a social schizophrenic straddling two cultures, but nevertheless the emerging middle-class Chicano is an individual who had accommodated himself to the dominant environment.

Everett Alvarez, the son of a plumber and metal worker, fits the mold perfectly. Unlike the other Mexican-American youngsters he grew up with, Alvarez was studious and athletic and ran with a circle of Anglo friends, which set him apart from the other Mexican-Americans. "Growing up was different for us," recalls Everett's older sister. "In those days, if you were a Mexican, you were a wetback. My brother and I, we had to 'white' in order to make it. It was like growing up between two cultures. We were afraid to get too brown."

What went on in that one decade that radically changed the Alvarezes' world? Much of the change came from the civil rights movement and the centuries-old dream of equality for black people in America that was rekindled in the 1950s and 1960s. In a single decade, an oppressive system of legal separation was struck down — a system that had stifled some of the most creative minds in the country, created a civil war, and tarnished the founding principles of the country. After decades of invisibility, blacks emerged into places of prominence and achievement in many areas of American life. Black income rose faster than white income while the number of blacks in college tripled. There was a dramatic expansion of the black middle class. All over America, public and private programs aimed at black advancement were launched.

The quest for equality was built largely around the ideal that tantalized a generation of lawyers and judges — the conviction that the courts of law could dismantle the grossest inequalities erected by politics and privilege. A long line of obscure citizens marched to that drum — Brown and Briggs, Gideon, Miranda, Baker, Shapiro, Serrano, others. Anonymous and powerless before they went to court, their pleadings changed the social fabric of America, from the practice of segregation to the protocol of police stations. Then, too, there was a heady spirit of upward and onward that dominated the federal domestic policy of the 1960s. It was a time when American democracy's traditional tenets of wisdom were under attack, when the prevailing assumptions toppled like trees in a storm and ambitious new ones sprouted in their place.

It is axiomatic that the profits and gains of one disadvantaged group will help other groups, and it was no surprise that Mexican-Americans were lifted up in the vacuum created by the black civil rights movement. The social programs created by equal rights legislation helped not only the Mexican-Americans in the *barrios* but also such Brown Middle American organizations as the American G.I. Forum, LULAC (League of United Latin American Citizens), and new groups.

Everett Alvarez returned home to find the world had passed him by, but Mexican-American servicemen of previous wars came home to find that things were unchanged—the doors that were closed when they went off to war remained closed when they returned. In 1948, the body of Felix Longoria, a Mexican-American serviceman killed in the battle for the Philippines, was returned to his hometown of Three Rivers, Texas, for burial. But a local mortuary refused to perform its services or to bury Longoria in the town cemetery. The incident quickly drew national attention. Finally, Lyndon B. Johnson, then the junior U.S. senator from Texas, intervened and secured permission to have Longoria buried in Arlington National Cemetery.

The Longoria-Three Rivers affair aroused the anger of Mexican-Americans in the state, and the next year a group met in Corpus Christi to bring together their protests of the Longoria incident and of other discriminatory treatment suffered by U.S. servicemen. Dr. Hector Garcia, a World War II combat surgeon who later served as an alternate delegate to the United Nations under President Johnson, organized the G.I. Forum, which eventually became the largest Mexican-American organization in the country.

Together with LULAC, organized in 1929 also in Corpus Christi, the G.I. Forum set up as goals the social, economic, and political rights of Mexican-Americans. In the wake of World War II, both organizations became active in seeking changes through the courts, and some of this litigation served as precedents in later school desegregation actions. Both organizations, though, drew membership from the middle and upper-middle class. Neither of them could claim to be the spokesman for the large majority of Mexican-Americans trapped in the *barrios;* and the advent of the civil rights and Chicano movements caught both LULAC and G.I. Forum on the defensive, rather than at the forefront of the cause. It is interesting that while both organizations maintained a commitment to upgrading the lives of Mexican-Americans, the local chapters tended to become social organizations, much like the country clubs that managed to exclude these same Mexican-Americans.

But in the 1970s Brown Middle America emerged, with greatly increased numbers of Mexican-Americans identifying themselves as middle class. Joined by hordes of college-educated professionals and businessmen, the older rank-and-file G.I. Forum and LULAC members revitalized their organizations to fit into the new situation. It was middle-class Mexican-Americans, after all, who held out the possibility of voting Republican and pressured the Nixon administration into naming a record number of Mexican-Americans to high government positions and into stepping up employment of Mexican-Americans at all levels of government.

Amazingly, the idea of a Brown Middle America suddenly became acceptable, even in the *barrios*, where in past years Mexican-Americans of middle-class status had been made to feel like outcasts with derogatory slurs such as *"Tío Taco"* or *"Tío Tomás."* Even the men in the *barrios* among Mexican-American activists realized that in the end, their activism and demands would result in a middle-class life.

An area that is trying to come to grips with social and economic development is East and Northeast Los Angeles, where scattered *barrios* house almost a half-million Mexican-Americans. Unincorporated East Los Angeles, for instance, is an old, physically deteriorating neighborhood with dense population, low incomes, high unemployment, and high drop-out rates in its schools. In 1968, fourteen labor unions established The East Los Angeles Community Union (TELACU), applying labor-organizing techniques to social, housing, business, and job development programs. Within five years, TELACU was a highly successful corporation backed not only by the usual "respectable" Mexican-Americans in the community but also by former street groups, whose purpose was altered when members gave up their street life to overcome social problems.

TELACU was active in various areas, but the greatest activity was in economic development, particularly housing and urban development. TELACU formed a general construction firm that built housing projects and assisted other Mexican-American contractors, mostly small subcontracting businessmen, in obtaining large building contracts that they could not bid for alone. TELACU hopes eventually to produce sufficient revenues from the construction firm and other ventures—including a mortgage bank, shopping center, and car dealership—to support social services in the *barrios*.

A major supporter of economic development in the *barrios* is the Southwest Council of La Raza, established by the Ford Foundation to act for the Spanish-speaking in much the same way as the NAACP has acted on behalf of blacks. Renamed the National Council of La Raza in late 1972, the council, working on the belief that "it is in the *barrios* that the Chicano cause will be won," organized a network of Mexican-American *barrio* groups to carry out the goals of community development. Among the council's most sweeping innovations was the creation of the nation's first Mexican-American-owned and operated minority enterprise small business investment corporation, named La Raza Investment Corporation, to provide loans and management assistance to *barrio* businessmen. In early 1972, Maclovio Barraza of Tucson, a four-term board chairman of the council, boasted that the council's economic-development efforts had "advanced the principle of self-determination from the stage of empty rhetoric to meaningful reality." Then, touching on the dream of a minority coalition, he urged the council to "respond to the times, even if it means building a new American pluralism involving *la raza* and our black brothers in manpower training—which will not only provide jobs, but show a troubled nation, struggling to live in harmony, how to build bridges of reconciliation."

Brown Middle America's very arrival on the scene has gone a long way toward destroying the old stereotype of the Mexican-American as a lazy, fat, mustachioed man with greasy hair under his hat and a pair of six-guns to help him steal. But there is also one Mexican-American group intended solely to end the stereotype and change the popular conception of the Mexican-American. Organized in 1967, the Involvement of Mexican-Americans in Gainful Endeavors (IMAGE) launched attacks on two popular television commercials—the Frito-Lay

Company with its patented "Frito Bandido" and the Bell Telephone Company and Bill Dana's portrayal of "José Jimenez." Although IMAGE met with limited success in immediately changing the advertising stereotypes, the significant point was that the new middle-class Mexican-Americans had awakened to the existence of an image and identity crisis.

Tony Calderon, the national executive director of IMAGE, himself suffered for years with an inferiority complex about being a Mexican-American. In the Army in 1953, Calderon turned down a chance for a commission because he couldn't picture himself as an officer. "Our contemporary image is usually projected as that of a social problem," Calderon said in one interview. "We have been stereotyped unjustly by the media as lazy, servantile 'flunkies' going around saying 'sí, señor,' or licking John Wayne's boots while he plays the big action hero. . . . Our brown skin does not permit us to identify with John Wayne or Doris Day."

In Hollywood, a Mexican-American group calling itself Justice for Chicanos in the Motion Picture and Television Industry took the film industry to task for a debasing image of Mexican-Americans and other Latins in motion pictures. In 1970, the group met with Charlton Heston, then president of the Screen Actors Guild, and received the guild's promise to review films and join Chicano picket lines if the films were found to be demeaning to Mexican-Americans. The Chicano group bitterly assailed the industry for producing such films as *One Hundred Rifles, Butch Cassidy and the Sundance Kid, The Wild Bunch,* and *El Condor,* claiming that these films showed Anglos who are vastly outnumbered gunning down whole armies of Mexicans and other Latin Americans. "Chicanos have for too long been portrayed as objects of filth, chicanery, and sexual perversion," the group charged. "We demand to know why the guild has sanctioned racist movies such as these for so long." Heston told a press conference: "We've got to go along with them. I don't see how we can challenge [the charges]. The Screen Actors Guild is now committed to unite the other creative guilds — the writers' and producers' and directors' — to find what steps can be taken to improve the image of *la raza.*"

In much the same way that Everett Alvarez found acceptance in the Anglo world in which he grew up, other Mexican-

Americans who have assimilated into Middle America have found themselves either precariously straddling two cultures and two languages or else suppressing their original language and culture. "Sometimes it's like living in a no-man's world," said the Reverend James Novarro of Houston, a Baptist minister who was co-leader of a South Texas farm workers' march in 1966. "Our cousins across the border stopped recognizing us long ago as one of them, and the Anglo environment has not yet fully accepted us."

Yet, if any characterization can be made of Brown Middle America today, it is that it seems to reflect many of the same traits as White Middle America—a moderate to conservative political stance; concern with uncontrolled inflation and spiraling costs; interest in their children's education and future; and uneasiness about drugs, crime, and the other urban ills.

As César Chávez's farm labor movement has shown, Brown Middle America depends strongly on the predominantly Anglo society. After all, it was only with help from organized labor, liberals, and the American consumer that Chávez was able to win the labor-organizing war with California's grape growers. And it was to those same Anglo friends that Chávez and the farm workers appealed for support in their later struggle with the growers and Teamsters, who threatened to put Chávez's United Farm Workers union out of business.

The rise of Chávez and his union was a classic example of lower-class Mexican-Americans trying to gain economic power—the first step toward achieving middle-class status. The example has been closely followed in El Paso, where organized labor successfully unionized the Farah Manufacturing Company. Farah, one of the nation's largest makers of men's pants and the biggest employer in El Paso, refused at first to recognize the union, which began its organizing drive in 1969.

In May 1972, about 2,000 Mexican-Americans—out of a total Farah work force of 9,000 in El Paso and four other cities—went on strike to protest unfair labor practices. At the heart of the struggle were issues of wages, benefits, and how employes were treated by management. The battle went into the courts; it influenced presidential politics, polarized the city, drew the Catholic Church into the fray, and stirred the sympathy and support of organized labor and liberals behind the strikers. In mid-1972, following the same course as in the farm labor situation, organized labor put its power behind the striking Farah workers when the AFL-CIO called for a nationwide consumer boycott of all Farah products. By mid-1973, the union and strikers were claiming to have crippled Farah. In 1971, Farah made a profit of $6 million on sales of $164 million. But the next year, the company lost $8 million and began showing a steady decrease in sales. By late 1973, in a generally declining market, Farah's stock on the New York Stock Exchange had dropped from a 1971 high of more than $49 a share to under $10 a share.

In the early 1970s, starting pay at the Farah plants was $1.70 an hour, 10 cents above the federal minimum wages; but workers complained they faced an uphill fight against unfairly high production quotas to earn a raise. The Most Reverend Sidney M. Metzger, the bishop of El Paso, quickly entered the struggle on behalf of the strikers and called on all U.S. Catholic bishops to support the boycott. According to Bishop Metzger's own study of the strikers' complaints, Farah employes in 1972 were taking home an average of $69 a week, while clothing workers at the unionized Levi-Strauss and Tex-Toggs plants in El Paso were netting $102 a week.

Farah strikers also drew support from the courts and the National Labor Relations Board. In the first year of the strike, the NLRB issued complaints charging Farah with unfair labor practices, including the surveillance and firing of union sympathizers; and it ordered the company to reinstate union supporters who had been dismissed and to stop interfering with lawful union-organizing activities. Three months after the strike began, U.S. Supreme Court Associate Justice Lewis Powell affirmed a lower federal court ruling declaring the Texas mass-picketing laws unconstitutional. He enjoined Farah and its agents and subordinates from interfering with the right of striking workers to "peacefully picket and protest against the defendant Farah."

While wages were among the issues in the strike, the conflict over money matters was overshadowed by complaints about company benefits and by what strikers described as "Dixie paternalism" on the part of Farah. The company operates buses to transport workers to its four plants in El Paso, and it offers hot lunches to employes who need them. Within the plants, the company provides medical, dental, and optical clinics and a pharmacy for employes' use. But Farah also had a personnel policy that allowed it to dismiss any worker judged to be an undesirable influence on other employes. An estimated 85 percent of the company work force is made up of women, and the strikers complained that the company offered no maternity insurance. The company's hospitalization policy, available to employes who have been with Farah five years, paid only $14 a day for hospital costs and imposed a $300 maximum on surgery expenses, and the union contended both aspects of the policy were inadequate in light of today's high medical costs.

Farah officials quickly became very sensitive about the strike and boycott. Supported by the El Paso business community, the chief executive William F. Farah called the boycott "un-American." Farah was quoted as describing Bishop Metzger as a member of the "rotten old bourgeoisie" and a man "lolling in wealth," and he made the strike out as a battle between his employes and those who had walked out. Indeed, the strikers were a minority of the work force, and it was understandably difficult to find workers within the plant who openly expressed differences with the company or supported the union. Farah's undaunted public position was that he owed his responsibility and allegiance to the wishes of the 7,000 or so employes who had not joined the strike and had remained loyal to him.

"It does smack a bit of the Old South paternalism," said State Senator H. Tati Santiesteban of El Paso, a longtime friend of some Farah officials who was a close observer of the union-organizing battle. "But I don't think Willie Farah is consciously trying to be some kind of Old Dixie paternalist. Economically speaking, Willie Farah would be better off if he'd rid himself of the pharmacy, the clinics, and the buses and let the union and the workers fend for themselves. But he's that much opposed to a union in his plant."

Antonio Sanchez, the El Paso Joint Board manager of the Amalgamated Clothing Workers of America, refused to describe the strike as a racial struggle, but he said the dispute with Farah went "to the very heart of what has been keeping the Mexican-American down" in the Southwest. "The workers have been deprived socially and educationally as well as economically," he said in an interview. "They're saying, 'Give us the extra money, and we'll find our own doctors and dentists, and we'll pay them out of our own pockets.' So long as you keep workers dependent on any company for their basic needs, you're going to keep them pent up politically and socially. You'll keep them in line, causing no trouble or what they would construe as trouble, in the community. And you'll keep them in place."

Finally, in early 1974, when his company was hurting financially and with no immediate end to the strike and economic boycott in sight, Farah capitulated and recognized the union as the bargaining agent of his employes.

Perhaps the most poignant aspect of the Farah strike is that it represented the decades-old struggle of Mexican-Americans in the Southwest to mix into the American melting pot, although today this traditional concept of assimilation has shown the need of a redefinition. Even for the European immigrants of yesterday, assimilation into American life was successful only to the extent that they could fill the gaps in the vast number of opportunities available. Not all the Irish became Kennedys, or, for that matter, middle-class Americans. Traditionally, the only opportunities available to immigrants into the Southwest have been low-paying, unskilled jobs, such as domestic work and farm labor, that locked these new Americans into a low-income class.

What finally did open the way for the emergence of Brown Middle America was a combination of factors — education, urbanization, the arrival of civil rights activism, and the quest by interested individuals for equality. And, of course, politics.

For years, Mexican-Americans, like blacks, voted Democratic in such disproportionate numbers as to allow political observers to generalize that the Mexican-American vote was locked up by the Democrats. Mexican-American politicos wore their Democratic party tags on their sleeves, and in Texas they proudly boasted about having carried the state's big electoral vote for John F. Kennedy in 1960. In short, it was safe for Democrats to assume that they could take the Mexican-American vote for granted; and, in fact, all too often, they did.

The new middle-class Mexican-Americans, however, threatened to loosen the Democrats' control of a brown bloc vote. It was characteristic of Brown Middle Americans, particularly those who had gone beyond middle-class status and attained some wealth, to be more conservative politically than Mexican-Americans of past years. In fact, it was from the heart of Brown Middle America that a new wave of Republicanism arose in the 1960s. This phenomenon undoubtedly aroused mixed emotions in such GOP strategists as Kevin Phillips, the controversial political analyst of the right, who wrote *The Emerging Republican Majority.* Phillips told skeptical hearers that just around the corner was an inevitable cycle of Republican dominance that would begin in the late 1960s and prosper until the turn of the twenty-first century. Phillips' theory was based on emotional or "gut" issues, mainly race and ethnicity. For instance, he saw a possible coalition built around the alleged hostility of Irishmen, Italians, and Poles, whose ethnic traits are conservative, toward Jews, blacks, and white liberals. On the basis of past political performance, Phillips wrote off the Mexican-American or Latin vote along with the blacks, figuring that a coalition in the South and Southwest of minorities and white radicals would drive the majority constituency of traditional white Democrats into the GOP. Phillips, however, was only partly right, because in 1972 a large number of Mexican-Americans joined traditional white Democrats in their flight away from the McGovern-Shriver ticket.

Indeed, in the fall of 1972, when the *Washington Post* took a look at the country's electorate, it singled out two Mexican-Americans as typifying the mood of the country. The lead of *Post* reporter Haynes Johnson's story follows: "Joe Medeiros and Santos Hernandez have more in common than their religion, Mexican-American ancestry and California residency. They are staunch Democrats who have worked hard all their lives. Now they are next-door neighbors on a pleasant street in a modest section of San Jose.

" 'To tell you the truth, this is the first election I don't care one way or another,' Joe was saying while standing on his front porch.

"A few minutes later, it was Santos Hernandez speaking. 'I was born in 1900, and I've voted Democrat in every election. I voted for Al Smith—remember Al Smith?—Roosevelt, Truman, Stevenson, Kennedy, God bless him, LBJ and old Hubert. But there is no more Democratic party any more. It's just fallen apart.'

"Just five weeks from now Santos Hernandez will vote Republican for the first time. He's voting for Richard Nixon because as he put it, 'I can't vote for that son of a bitch McGovern.' His friend Joe Medeiros is reacting equally negatively to his first presidential election of the 1970s. He doesn't like McGovern either— 'To me, he's almost a stranger' —but will vote for him."

Such a departure from past tradition rivals the phenomenon of Brown Middle America's emergence. Clearly, the latter was at least partly responsible for the swing of traditionally Democratic Mexican-American voters into the Republican ranks. But in the 1972 election, there was another, even more important, factor at work.

In much the same way that the American political system and the American electorate were corrupted and victimized in 1972, the Mexican-American electorate—and particularly the potential GOP voter amidst the new Brown Middle America—became the target of a secret, well thought-out political plan not unlike other plots that were unfolding elsewhere in the country.

Even in that sense, Brown Middle America had arrived home.

12 THE CHICANO STRATEGY

In historic San Antonio, the cradle of animosity between Mexican-Americans and Anglos, they joke that the Mexican-Americans in 1968 dealt Richard Nixon the worst defeat of a gringo since the Battle of the Alamo. That year, the San Antonio Mexican-Americans gave the Republicans 6 percent of their votes. This was just one percent more than the Mexican-American vote Barry Goldwater received in 1964, and it was 11 percent less than Nixon won against John F. Kennedy in 1960.

It's clear that the Mexican-American vote cost Nixon the twenty-five Texas electoral votes in 1968. Even GOP strategists conceded later that they were wrong to write off the Mexican-American vote, and their own figures showed that Nixon could have taken the state away from Hubert Humphrey if he had won only another 5 percent of the Chicano vote.

When the 1972 elections rolled around, President Nixon and the Republicans were determined not to make the same mistake in Texas and four other Southwestern states. Their plan was simple: to woo Brown Middle America by providing high administration positions and more government jobs to Mexican-Americans and by doling out a bigger share of federal dollars to programs aimed at Mexican-Americans. Observant GOP officials saw the potential bloc of voters, and the Mexican-Americans, encouraged by the presence of some brown faces in the Nixon administration, had become disgruntled with the Democratic party.

Call it the Chicano Strategy, or better, in the peculiar jargon of the Nixonites, the Republicanization of the Mexican-American. It was a political move that aroused mixed feelings. On the one hand, Mexican-Americans were making unprecedented gains in the Nixon administration. Without a doubt, the GOP showed up the Democrats in getting things done for *la raza*. But on the other hand, there were strong, nagging doubts as to how long the trend would last. Indeed, the strategy came from the master of politicians, and one couldn't help but wonder whether the appointments, the jobs, and the federal money wouldn't suddenly develop a problem like the proverbial used car that you wouldn't dare buy from the man.

Clearly, even the administration's record of dealing with Mexican-Americans left room for suspicion.

When President Nixon came to office in 1969, with a minimum of support from the Mexican-American electorate, his administration inherited something called the Inter-Agency Committee on Mexican-American affairs, created during the Johnson days to deal with complaints from Mexican-Americans in the Southwest. During Mr. Nixon's first year in office, Congress passed legislation changing the agency into the Cabinet Committee on Opportunities for Spanish-Speaking People — this was supposed to strengthen and broaden the scope of the agency to include Puerto Ricans and Cubans. Instead, the newly formed Cabinet Committee took a siesta that lasted for a year and a half. The committee chairman had intended to meet with members of the President's cabinet to discuss problems, and an advisory council was supposed to be established. During the siesta, those parts of the law were not carried out.

It was also during the Cabinet Committee's siesta that one of President Nixon's first high-ranking Mexican-American appointees, Martin Castillo, resigned as chairman of the committee along with committee executive director Henry Quevedo. Both resignations reportedly came under pressure from the White House, as a result of the Mexican-Americans' heavy Democratic vote in the California and Texas senatorial elections in 1970 in which the President and the Republican candidates were rebuffed. In 1970, both President Nixon and Vice-President Agnew campaigned for George Bush, a former congressman and a promising face within the GOP, who made an all-out effort to become Texas' second Republican senator. In California, the President lent his weight to the incumbent, former actor George Murphy, who was challenged by John V. Tunney, a young liberal Democratic member of the House and a close friend of Senator Edward Kennedy. In 1968, Mr. Nixon had carried his home state of California and had come close to winning Texas; but despite the President's active support two years later, both Murphy and Bush were beaten. Those elections were tests for the GOP's Chicanos, and the White House quickly made known its displeasure with their performance.

The California and Texas senatorial elections, however, were but a sampling of the problems facing the Republicans and President Nixon as he moved into the second half of his first term. In mid-1971, while everyone still looked to Senator Edmund Muskie as the likely Democratic challenger the following year, Mr. Nixon hardly gave the appearance of becoming a landslide winner. He was surrounded by the same problems that had engulfed President Johnson.

At this point, while the Gallup and Harris polls weren't providing pleasant reading, the President suddenly decided to awaken the Cabinet Committee from its sleep. On August 5, 1971, President Nixon announced the appointment of Henry M. Ramirez, an educator from Mr. Nixon's hometown of Whittier, California, as the committee's new chairman. At the same time the President directed administration officials to step up the hiring of Spanish-speaking persons and to fund government programs for the country's Spanish-speaking population.

In the months that followed, Ramirez was joined by a flood of other Mexican-American appointees. Phillip V. Sanchez, an unsuccessful GOP candidate for congress in California, was named national director of the Office of Economic Opportunity, thus becoming the highest ranking Mexican-American official in the administration. Mrs. Romana A.

Banuelos, a Los Angeles businesswoman, was appointed treasurer of the United States, the first Mexican-American woman ever named to such a high post. White House Counselor Robert H. Finch, Mr. Nixon's longtime political ally, was assigned to be the President's own liaison with the Cabinet Committee, and he was given responsibility for handling Mexican-American relations. The White House even directed a Spanish-speaking Japanese, staff assistant William H. Marumoto, to develop a government recruitment system for Spanish-speaking Americans. By election time in 1972, there were at least fifty high-ranking Mexican-American officials who owed their jobs to the administration's Chicano Strategy.

Why did the Mexican-American vote require a strategy all its own? Obviously, in his lopsided *mano-a-mano* with McGovern, Nixon could have spotted the Democratic candidate all the Chicanos in the country and it wouldn't have made a difference in the results. In mid-1971, though, it appeared that the President was going to need every vote he could get, and in several of the key states, it was the Mexican-Americans who made up the balance of power.

Texas and the 1968 election were one example of how the Chicano vote could mean the difference; if the Republicans made little effort to go after the Mexican-American vote, they were likely to receive only a small percentage of it. California was another state where the Chicano vote could mean the difference. Mr. Nixon carried the state easily in 1968, but he remembered a close call in 1960, when he won by only 35,000 votes. Adding to the Republicans' doubts were Mr. Nixon's disastrous loss in the 1962 California gubernatorial election and Senator Murphy's loss in 1970. Indeed, the stakes were big. One study showed that a switch of only 6 percent of the Mexican-American vote could affect the elections not only in Texas and California but also in New Mexico and Illinois, four states with 101 electoral votes out of the 270 needed to elect a president.

By early 1972, the number of Mexican-Americans in the upper echelons of the administration left little doubt about the White House's intention of going after the Mexican-American vote. On the surface, the strategy appeared positive and well-meaning: first, there were the appointments, the jobs, and the money that would be going to Mexican-Americans and their programs. Second, and more important, there was the exposure of the administration's good deeds, to be accomplished by appointees acting as the President's Spanish-speaking surrogates.

But this was only a part of the story. Just as the Watergate scandal revealed the espionage, subversion, and other "dirty tricks" used in the covert political strategy to reelect the President, there were hints of questionable tactics woven into the Chicano Strategy.

The Committee to Re-Elect the President, with all its complexities and political labyrinths, included a division assigned to woo the Spanish-speaking voter. In charge of it was Alex Armendariz, head of a campaign-management firm in South Bend, Indiana, who prepared a memo recommending strategy for the Chicano as well as the Puerto Rican vote. The memo, dated June 16, 1972, went to Frederick Malek, deputy director of the committee. In it Armendariz mapped out a strategy that the Democrats later attacked as a "model of bigotry" against Spanish-speaking voters and as a "plot to sabotage the Spanish-speaking vote." GOP campaign leaders declined to confirm or deny that Armendariz's proposed strategy had been adopted, but the memo contained suggestions and recommendations that certainly were employed, then or later, to woo *la raza*.

The memo shows that Armendariz planned to use negative tactics in either attracting or neutralizing the Mexican-American vote. For example, he suggested that the GOP provide secret assistance to the fledgling La Raza Unida party in Texas as an effort to pull votes from the Democrats. Also, he recommended capitalizing on the criticism by Chicanos of the President's appointees, particularly Mrs. Banuelos. This is how Armendariz outlined the strategy:

Any analysis of this area [Texas] would be incomplete without special mention of La Raza Unida. It is unique in that it is not just a supportive organization, but desires to be an effective political party. The party is working on its own political organization, caucuses, slates, and the signatures necessary to present its own ballot. The rationale it presents is that if enough votes are siphoned away from the Democrats, there will be more of a power balance and La Raza could cast conclusive votes, or at least achieve bargaining power. *Republicans are in a good position to help to attract to La Raza as voters the 62.3 percent who already approve of that party.* La Raza's strategy usually is denouncement of old party politics. *Any help given them would not be identifiable as Republican.* McGovern could be exposed as an old-style party politician especially since his recent visit to [Alabama Governor George] Wallace, who is vastly unpopular among Mexican-Americans. Humphrey is easily attacked in this manner. Kennedy would present an enormous problem as his whole family is loved by Mexican-Americans. *Republicans would have to lay off him entirely and expend all negative efforts in the Spanish-speaking community helping La Raza.*

On the other hand, the 19.4 percent who disapprove of La Raza may be the most conservative of the group, making them a natural Republican target. It would be well to try to get a beat on the Mexican-American group opinion of Governor Connally to determine whether he can make a pitch for us. After all, he was shot too in Dallas. Furthermore, *it will be our job to try to crystallize the remaining 33 percent of the Spanish-speaking who have never heard of La Raza, or who have no opinion of it, toward La Raza, the Republican party, or staying at home.*

There is a real chance here to influence some middle-class people by careful use of presidential surrogates. This program so far has not been completely successful. Indications are that they are speaking to the wrong audiences and press coverage is sparse. Henry Ramirez, who has over-all done the best job of presenting the President, has been spread too thinly over the country. These people are not reading the *New York Times* or Florida papers! Given indices so far presented, *Mrs. Banuelos, who is most easily identified by the Spanish-speaking group in general, is probably in this position due to attacks made on her, and the coverage thereby generated by the liberal press. This is not entirely bad.*

They spelled her name right and Mexican-American men are probably not too pleased by attacks on a woman of their own background.

Someone must come up with a slick advertising package showing the President doing, or having done, something about jobs and housing. Anything prepared for the country in general would do here. If he could be directly and personally identified with a push for bilingual education, we would have a strong positive issue. [Italics mine]

It is not particularly surprising, then, that George McGovern, during the last month of the campaign, accused the Republican party of bribing activist minority leadership, namely La Raza Unida in Texas, to hold down the vote among Mexican-Americans. Through his Illinois coordinator, Gene Pokorny, Senator McGovern accused José Angel Gutiérrez of espousing neutrality in the presidential election in exchange for a $1 million health clinic for his hometown of Crystal City, Texas. Pokorny got his information from Dr. Jorge Prieto, a Chicano doctor who said he was offered a job at the new health clinic by Gutiérrez's wife. "She indicated that such funding had been made available because of an arrangement between La Raza Unida and Republican party officials," Pokorny said.

At its national convention in El Paso, La Raza Unida refused to endorse either Senator McGovern or President Nixon, and party leaders instead urged their followers to forego national politics and concentrate on races involving La Raza Unida candidates, such as Ramsey Muñiz, the party's gubernatorial nominee in Texas. This move came as a surprise and a disappointment to McGovern backers and other liberals, who counted on the support of Chicano activists. At the convention, Muñiz declared that the only way he would favor endorsing McGovern would be by securing a return endorsement of his own candidacy from the Democratic nominee.

McGovern's accusation against La Raza Unida evoked a rash of angry denials and denunciations. Muñiz charged that McGovern was "playing politics with the health needs of Chicanos." And Mario Compean, La Raza Unida's state chairman in Texas, replied: "We still maintain our position that there is no difference between George McGovern and Richard Nixon. It really doesn't make any difference to us who gets elected."

Meanwhile, the federal health grant to Crystal City ran into some red tape, and a group of Crystal City citizens wound up lobbying for the grant in Washington. At a press conference, Crystal City Mayor Francisco Benavides called Mc-Govern a liar for alleging that "this grant was only a political arrangement between our city and the Republicans in return for the Chicano vote." And in a letter to Dr. Prieto, Gutiérrez's wife, Luz, wrote: " . . . since 1970, this community has been and continues to be demanding, threatening, and fighting to get not one million dollars for one clinic in Crystal, but $25 billion for clinics in Chicano communities throughout the Southwest. . . . Nothing is going to deter us from continuing our struggle for health care. Gringo bullets and ballots haven't stopped us yet, so little political schemes designed to promote the presidential aspiration of a gringo will certainly not get in our way."

In the home stretch of the Texas gubernatorial campaign, there occurred a second major incident that looked like another GOP-La Raza Unida "arrangement." Four days before the election, Muñiz charged that the Democratic nominee Dolph Briscoe had undergone electric shock therapy for "severe depression" twice during the past eighteen months. Muñiz acknowledged that he had no documentation for his charge, but the allegation still made the front pages of several newspapers. Much earlier in the year, another rumor about Briscoe's mental health had made its rounds in political circles, but a careful check by several newspapermen failed to confirm that story. Briscoe denied Muñiz's charge, but he could not be sure what impact it would have. One effect came clear on election night, when Senator Henry C. Grover, the GOP candidate, ran a surprisingly strong race in the closest gubernatorial election in the state's history.

Grover's strong showing led Democrats to speculate that Muñiz's shock therapy charge, which might account for the drop in Briscoe's expected total, might have been planted to help the Republican candidate. Briscoe certainly did not stand to gain from it, and Muñiz, as it turned out, wound up actually getting hurt because the charge disappointed some followers of his quixotic campaign. Grover condemned Muñiz's charge, making himself appear to be above such tactics, and his own personal integrity suggested that he would not have taken part in a deal with La Raza Unida. But some Grover backers and Raza Unida activists admitted that at least one meeting took place between them, although they refused to say what they had discussed.

But a Republican-Raza Unida "arrangement" was only one of the charges Democrats made against the GOP's Mexican-American ranks after the election. In the year leading up to the election, the Cabinet Committee and its chairman Henry Ramirez were extremely active in playing up the administration's pro-Spanish-speaking posture, and Democrats were quick to charge that both the Cabinet Committee and Ramirez had overstepped their boundaries by getting involved in the campaign. The Democrats also charged that the White House used some of the Mexican-American appointees, whom the Hatch Act prohibited from becoming active in politics, as spokesmen for the President's campaign.

In 1973, while Watergate and Senator Sam Ervin's investigating committee captured the national spotlight, Representatives Henry B. Gonzalez and Eligio (Kika) de la Garza, both from Texas, worked quietly to force changes in the Cabinet Committee or else curtail its funding by Congress. At the same time, the Cabinet Committee came under additional pressures at hearings conducted by the Government Operations and the Judiciary Committees of the House of Representatives. Representatives Gonzalez and de la Garza were a strong threat, but the man the people at the Cabinet Committee feared most was Representative Chet Holifield, a Democrat and dean of the California delegation. Holifield left little doubt that he wanted to shelve the Cabinet Committee; all he was looking for was ammunition.

Ultimately, the House Judiciary Committee got the necessary weapons to use against Ramirez and the Cabinet Committee. For example, the Judiciary Committee learned that Ramirez had attended the GOP National Convention in Miami Beach on Cabinet Committee funds, and it was not until a few days before their hearings that Ramirez finally corrected his error. Using records belonging to the Cabinet Committee and to the Spanish-speaking division within the Committee to

Re-elect the President, the Judiciary Committee staff un-covered more than 500 pages of memorandum, which told a good deal about the roles of Nixon's Mexican-Americans in the campaign.

Among the documents in question—which later fell into the hands of Senator Ervin's Watergate committee—was an intriguing hand-written letter from New Mexico's Tijerina to Ramirez: Tijerina was acknowledging he'd been offered an executive pardon for a federal felony conviction in return for his support of President Nixon. Certainly, Tijerina had dras-tically toned down his rhetoric since being released on parole from a federal penitentiary. And the activists no longer looked up to him as a top movement leader, although Tijerina re-mained influential in New Mexico among the Indo-Hispanos, as he called them, whose hopes he had once lifted with the possibility of some day regaining the ancestral Spanish land grants.

In his letter to Ramirez, dated August 14, 1972, Tijerina wrote: "I'm very glad that I got to know you. I also want to make it very clear that I am very thankful of what you men-tioned to me in your office concerning my probation, parole, and the possibility of a full executive pardon. As I said before while I was in your office, I want to repeat it in writing, most of the Spanish-speaking people in the United States would feel grateful if an executive pardon would be granted."

Ramirez forwarded Tijerina's letter to Armendariz along with a memorandum: "Please see attached letter with specific reference to the third paragraph (concerning executive par-don). Mr. Tijerina indicated that he would work for us in return for due consideration."

All through this controversy there were references to Henry Ramirez, Brown Middle America's answer to the likes of Tijerina, José Angel Gutiérrez, and Corky Gonzales. In 1972, Ramirez, a distinguished, balding man in his forties who gives the appearance of a Spanish señor, established himself as the Nixon administration's leading Mexican-American spokesman. Ramirez claimed the administration moved him up to the Cabinet Committee chairmanship because he had credibility in the Mexican-American community and was from the *barrio* himself. The son of Mexican immigrants who began as migrant workers in California, Ramirez studied for the priesthood but instead wound up a language teacher in a high school in Whittier, the President's hometown. Later he worked for the Republican party on the precinct level in California, closely allied with Robert Finch, then a rising star in California GOP circles. Despite his political activities, Ramirez considered himself an educator, and he became director of the U.S. Civil Rights Commission's Mexican-American Studies Division where he headed up the commission's exhaustive study of Mexican-American education in the Southwest.

Then in August of 1971, the President elevated Ramirez to the chairmanship of the Cabinet Committee. By the end of the 1972 election campaign, the Cabinet Committee boasted that Ramirez had traveled more than 135,000 air miles in telling the story of the administration's good works. One of Ramirez's first trips was a two-day swing into Texas and the Lower Rio Grande Valley along with a host of other Mexican-American appointees, including OEO Director Phillip Sanchez and Treasurer Mrs. Romana Banuelos. Ramirez's rhetoric on that trip set the pace for the spiels by the administration's Spanish surrogates during the next few months. "No other administration has placed such a heavy emphasis on solutions to the problems of the Spanish-speaking," Ramirez told a press conference in Houston. "Next to the American Indian, Spanish-speaking rank lower than any other single group in such areas as educational attainment, housing conditions, employment, etc. Under the present administration, we have witnessed a new awareness of the problem and a willingness to take steps to alleviate these conditions within the Spanish-speaking community."

But by far the most revealing thing Ramirez said came at a press conference in Dallas during the last days of the campaign. Pressed by a reporter, Ramirez lashed back with a thinly veiled threat: If the GOP's presidential ticket failed to win at least 20 percent of the Chicano vote, President Nixon would cut off all "concessions" to the Spanish-speaking, meaning the end of federal appointments and the flow of federal funds into Mexican-American projects. But if the Chicanos did produce the required vote quota, "it will place us in a good negotiating position for further appointments and funds from the administration."

Ramirez's warning looked like the blackmailing of a

Democratic ethnic group. Surely there was a cruel irony in the President's rejection of hiring quotas while on the other hand demanding a specific vote quota from Mexican-Americans. Possibly the incident reflected some late doubts about the Chicano Strategy including the buttons and bumper stickers reading *Presidente Nixon: Ahora mas que nunca!* (President Nixon: Now more than ever!), and also the impact of the administration's Chicanos. Incidentally, the Republicans, including some of the Mexican-American appointees themselves, preferred calling Ramirez and the other Spanish-speaking appointees "Nixon's Hispanos," believing that such a term was less grating than "Chicanos" for Anglo voters.

Besides Ramirez, Sanchez and Mrs. Banuelos were the other two Hispanos most visible in the campaign. Mrs. Banuelos, no doubt, strengthened the administration's support among Mexican-Americans who were offended by the Chicano activists' demonstrations against her. In San Antonio, for instance, Chicano activists and supporters of the farm labor movement, including Bishop Patricio Flores, picketed an appearance by Mrs. Banuelos. The next day, the *San Antonio Express News* carried the story and a front-page picture of Mrs. Banuelos, a bouquet of roses in her arms, confronted by a young demonstrator pushing at her with a sign saying, "Go Back to Nixon." In some quarters, however, Mrs. Banuelos became a liability when immigration authorities discovered a number of illegal aliens working for low pay at her Mexican food business in Los Angeles.

Meanwhile, Sanchez, as national director of OEO, represented the pinnacle of Mexican-American success within the executive branch. OEO, Lyndon Johnson's brainchild for administering the War on Poverty, is ranked just under cabinet level, and in 1972 Sanchez was the highest-ranking Mexican-American presidential appointee in the nation's history. Although overshadowed by Ramirez, Sanchez played the administration's ball game well. But within three months of the election, Sanchez's lofty world came tumbling down.

In early 1973, the Nixon White House, which was never fully sympathetic with the Johnson dream of a war on poverty, announced its intention to dismantle OEO. The move, which caught Sanchez by surprise, no doubt cast a dark shadow over how he saw his role and influence within the administration in the previous year. But an even more crushing blow was the way he was relieved of his duties. To dismantle OEO, the White House selected a young conservative firebrand named Howard J. Phillips, who described himself as "this country's Cato" after the Roman senator who demanded the destruction of Carthage in the Third Punic War (149–146 B.C.). According to other OEO officials, on the day Phillips was appointed acting director of the program, he walked in and told Sanchez to move out at the close of the day—and not to go home in the chauffeured car assigned to the director because he would be using it instead.

Sanchez, Banuelos, Ramirez, and the other high-ranking Hispano appointees represented only a fraction of the Mexican-Americans who became government employes under the Nixon administration. In November of 1970, the White House announced what came to be known as the "Sixteen-Point Program" for assisting Spanish-speaking Americans in getting more lower- and middle-level federal jobs. But the president failed to set out any specific goals or timetables in the program, thereby creating a point of conflict between the administration and Mexican-American groups seeking a massive job-assistance effort.

In mid-1972, a year and a half after the President had launched the Sixteen-Point Program, five major Mexican-American organizations still saw it necessary to call for an "affirmative moral commitment" from the White House to step up federal employment of the Spanish-speaking, accusing Mr. Nixon of trying to woo the Chicano vote "with flowers but not with tortillas." The organizations, including LULAC, the G.I. Forum, and the Mexican-American Political Association, asked the Equal Employment Opportunity Commission to set specific goals and timetables for employing the Spanish-speaking. The leaders of the organizations said that for almost two years they had sought unsuccessfully on ten separate occasions to meet with the President to discuss such goals and timetables. They claimed that Mr. Nixon's failure to ensure population parity in government employment to Spanish-speaking Americans cost Mexican-Americans 101 federal jobs and $950 million in 1971. According to statistics compiled by the organizations and their representative, the Mexican-American Legal Defense and Education Fund, Spanish-speaking Americans represented 7 percent of the nation's population but only 2.9 percent of the federal government's civilian full-time employees.

While the administration undoubtedly increased the number of Mexican-Americans within the lower- and middle-level ranks, there was no significant increase in the percentage of Spanish-speaking persons among federal employes. Then, shortly after their appeal to the EEOC, the Mexican-American organizations heard that President Nixon was repudiating quotas in government hiring and employment.

One aspect of the Nixon Chicano Strategy that did stand out, though, was the amount of money the administration poured into Spanish-speaking projects. In the year preceding the election, an estimated $47 million was channeled into programs for the Spanish-speaking, many of them funded on a one-year-only basis. Administration officials admitted that at least $11.4 million was used to fund projects that ordinarily would not qualify for funding because the programs or the proposals were deficient—and they stood little chance of being re-funded the following year. An additional $24 million to $26 million was set aside through the Department of Housing and Urban Development for low-cost housing for Spanish-speaking groups.

The total amount spent in the Spanish-speaking communities was a figure the Nixon Hispanos hesitated to discuss. But there were indications that the $47 million figure was actually far below the total expenditure for the Chicano vote. Documents in the Cabinet Committee showed that at least $20 million was invested in Spanish-speaking projects in the Texas region and another $17 million in the California region, and these funds were in addition to what Mexican-Americans received through regular federal programs.

By the end of the campaign, the GOP's Chicano Strategy, despite its shortcomings, had the Democrats on the run. From the beginning, Democrats had taken the administration's wooing of the Chicanos lightly, and they appeared to disregard the discontent among Mexican-Americans even within their own ranks. Meanwhile, the Republican effort went beyond rhetoric, and it was hard for Democrats to argue with the Hispano appointments, the Spanish-speaking employment program, and the federal dollars flooding Mexican-American projects. In the wooing, the President even used his daughter Tricia, who attended the national convention of LULAC on behalf of her father and told the 1,000 convention delegates: "With the government today, *no es solamente que viva la raza, pero que cuente la raza.*" (It is not only that *la raza* live, but that *la raza* count.)

By all indications, the strategy worked. Although the Republican ticket wound up winning with plenty of room to breathe, the President's Chicano Strategy succeeded in winning so many Mexican-American votes as to raise the question whether the Chicano vote would ever return to the Democratic fold in the one-sided proportions of past years. In Texas, where President Nixon had received only 10 percent of the vote in 1968, the Nixon-Agnew ticket made sweeping gains among Mexican-American voters, with predominantly Mexican-American counties in South Texas and the Lower Rio Grande Valley giving the President as much as 65 percent of the vote. According to a CBS analysis, President Nixon carried 49 percent of the Spanish-speaking vote in Texas and Florida and 11 percent of the Spanish-speaking vote in California. Demographic studies are an uncertain science, and the CBS analysis — which on the basis of methodology appeared to be the best — also showed that the President received 31 percent of the Spanish-speaking vote nationally, which, in addition to the Chicano vote, took into account the Puerto Rican vote in New York and the Cuban vote in Florida.

The Committee to Re-Elect the President made its own check of Mexican-American voting trends, and in San Antonio it took a sampling of three predominantly Mexican-American precincts, which showed the relationship between income and voting tendencies. President Nixon received 20 percent of the vote in a low-income precinct, 49 percent in a middle-income precinct, and 68 percent in a high-income precinct. Similar precinct samplings in Los Angeles showed that the GOP ticket ran well, beating the Democrats in some places, and suggested a much stronger Nixon vote among Mexican-Americans in the state than was indicated in the CBS analysis.

On election night, Nixon's Hispanos celebrated along with everyone at Four More Years, Inc., but the landslide victory and the success of the Chicano Strategy were both in for an abruptly short honeymoon. Just weeks after the inaugu-

ration, President Nixon and his administration found themselves entangled in the Watergate matter. And it was at
about this same time that the Nixon Hispanos and others who
had been wooed to the Nixon camp awakened to political
reality.

The White House decision to dismantle OEO and the
subsequent humiliation of Phillip Sanchez were representative of what some Mexican-American leaders felt was their be-
trayal by the administration. After the election, the number of
high-ranking Spanish-speaking officials leveled off and
actually dwindled a bit. Talk ended about stepped-up government hiring of the Spanish-speaking, and the President instead announced budget cutbacks in housing, manpower
training, and health and education. Sanchez was shipped out
as ambassador to Honduras, and the White House itself was
soon cleaned of token Hispanos when two Mexican-American
staffers were sent back to the minor leagues.

The only rising brown star still in the administration in
1973 was Alex Armendariz, who was named director of the
Office of Minority Business Enterprise within the Commerce
Department. Suddenly there was a change in the rhetoric
coming out of the mouths of the Nixon Hispanos. "This
country is based upon the principle of private enterprise—
competition in business—and we will not be in the mainstream of American life until we, the Spanish-speaking, get
into business on the same footing as everyone else," Ramirez,
still chairman of the Cabinet Committee, told the National
Spanish-Speaking Business Development Conference in
Chicago. "I believe we should be in everything, but I do want
to stress that we have more to gain in furthering the cause of
the Spanish-speaking by increasing our opportunities in economic development than through any other single route."

But the rhetoric overlooked the major problem—the extremely high failure rate of small businesses. And, as much as
the campaign strategy, the message was aimed at Brown
Middle America rather than the masses in the *barrios* who
were in much greater need of federal assistance. "Spanish-
speaking voters gave the President a vote of confidence,"
observed Tony Gallegos, national chairman of the G.I. Forum,
"and we've been left out in the cold."

The Mexican-Americans showed their participation in

the mainstream of American life by joining other groups in expressing their discontent. In the year following his great victory, President Nixon, it would seem, stood in an enviable position. He had a chance politically both to build on his massive electoral majority and create a dominant Republican coalition, and also to lead America toward a new era of peace abroad and reconciliation at home. Yet those were not reassuring times for the President. He was in trouble with the American public, and it began to look as though Richard Nixon was in danger of being consumed by domestic problems just as Lyndon Johnson had been by foreign ones after a similarly overwhelming triumph.

If the 1972 presidential election turned out to be a shattering experience for the country's faith in the political process, it was a stunning blow to the Mexican-American electorate for other reasons. The Chicano Strategy went beyond political folly and became a political lesson not limited entirely to the Chicanos themselves. The Mexican-Americans who moved to the GOP aren't likely to scurry back to the Democrats; on the other hand, neither is the Chicano exodus to the Republican ranks likely to continue. The lesson is that the Chicano Strategy produced a remarkable transformation in the politics of Mexican-Americans from a predictable, homogeneous bloc into a fluid, ticket-splitting electorate that—much like the rest of America—has become disillusioned with politicians and the parties, weary of political promises and slogans, and eager to find a better way to solve its problems.

13

THE
POLITICS OF
INCLUSION

Watergate and the nationally televised hearings of Sam Ervin's investigating committee gave the nation a shattering exposure of the corruption that surrounded President Nixon's reelection and, at the same time, offered the electorate a thorough look at the men who belong to the country's most exclusive club—the United States Senate. Watergate made a legend out of Senator Ervin, the club's most knowledgeable constitutional authority. Howard Baker, the good-looking Tennessee senator who continually asked for the "whys" behind the dirty tricks, the wiretapping, and the dishonesty, emerged as presidential timber, possibly the GOP's answer to Edward Kennedy or whoever carries the Democratic banner in 1976.

Then there was New Mexico Senator Joseph M. Montoya, the highest elected official of Mexican-American ancestry in the country, whose inept performance certainly went against the assertive, anything-Anglo-can-do-I-can-do-as-well-or-better image that the Chicano movement sought to project. Montoya's underwhelming performance was nothing short of painfully embarrassing for anyone trying to sell the competence of minority leadership. Montoya even became the butt of the Watergate press corps, as *Rolling Stone* contributing editor Timothy Crouse described in writing about the hearings:

> Their [the reporters'] attention, even at the best of times, ebbs and flows according to the witness in the chair and the senator conducting the cross-examination. The tide invariably goes out during the turn of Senator Montoya, whose question periods are universally recognized as the best time for voiding the bladder. The senator from New Mexico has become so thoroughly associated with the lavatory that several network people refer to him as "Montoilet," prompting frantic rebukes from their producers who are afraid that they will someday slip and use the name on the air.
>
> People who know Montoya say that he is not as stupid as he looks. He just freezes on camera, they say. His brain jams with stage fright, and he cannot concentrate on whatever the witness is telling him. Chairman Sam has made repeated attempts to help him overcome this disability. On one occasion, Ervin had a committee staffer kneel on all fours next to Montoya's chair, popping up to hand him a fresh question whenever a nearby monitor showed that the camera was on the witness. But nothing seemed to work. Every time Montoya gets the microphone, the reporters begin to pass notes to each other, making fun of the wretched senator. The most famous note, an instant classic, contained a mock dialogue in which Montoya asked the witness, "Now, would you like to meet my *seester?*"

The problem was one of image and style. Clearly, Montoya, a competent, well-respected, hard-working senator in his own right, was out-classed. It was not as if he had carried the hopes and aspirations of the nation's Mexican-Americans into the committee hearings and gambled them away. But, at the very least, Montoya was carrying the Chicano colors into battle, and in a race-conscious country where color has historically made a difference, he was showing that brown isn't up to white. At least not this time.

The case of Senator Montoya and the Watergate hearings points up the challenge inherent in being Mexican-American, and it suggests the test that lies ahead for Brown Middle America and for Mexican-Americans in general. Brown Middle America, like Black Middle America, has reached the zenith of assimilation. The melting pot, if there is such a thing, has done all it can for Brown Middle Americans. Maybe they will become wealthier, smarter, taller, or prettier. But they are not going to become any less brown.

That is the crux of the matter. If Senator Montoya had been some WASP senator with all the right characteristics (meaning white with no accent), there would never have been any *seester* joke and probably few people would have given much thought to his performance. Mediocrity, even if it is only in style or image, is generally acceptable and taken for granted in White Middle America.

The inherent challenge is that, regardless of wealth, position, or assimilation, any Mexican-American in the public eye will be judged in everything he does not only by the normal standard of his business but also on the basis of being Mexican-American. And any failure or shortcoming on his part will be judged as a failure or shortcoming of his nationality. In that sense, Mexican-Americans, like blacks, cannot really follow in the footsteps of the European immigrants who entered American life before them and popularized the myth of the melting pot. A third- or fourth-generation middle-class German-American does not face the problem of the middle-class well-assimilated Mexican-American because on the surface he is no more readily identifiable than, say, a Swedish-American.

In the 1970s, the Mexican-American may face a somewhat compromised position in American society, but it certainly is a much better place — with far greater prospects — than he held in the early 1960s. No one Mexican-American group or individual has been totally responsible. Certainly César Chávez's farm labor movement was a triggering agent, and that's not to say that the militant rhetoric of Reies López Tijerina, Corky Gonzales, and José Angel Gutiérrez didn't make the requests and demands of Brown Middle America — say, the Henry Ramirezes — much more palatable to the establishment. On one level, the Chicano movement was a narrow assertive effort at ethnic identity; and on another plane, it was a drive by a broad spectrum of voices and philosophies all seeking a better life. The one thread that seemed to tie it all together was politics.

Since de Tocqueville, it has been understood that the passion for equality would be a central theme of American life, but that it would take the form not of leveling but of diffusing of what had theretofore been privilege. In part, American politics has been a long process of including new groups in this manner. The era ushered in by the 1960s began with the election of a Roman Catholic to the presidency, resolving an issue in English-speaking politics that began with Henry VIII. Fittingly, John F. Kennedy's election was followed by the great black assertion of the 1960s, and then what some described as "the fever of ethnicity," not the least of which was the Chicano movement, clamoring for inclusion.

In that sense, the Mexican-American has aroused American politics into an orgy of inclusion. The Nixon Chicano Strategy and the strong response it triggered among the Democrats were unparalleled in recent history, and despite their political motivations, they made an impact because the Hispanos were as opportunistic as the politicians themselves. Certainly, too, the bargaining power of the middle-class Mexican-Americans with the major parties was not hurt by the political emergence of La Raza Unida. No, La Raza is never going to make it big in national politics, but the continuing growth of the party in places like South Texas and the harassing campaigns such as Ramsey Muñiz's gubernatorial effort in Texas make the politics of inclusion a much more desirable alternative for the major parties. But the politics of inclusion need not be instantly successful. Had Kennedy lost in 1960, Catholics would not have given up on America. The mere fact of the nomination was an achievement. A similar sequence appears likely for the Mexican-Americans.

Though in recent years politics have been kind to the Chicanos, there remains some question as to how effectively the political gains will be expressed in the *barrios* of the Southwest, where life still goes on, and sometimes still ends quickly, with the same senseless killing that claimed many other Mexican-Americans in the past. Take, for instance, the Chicano *barrio* of Dallas known as "Little Mexico," just north of the downtown area.

In the summer of 1973, while Watergate was deafening the ears of the country and Senator Montoya was doing slightly less, a truly unbelievable killing took place in Dallas. Sitting handcuffed in the back seat of a Dallas police car in the early hours of the morning, Santos Rodriguez, a twelve-year-old youngster who had been picked up on suspicion of burglary, was shot in the head and killed by a police officer playing Russian Roulette in an attempt to make the boy talk. Santos' thirteen-year-old brother, who was also in the car, saw the shooting, as did the police officer's partner. The local authorities filed first-degree murder charges against the officer, Darryl L. Cain. The killing aroused anger in Dallas' normally passive Mexican-American community, which, compared to the restlessness of other Chicano communities, in general reflects the conservatism of the city. Four days after the shooting, several thousand Mexican-Americans and black and white sympathizers marched through downtown Dallas to City Hall, where the angry mood grew to a fever pitch and erupted in attacks on nearby policemen and a window-breaking and looting rampage. City officials were reluctant to describe the event as a "riot," but this was unquestionably the most violent disruption in the city's history.

If the Chicanos have taken to the streets in Dallas, where Mexican-Americans enjoy the highest standard of living of any city in the country, you can count on restlessness among the Mexican-Americans elsewhere in the Southwest. The dual system of justice still stands out as one of the crucial social problems that beset Chicanos. The passion for equality, which underlies the Chicano Strategy and the politics of inclusion, sometimes seems only to heighten the frustrations of the poor and the excluded by dramatizing how unequal people really are. Events like the Dallas shooting pose the uncomfortable question of how far Americans really are willing to go in changing the basic differences of income and status. Even the skimpy successes of the Great Society's social programs suggest that the federal government's promise of "equality of opportunity" implies results which government cannot deliver, short of radical economic change — short of altering human nature itself.

Having ridden the crest of the civil rights movement, the Chicanos and other minorities now have to face an uncertain future: they have to deal with the same concerns that arose among the old guard of the civil rights movement in December 1972, when they gathered for a nostalgic two-day symposium at the Lyndon B. Johnson Library in Austin. The symposium marked one of former President Johnson's last public appearances and the dominant theme was whether the legal victories over segregation and discrimination can finally be translated into economic improvement for millions of poor blacks, Mexican-Americans, and other minorities. There was general agreement that if the civil rights movement is to have a future, it must now deal with the problems of political and economic power, health care, welfare, housing, and employment. It was the old story about the hard-won right to sit at a lunch counter not being worth much if you don't have the money to buy a sandwich.

And, of course, the way you deal with these big problems in the American system is through politics and its impact on government and public policy. The impact of the Chicanos' achievement in the early 1970s on improving life in the *barrios* is something that can only be measured in long-range terms.

In 1972, Mexican-American political activists in the two major parties extracted unprecedented platform concessions from both the Democrats and the Republicans, with the parties pledging commitments to programs affecting the lives of the nation's Spanish-speaking minorities. The Democrats' commitment was more far-reaching than the GOP's, although essentially the major dispute between the two parties' commitments was the Democrats' support of Chávez's farm labor movement in his struggle with the California growers and the Teamsters. The Democrats, however, were backed into their position by the Republicans' own concerted effort—the Chicano Strategy—and they were even further pressed by the emergence of a Democratic National Latino Caucus. The discontent among Democratic Chicanos grew stronger several weeks after the national convention over a dispute in the Democratic National Committee. Polly Baca Barragan, special assistant to then Democratic National Chairman Jean Westwood and director of the DNC's Office of the Spanish-Speaking, became bitterly angry when Mrs. Westwood proposed dismantling her office. Along with the Latino Caucus, Ms. Barragan saw this bureau as the only real Spanish-speaking advocate within the DNC. She resigned her position and later was named national committee member from Colorado.

At the party's national convention at Miami Beach, the Latino Caucus totalled 151 convention delegates and 72 alternates, quite a difference from the 1968 convention in Chicago, where there were 56 Spanish-speaking delegates. The Chicanos, of course, were among the groups that profited from the Democrats' reform measures, particularly the controversial quota system of delegate selection, which apparently went by the wayside when the party decided to reform the reforms. The immediate reaction to doing away with the quotas in delegate selection was fear that the party would immediately revert to the way it had been in the past, with minorities left on the outside. On later reflection, however, it was clear that the political awakening of the Chicanos and others was not to be so easily undone.

The situation was similar for La Raza Unida in Texas. Running a slate of statewide candidates, getting on the ballot, and winning 6 percent of the vote in the gubernatorial race were all achievements. When the election returns began to come in, the obvious reading of them was as a sound defeat of the party. But then, returns showed that the winner had less than a majority of the votes and that this was the closest gubernatorial contest in the state's history. La Raza Unida's impact became clear. Indeed, the party could boast of being the balance of power, and in the politics of inclusion that claim is virtually the same as winning.

As a statewide political party, La Raza Unida not only showed considerable influence but indicated it would be around for a while. In future years, Muñiz and other statewide candidates stood the chance of increasing slightly their percentage to 10 or possibly even 12 percent of the vote. These are the immediate goals, but the possibility of La Raza Unida emerging as a true statewide party is too remote to consider seriously. By its very nature, La Raza Unida is a minority party in the state, although in its own way the party has played much the same role as the Nixon Hispanos and the Democrats' Latino Caucus. The strategy of all three groups has been essentially the same: to parlay their numbers and strength into concessions from the powers that be. The best that La Raza Unida could have done in Texas in 1972 was to take enough votes away from the Democrats to elect a Republican governor. La Raza almost did that, but even in failing, it presented the Democrats with the very real threat of a similar alignment occurring at some point in the future. In much the same way that the Nixon Chicano Strategy aroused the national Democratic party, La Raza Unida's showing awoke the Texas Democratic establishment from its own siesta.

Implicit in all the hue and cry for inclusion in the political process is the activists' age-old ideal of nationalism. Perhaps because of its name, La Raza Unida appears to be a nationalistic party. There is no quarreling with the rhetoric that came out of the party's 1972 national convention, where activists indeed organized a national Raza Unida party along highly nationalistic lines. But the national party was so badly fragmented that it was hard to be sanguine about its future. Muñiz, Gutiérrez, and the Texas organization broke ties with the national party's steering committee over a disagreement on priorities and direction, and Gutiérrez, elected national chairman of the party at the El Paso convention, put aside, at least temporarily, his dream of a national organization to concentrate on the redevelopment of Crystal City and on strengthening the party base in Texas.

In Denver, Corky Gonzales remains the leading apostle of Chicano nationalism, and he is at the controls of La Raza Unida's national organization. Gonzales was openly critical not only of the Mexican-Americans working directly with the Republicans and the Democrats but also of La Raza Unida in Texas, where, as in the case of Crystal City and the health clinic funded by the Nixon administration, party activists have worked closely with the political establishment.

Ramsey Muñiz's gubernatorial campaign, for instance, actually turned into a brief attempt at coalition politics. Muñiz got the support of blacks, students, and liberals, who were disenchanted with the leadership of the state Democratic party and were looking for a protest outlet. Understandably, Gonzales and other nationalists were outraged, and there were splits over the issue among party activists even in Texas.

Indeed, factionalization is a problem that has long plagued the Chicano movement. The rifts within La Raza Unida are similar to divisions within other Chicano groups. Strangely enough, the closer different groups within the movement have tried to get to each other, the wider their differences have become. But this phenomenon only parallels a similar process within the black movement as it sought to organize an independent political force with its own political strategy. The factional struggles of the Chicano and black movements raise general questions about the local versus the national in political movements. Today most blacks have accepted the fact that leadership on the magnitude of a Martin Luther King is uncommon in any race or time. Although blacks were never in full agreement with all of King's tactics, they look back on his years at the head of the movement with nostalgia for a time of clear issues and programs. Even so, they now look less longingly for any single man to provide a sense of unity that, however uplifting, must necessarily be an illusion when applied to a people who are as diverse as any other in their talents, interests, intellects, and philosophies. The Chicano movement has only begun to come to the same realization.

While the Chicano movement today is splintered, many Mexican-Americans would argue that it always has been so but that the condition is now more readily recognized by all Chicanos as a positive asset. Strongly linked by a fierce pride in their culture and language, the movement's leaders are pursuing progress on many specialized fronts. More than in the past, the assault on inequality, the use of brown pride and power, is taking place on the local community level. The lack of national voices makes the decibel level of Chicano protest seem lower. Actually, the many local voices have been speaking loudly, but white America has not always been listening.

This new localism draws much of its strength from the intense feelings and aroused energy of an increasingly activist and impatient generation of Chicano youth, who reflect the assertiveness and independence of their peers across the nation. It also coincides with a philosophical and pragmatic fragmentation of the entire Chicano movement. There is sharp disagreement among the traditional leaders, who can be divided into three main groups. First, there are such near-Establishment figures as César Chávez and Democratic and GOP Hispanos; next, the Chicano nationalists, of whom Corky Gonzales and José Angel Gutiérrez, though themselves divided on methodology and philosophy, are leading spokesmen; and, third, the Marxist-oriented revolutionaries, limited to a small number of Chicanos, most of them in California. The traditionalists continue to hold to the classic techniques of progress through the courts, the Congress, and the federal government. The nationalists, who appeal to Chicano pride and push for Chicano studies, local control of communities, and Chicano political and economic power, are slowly gaining strength. At the same time, more Chicanos are becoming radicalized. Though still a minority within the minority, the radicals who lean toward a militant concept of class struggle, sometimes in alliance with other revolutionaries, to overthrow the present capitalistic system are beginning to gain attention.

For Chicano leaders, all three courses pose risks. A complete return to purely passive, conventional protest would destroy the morale and thrust of the Chicano movement. Chicano nationalism, if carried to extremes, could lead to separatist schemes and policies that are unrealistic for a small minority who must live in a predominantly white society. As for revolution, it is clearly impossible, and irresponsible talk about it, however justified the anger that prompts it, can be dangerous because it may mislead Chicanos about the extent of their power and may serve to confirm whites in fear and repression. The most hopeful strategy thus seems to be the determined use of political organization and economic pressure that have been used countless times before within the American system. Such a strategy can make full use of Chicano nationalism to build pride and spirit.

Crystal City in South Texas stands out as the prime example of how Chicanos are uniting on the local level to assert their political and economic strength against a white-controlled status quo. The redevelopment of Crystal City was the brainchild of Gutiérrez, who returned home to apply his considerable intelligence to what he believed was an unchallengeable moral cause. More often, however, the new Chicano localism is the work of lesser-known figures who are learning how to create Chicano self-help groups, to bring off coalitions with whites where necessary, and to work among the Chicano poor to give them hope and the techniques to improve their living conditions. This is hard, painstaking, unromantic work in which success seldom comes swiftly, but once achieved, can have lasting effect.

The most enduring aspect of Chicano localism is to have

hardened the attitudes of Mexican-Americans into a pattern that will shape the brown-white racial crisis for years to come. For Mexican-Americans, pride in themselves and their culture, so long smothered in a predominantly white society, is now a pervasive reality. Still-unbroken barriers of prejudice, discrimination, and inequality are clearer targets for Mexican-Americans than ever before. All the bitterness and frustration notwithstanding, Chicanos in America express strong confidence that life is improving for them and will improve further in the days ahead. The vast majority want to work through the existing system for further gains. But most of all, Mexican-Americans see their own militance and strength winning the battle for equality over a white-run system, which they increasingly distrust as a whole. Attempting to work within a system one distrusts might appear contradictory, but this is a program all radical reformers have to follow.

There is a New Consciousness in Brown America, which today remains much like Black America, still struggling, still largely separate and unequal—and still fairly isolated from the centers of politics and power in the country. The Chicanos have profited from what Daniel Moynihan describes as the "positive, heartening social change in the last decade," and recent major strides in the political system make their progress seem even more impressive.

But Chicano progress must be considered against a national landscape in which the locus of American politics has shifted to the counter-revolution discovered by George Wallace and mobilized by Richard Nixon—to a mostly white majority numbed by Vietnam, pinched by taxes and inflation, frightened by militancy and violence, and weary of demands for change. It is a different national climate from the one during which the Chicano movement began, and at the same time the distance between the *barrios* and the world outside has been widening as well. Thus, any look back at the Chicano movement discloses a confused collage of verbal combatants, seeking change in the status quo but often not knowing where to look for it in all the rhetoric.

Often change hung on a matter of form or style—the element that eluded Montoya. For that, the Chicanos perhaps can blame one of their own champions. John Corry offered this recollection in *Harper's:*

It happened sometime in the early 1960s and although no one can say exactly when, it may have begun in that magic moment when Robert Frost, who always looked marvelous, with silver hair, and deep, deep lines in his face, read a poem at the inauguration of John F. Kennedy, and then went on to tell him afterwards that he ought to be more Irish than Harvard, which was something that sounded a lot better than it actually was. Hardly a man today remembers the poem, which was indifferent, anyway, but nearly everyone remembers Frost, or at least the sight of him at the lectern, which was perhaps the first sign that from then on it would not matter so much what you said, but how you said it.

Ah, the style. What Senator Montoya lacks has been made up by a mosaic of Mexican-American moderates and militants, nationalists and assimilationists, a handful of national celebrities, and a thousand anonymous store-front organizers.

Chicano style was César Chávez holding a news conference on Capitol Hill and charging that the California growers and the Teamsters were involved in a "conspiracy" to crush his union. In the beginning of the farm labor union fight, the rhetoric had been entirely different, though the growers were as strongly committed then in their opposition to the union. But in 1973, when the word had been baptized into the world of chic, "conspiracy" could be bandied about, though the charge is one of the hardest to prove in any court of law. But that was style.

To the extent that the Chicano movement celebrates brown culture and nourishes brown pride, it is a positive, important, undoubtedly permanent phenomenon. To the extent that Chicano nationalism represents a retreat in hatred from U.S. society, it may be only a temporary phase. The hope is that the Chicano movement, aspiring to deal with white America on more nearly equal terms, actually seeks the good things in life; and it thus makes the Chicanos indeed faithful dreamers of the American dream — but scandalously hampered in turning that dream into reality for themselves.

The way American society, particularly in the Southwest, reacts in the future to the Chicanos and other minorities and their demands for equality will define for decades what kind of country America really is. How America deals with the Chicano movement, and therefore with itself, will show it to be either the nation seen by its detractors — selfish and oppressive — or else the country seen by its defenders — painfully troubled but still holding to its original moral purpose and promise. It may be the Chicano's role not only to struggle for his rightful share of his heritage, but also to recall white America to its own sense of conscience and destiny.

BIBLIOGRAPHY

ACUNA, RODOLFO. *Occupied America: The Chicano's Struggle Toward Liberation.* San Francisco: Canfield Press, 1972.

BARONE, MICHAEL; UJIFUSA, GRANT; and MATTHEWS, DOUGLAS. *The Almanac of American Politics.* Gambit, 1972.

BERGER, PETER L., and NEUHAUS, RICHARD J. *Movement and Revolution.* Garden City: Doubleday & Co., 1970.

BRINTON, CRANE. *The Anatomy of Revolution.* New York: Prentice-Hall, Inc., 1965.

BRODER, DAVID S. *The Party's Over: The Failure of Politics in America.* New York: Harper & Row, 1971.

COLES, ROBERT, and ERIKSON, JAN. *The Middle Americans.* Boston: Little, Brown & Co., 1971.

DAY, MARK. *César Chávez and the Farm Workers.* New York: Praeger, 1971.

DIAMOND, ROBERT A., and ALLIGOOD, ARLENE, eds. *Civil Rights: Progress Report, 1970.* Washington: Congressional Quarterly, Inc., 1971.

FUCHS, LAWRENCE H., ed. *American Ethnic Politics.* New York: Harper & Row, 1968.

GALARZA, ERNESTO; GALLEGOS, HERMAN; and SAMORA, JULIAN. *Mexican-Americans in the Southwest.* Santa Barbara: McNally & Loftin Publishers, 1970.

229

GARCIA, F. CHRIS, ed. *Chicano Politics: Readings.* New York: MSS Information Corporation, 1973.

GLAZNER, NATHAN, and MOYNIHAN, DANIEL PATRICK. *Beyond the Melting Pot.* Cambridge: MIT Press, 1963.

GREBLER, LEO. *The Mexican-Americans.* New York: The Free Press, 1969.

GUTIÉRREZ, JOSÉ ANGEL. *El Politico: The Mexican-American Elected Official.* El Paso: Mictla Publications, Inc., 1972.

GUTIÉRREZ, JOSÉ ANGEL. *La Raza and Revolution: The Empirical Conditions of Revolution in Four South Texas Counties.* Unpublished master's thesis presented to the faculty of the Graduate School of St. Mary's University, San Antonio, Texas.

HANSEN, MARCUS LEE. *The Immigrant in American History.* New York: Harper & Row, 1964.

HELLER, CELIA. *Mexican-American Youth: Forgotten Youth at the Crossroads.* New York: Random House, 1966.

HOLLINGS, ERNEST F. *The Case Against Hunger.* New York: Cowles Book Company, 1970.

KOTZ, NICK. *Let Them Eat Promises: The Politics of Hunger in America.* New York: Doubleday & Co., Inc., 1971.

LUBELL, SAMUEL. *The Future of American Politics,* 3rd ed. New York: Harper & Row, 1965.

MC CLESKEY, CLIFTON. *The Government and Politics of Texas.* Boston: Little, Brown & Co., 1969.

MC WILLIAMS, CAREY. *North From Mexico.* New York: J. B. Lippincott Co., 1949.

MADSEN, WILLIAM. *Society and Health in the Lower Rio Grande.* Austin: University of Texas Press, 1961.

MATTHIESSEN, PETER. *Sal Si Puedes: César Chávez and the New American Revolution.* New York: Random House, 1969.

MEIER, MATT S., and RIVERA, FELICIANO. *The Chicanos.* New York: Hill and Wang, 1972.

MOQUIN, WAYNE, and VAN DOREN, CHARLES, eds. *A Documentary History of the Mexican-Americans.* New York: Praeger, 1971.

MOORE, JOAN W., and CUELLAR, ALFREDO. *Mexican-Americans.* Englewood Cliffs, N.J.: Prentice-Hall, 1970.

NABOKOV, PETER. *Tijerina and the Courthouse Raid.* Albuquerque: University of New Mexico Press, 1969.

NAVA, JULIAN. *Mexican-Americans: Past, Present, Future.* New York: American Book Company, 1969.

NEWFIELD, JACK, and GREENFIELD, JEFF. *A Populist Manifesto.* New York: Praeger, 1972.

NOVAK, MICHAEL. *The Rise of the Unmeltable Ethnics: Politics and Culture in the Seventies.* New York: The Macmillan Co., 1971.

PARKES, HENRY B. *A History of Mexico*. Boston: Houghton-Mifflin, 1966.

PEIRCE, NEAL R. *The Megastates of America*. New York: W. W. Norton & Co., Inc., 1972.

PEIRCE, NEAL R. *The Mountain States of America*. New York: W. W. Norton & Co., Inc., 1972.

PHILLIPS, KEVIN P. *The Emerging Republican Majority*. Garden City, N.Y.: Doubleday & Co., Inc. 1970.

PYE, LUCIAN W., and VERBA, SIDNEY, eds. *Political Culture and Political Development*. Princeton: Princeton University Press, 1965.

RENDON, ARMANDO B. *Chicano Manifesto*. New York: The Macmillan Co., 1971.

RUIZ, RAMON E. *The Mexican War: Was It Manifest Destiny?* New York: Holt, Rinehart and Winston, 1963.

SAMORA, JULIAN. *La Raza: Forgotten Americans*. Notre Dame: University of Notre Dame Press, 1966.

SANCHEZ, GEORGE I. *Forgotten People: A Study of New Mexicans*. Albuquerque: University of New Mexico Press, 1940.

SCAMMON, RICHARD M., and WATTENBERG, BEN J. *The Real Majority: An Extraordinary Examination of the American Electorate*. New York: Coward-McCann, 1970.

STEINER, STAN. *La Raza: The Mexican-Americans*. New York: Harper & Row, 1970.

Texas Almanac. Dallas: *The Dallas Morning News,* annual.

U.S. Civil Rights Commission, Mexican-American Studies Division. *Ethnic Isolation of Mexican-Americans in the Public Schools of the Southwest*. Washington, D.C., 1970.

U.S. Civil Rights Commission, Mexican-American Studies Division. *Mexican-Americans and the Administration of Justice in the Southwest*. Washington, D.C., 1970.

U.S. Civil Rights Commission, Mexican-American Studies Division. *The Unfinished Education: Outcomes for Minorities in the Five Southwestern States*. Washington, D.C., 1971.

WRINKLE, ROBERT D., ed. *Politics in the Urban Southwest*. Albuquerque: University of New Mexico Press, 1971.

Other sources: Ongoing coverage of the *Dallas Morning News,* the *Los Angeles Times,* the *Washington Post,* the *New York Times,* the *Wall Street Journal,* the *National Journal,* the *Denver Post,* the *Texas Observer,* the *Houston Chronicle,* and the *Houston Post.*

INDEX

Abernathy, Ralph David, 35, 102, 126, 174
AFL-CIO, 86, 92, 93, 98; Farah involvement and, 193; UFWOC support, 89; UFWU support, 82, 105
Agnew, Spiro T., 67, 68, 200
Agricultural Workers Organizing Committee, 86
Alamo, the, 21
Alatorre, Richard, 171
Alianza Federal de Mercedes, 119
Alianza Federal de los Pueblos Libres, 113–119; end as political threat, 117; militancy of, 119; as populist movement, 113; pressure against, 121
Alinsky, Saul, 84
Allee, Captain A. Y., 50
Alvarez, Delia, 185
Alvarez, Everett, Jr., 185–188, 191
Alvarez, Madeleine, 185
Alvarez, Soledad, 185
American Coordinating Council of Political Education (ACCPE), 27
American Farm Bureau Federation, 90
American Farm Committee, 81, 90
American G. I. Forum, 137, 170, 213; appeal to White House, 210;

convention of, 4; goals of, 188; organization, 188
Amalgamated Clothing Workers of America, 194
Angel, Judge José, 123
Anglo-American movement to Southwest, 113–115
Anti-union legislation, introduction in states, 90
Armendariz, Alex, 202, 207, 213
Arredondo, Domingo, 50
Arriola, Roland, 180
Assembly of God Institute, 118
Assimilation: through education, 186; of Mexican-American in Farah dispute, 195; in Brown Middle America, 217
Austin, Moses, 113
Austin, Stephen F., 50, 114
AWOC role in Delano Grape Strike, 92
Aztecs, 131, 132
Aztlan, 132, 133

Badillo, Herman, 24
Baker, Sen. Howard, 215
Banuelos, Mrs. Romona A., 200–202, 203, 208, 209
Barnes, Rep. Ben, 177–178
Barnes, Ken, 30

233